I0104285

# A MEETING IN THE RAIN

*Tales of Multigenerational Homelessness and the Struggle for Homeless Rights in America*

## NANCY MCCRADIE

Edited by
**BRYAN SNYDER**

Moreton Bay Freedom Press

Copyright © 2025 by Nancy McCradie

All rights reserved.

No part of this book may be reproduced in any form or by any electronic or mechanical means, including information storage and retrieval systems, without written permission from the author, except for the use of brief quotations in a book review.

Paperback: ISBN 978-1-958860-12-0

Ebook: ISBN 978-1-958860-11-3

Cover art by Jeffrey Hess

*To Robert Allen Hansen, a.k.a. Protest Bob, and to my children, Robyn Hall,*
*Krystal Freedom and Sean Ross McCradie.*

# CONTENTS

# INTRODUCTION

My name is Nancy McCradie. For over forty years, I woke before dawn and delivered the Los Angeles Times, the San Francisco Chronicle, the New York Times and the Santa Barbara News-Press to newspaper vending boxes across Santa Barbara County. I am now retired, but writing my memories down in this book has kept me busy during the twilight period of my life.

This is the story of a woman who grew up in a middle-class family in an affluent town and found herself homeless at the end of a very rocky marriage. The bulk of this tale focuses on my two decades of homelessness where I struggled to provide stability for myself and my children while dealing with cops, predators and the apathy of politicians and the general public. It is also the story of the joys found along the way and our victories in fighting for self-determination.

While reading these pages, strong emotions may come to the surface and you will undoubtedly be tempted to pass judgment. Will you feel anger toward me for the choices I made in life, or will you see a woman who followed her life's calling? I hope you might find compassion in your heart for those who have had to flee into the streets to escape domestic violence. Perhaps you will feel a measure of sorrow for those who seek solace from that kind of conflict but soon find themselves trapped in even scarier situations.

For most people, the experience of homelessness is a slow spiral where bad luck and inconveniences lead to greater hardships, sadness, anger and depression. Adapting to life on the streets can be too much for some people to bear. But my father once gave me advice that guided me through those perilous decades: "Whatever situation you find yourself in, Nancy, you need to hold your head up high and view every experience in life as a given adventure. So stay strong, will you?"

"Yes! I surely will, Papa," I told him.

And I would like to think that I did. This book details the battles I fought alongside my homeless friends against the onslaught of persecution enacted against us by the city and county governments as they erratically strove to combat the proliferation of a class of people that they feared and hated.

With little knowledge of why homelessness is increasing, cities across America are reacting recklessly by criminalizing this behavior. *Let's just put them in jails and let the courts and the police handle it.* Strong emotions and ignorance of the underlying conditions are common among those lucky enough to have purchased housing when it was affordable.

It has always been up to us - the ones who have experienced homelessness firsthand - to call attention to our plight. So this is a story about community organizing, speaker bureaus, street theater, civil disobedience and countless meetings with government officials. Our city and county representatives were disgusted by our behavior, but for every obstacle they placed in our path, we found the resources to push back with three times as much force.

Back in the 1980s, the citizens of Santa Barbara were amazed that the homeless were organizing. The hardened assumptions that homeowners had about the houseless began to crack. It started with the evolution of the Homeless People's Association into a community-based advocacy group that renamed itself the Santa Barbara Homeless Coalition. Importantly, this organization brought the homeless on board so that we could collaborate with each other. Spokespeople for the rich and the poor, along with countless attorneys, gathered monthly to try and get a handle on the burgeoning issue.

We struggled to win the right to vote. It was a long journey... one that parallels the actual trek we took in the presidential election year of 1988, walking across the entire United States to draw attention to homeless rights.

One of my goals in writing this book is to show how criminalization does not work and does nothing to stop the onslaught of development, real estate speculation, price-gouging and the tearing down of affordable housing options. Our government leaders do not get it. Too often, they choose to punish only the victims of the housing crisis, not those who perpetuate it.

I hope you will enjoy these writings... the stories that make up my adventurous and complicated life. My wish is that you will look at this class of society in a new light by the time you finish the last chapter. This book is a call for compassion and decriminalization... a push for affordable housing for everyone.

*Nancy McCradie*
*January 2025*

# PROLOGUE

After the Second World War, when I was barely six months old, my parents and I drove from Connecticut to Santa Barbara, California, seeking a fresh start in the town where my father grew up. Despite both my parents having enlisted and supported the war effort, they were completely unable to find housing they could afford, even as a rental. After spending a few weeks searching for a home and sleeping in their Buick at night, my mother wrote a letter to Santa Barbara's main newspaper. It was printed in the spring of 1946 and read:

*Editor of the News-Press,*

*We wonder if Santa Barbara residents are truly aware of the problems that have confronted the Veteran since the war ended.*

*We fought the war and we were glad to, most of us, if it meant ultimate security, peace, and a way to a better life for all of us. It is like a deep crying ache inside that will not stop, to find it did not end with the assurance that those things we held so dear and dreamed of and worked for and remembered, always remembered, were ours.*

*Santa Barbara is our home. We lived here before the war broke out. We went to school and we worked here. We attended college and looked forward to a good future with the brightest of hopes. When the war came, those hopes had to be put aside to "save our country, even humanity itself," they said. It lasted four years, and four years is a long time to take from the lives of young people. Really it was longer than that. Days of miserable living and loneliness and hopelessness and disquiet stretched interminably in the human heart.*

*Now we are back. We are older, and we've changed. But Santa Barbara is the same. The palm trees still stand tall on each side of its streets, the ocean still washes onto its shores and it is beautiful. We walk along the streets at night and see people sitting in their homes, relaxing because the day is over. Some of them have worked hard. We like to watch them because our own windows gleamed with lamplight once and we sat with our families, and we are remembering again how it was.*

*Can't we have it back? Can't we have a place to live in that we know will be ours at least for a while? Can't we work and know that those we work with appreciate the fact that we are starting all over again? Most important, can't we have the security of being family units in our own right? We need it so our love can survive. We need it to have the patience to bring up our children wisely. We need it to keep our very faith in God. And we need it now!*

*We aren't griping. We are reaching the end of human endurance and are asking for help.*

My mother pulled out this letter and showed it to me for the first time in the 1980s after I had written my own letter to the Santa Barbara News-Press. She explained that she had also worked to find housing for the homeless, although in her case, the people in need were often veterans returning home after World War II. It was an eerie parallel to my own efforts. Reading her words, I realized that housing issues were not a new occurrence in our city and that solutions from history could potentially be used to solve modern-day problems.

I still believe it. I am my mother's daughter, and the fight goes on.

## ❧ I ❧

## AFTER THE WAR

I was born in Bristol, Connecticut to Herbert and Dorothy Fredlund on August 13th, 1945. Atomic bombs had fallen on the cities of Nagasaki and Hiroshima during the week prior, though it took years for Americans to become aware of the horrors that befell the people there. The news of Japan's surrender came much earlier, on August 14th. Cheers of joy erupted in the streets of Bristol, reaching the windows of the maternity ward where my mother rested with me, her firstborn child, in her arms.

My parents had both enlisted in the Coast Guard and were stationed in San Francisco during the final stages of the war. My father served as the chaplain's assistant on a supply ship docked in the Bay. He played the organ during church services, while my mother sang in the Coast Guard choir when she was not tending to her secretarial duties.

Music was their first bond. She noticed her future husband among the musicians playing in the supply ship jazz band - a tall, Swedish-looking gentleman who played the saxophone. Herbert admired her strawberry-blond hair and hourglass figure, and soon Dorothy was showing him pictures of her life on her grandparents' farm in Vermont. Everything clicked, and six weeks later, they were married. Nobody waited to get married during World War II because no one truly knew how much time remained to them. In my father's case, his supply ship was being deployed to the Southwest Pacific, and time was very short indeed. They honeymooned in San Francisco, during which time I was conceived. My mother didn't realize she was pregnant until long after my father had left. She received an honorable medical discharge and decided to return to her mother's house in Bristol, Connecticut to await my arrival.

Herbert was not released from the military until I was ten weeks old. We were still living in my grandparents' home, a two-story white house with blue trim surrounded by birch trees, when my father walked wearily through the front door. His reunion with my mother was joyous, but she was a bit sad that he failed to gush over me, his firstborn child. War changes everyone, and my dad was not immune to its impact.

Later that evening, however, my mom discovered that Herbert was missing from their bed. She found him leaning over my bassinet, watching me sleep. That moment of bonding was the beginning of a long and wonderful relationship with my father.

As the weeks went by, Herbert trudged through the snow looking for work in Bristol. He got a job with the local Red Cross, but the pay wasn't enough for us to be able to afford a home away from my grandparents. He really craved independence, and at the same time, he missed his hometown of Santa Barbara - the oceanside city that lay three thousand miles distant on the West Coast. So when I turned six months old, my father deemed me healthy enough to make the journey. We packed up the Buick and drove across the continent, keeping the detours minimal until the sparkling waters of the Santa Barbara Channel finally came into sight.

Herbert felt ecstatic to be able to hop out of the car and sink his toes into the sand once more. If it weren't for my mother, my dad would have probably been content as a beach bum or a sailor. He loved being out on the water, undoubtedly due to the Viking blood that coursed through his veins.

Unfortunately, Santa Barbara had a distinct housing shortage. We had to sleep in the back of the Buick for several weeks while we searched fruitlessly for a new home. In desperation, my mother sent out her plea to the Santa Barbara News-Press, which had an extensive readership. I'm not certain how much political impact the letter had, but soon afterward, we were invited to move into a newly-established group home for veterans off of Mission Hills on the Riviera.

*Dorothy, Herbert and Nancy*

Living with nine other families and having to share kitchen and bathroom facilities was far from ideal. My parents were grateful to get off the streets, but they still lacked the independence they were craving. It took six months before another housing opportunity opened up: a converted World War II hospital called Hoff Heights.

The predecessor to Hoff Heights, Hoff Hospital, was built just five years earlier, in 1941. Contractors worked through a brutally wet rainy season that dumped forty-one inches of rain on Santa Barbara, toiling through the mud to build one hundred temporary buildings, a commissary, a linen supply depot and several mess halls in addition to the surgical and medical wards. It was located on Las Positas Road where the Municipal Golf Course currently resides, and 1,300 beds were installed to give injured war veterans a place to recover from their wounds. During the four years of its operation, the hospital treated more than 27,000 military patients, but once Japan surrendered, it was not deemed to be necessary any longer.

In November of 1945, over two hundred German prisoners of war, against the dictates of the Geneva Convention, were sent from Camp Cooke to dismantle and crate up the contents of the hospital before they were allowed to return home. The preparation for demolition proceeded through the winter until it was suddenly halted on orders of the Ninth Service Command. The News-Press soon reported that Santa Barbara County's interest in using the buildings for emergency housing was responsible for the federal action.

On February 9th, 1946, a congressional letter arrived at the newspaper office declaring that the Hoff Hospital had been declared surplus and would be transferred to the Federal Public Housing Authority for disposition. The Authority then agreed to convert some of the Hoff buildings into seventy emergency housing units. A surprising amount of red tape was cut through in short order due to the post-war housing crisis, so after six months of living in the shared veterans' home on the Riviera, my mom and dad were able to move into the newly-christened "Hoff Heights".

The residence was little more than a converted barracks, but "H67 Apartment #111" provided a lot more freedom than their previous accommodations. Priority had been given to veterans who were using the GI Bill to attend university in Santa Barbara. That worked for my dad; he immediately enrolled in a program to become certified as a music teacher. On the side, he performed in the Lamp Lighters Dance Band and the Santa Barbara city band, but for employment, he took a job at a drive-in restaurant called the Blue Onion. Today, the building still exists as an International House of Pancakes, but back in the 1940s, they served onion rings, french fries, hamburgers and other sandwiches.

In later years, my mother also attended UCSB and earned a degree in English, but during my childhood, she looked after me and my siblings as a dutiful housewife and mother. Just before my second birthday, she brought my sister Ann Elizabeth into the world. Dealing with a newborn, plus a highly active two-year-old, was an exhausting task, so my Nana hopped on a passenger train in Connecticut so she could travel to California and help mom and her grandchildren.

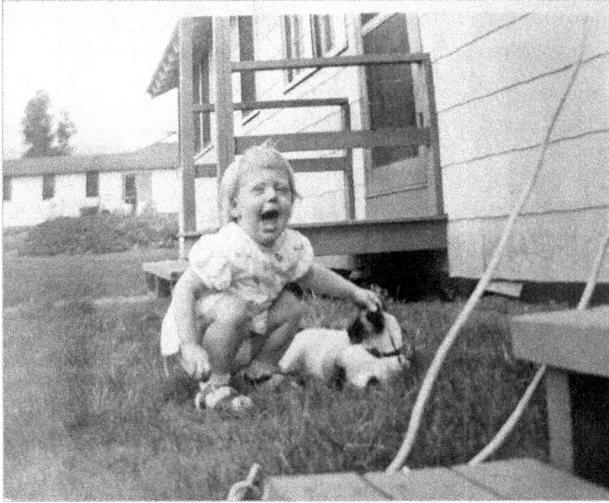

*Nancy at Hoff Heights*

Nana was just coming out of the other side of a nervous break-down. She had experienced an immense tragedy recently; she and her husband had been struck head-on by a drunk driver while on a visit to their farm in Vermont. Grandpa did not survive long enough to reach the hospital. He was the love of her life, and she was devastated.

Nana's physical wounds healed, but it took a while for her soul to recover. Perhaps looking after me gave her a renewed sense of purpose. She brought her camera to the West Coast with her, for she loved to take pictures. I still have relics from our time together - a set of faded photographs of me at the Historical Museum, the old Mission and the Courthouse. She took me to every corner of the city. My favorite place of all was the train station. Clutching Petey, my favorite stuffed bear, I played with Nana in the triangular park nearby while we waited for the "choo-choo trains" to arrive.

By now, so many veterans at Hoff Heights were having children that it generated a strong demand for daycare. Thankfully, twelve of the residents persuaded the County Housing Authority to let them use the former Officers' Recreation Hall as a nursery school. The redesign of the building and the creation of the program took a great deal of collaboration. The veteran fathers, the Women's Volunteer Service and the Red Cross all pitched in, providing enough labor, equipment and financing to make the project a reality. It functioned successfully for the nine years that the housing complex lasted, thanks to the county being persuaded not to charge utilities or rent.

My Nana returned to the East Coast once my mother adjusted to having two little girls around, and I began attending the brand-new nursery school. One of my very first memories was forged there. I remember leaving the building at the end of a school day in possession of a large yellow balloon. I was so proud of this treasure, but alas, it popped on the way back to my apartment. It was a devastating event for a three-year-old.

My father took four years to graduate from UCSB with a B.A. in Music and Junior High Education, but once he held the diploma in his hands, he knew it was time to say goodbye to Hoff Heights. Finding an entry-level teaching job in his field in Santa Barbara would have been even more of an ordeal than finding housing had been. He needed to look further afield.

We couldn't have stayed in our apartment for much longer anyway. Hoff Heights would be demolished within five years so that the city government could build a municipal golf course. The nursery school would move to the Riviera Campus of UCSB for two years before transitioning to its final location on Junipero Street where it still operates as the Oak Parent-Child Workshop today.

~

MY FATHER'S CAREER AS A MUSIC TEACHER LASTED THIRTY-FIVE years, but his first job offer disintegrated before it could become realized. Harlan County in Kentucky needed a music supervisor, and they were about to fly my father out for a final face-to-face interview when the school itself burned down. A few positions materialized in the Bay area, however, so my parents drove up to San Francisco and took a tour of the neighboring communities that had openings. The location they liked the most was located east of Santa Rosa in vineyard country - a town on the north side of Napa County called Calistoga.

We packed up our most important belongings at Hoff Heights, gave the rest away and then drove to our first residence in Calistoga - a motel. It was an affordable option because it was the winter off-season... and possibly because the place *stunk*. The motel used water from a natural hot springs to provide bathing opportunities for its patrons. Unfortunately, the ambient smell of dissolved sulfur and other minerals gave the premises a hellish atmosphere. There had to be better options out there.

Our next home was a ranch house in Franz Valley, a few miles outside of Calistoga. It lay along a winding road that twisted its way through a pine forest. My mother tended the family garden, and I helped pull weeds and collect vegetables when asked. Gardening was my mother's passion. She canned as many fruits and vegetables as she could, then allowed our neighbors to come onto the property so they could glean the rest, free of charge. Our family knew what poverty was like, so sharing resources only made sense. And because my father made only $2,700 a year, the extra food from the garden helped sustain us, too.

We acquired a new addition to the family - a rascally fox terrier named Pal who helped chase critters out of the garden. Whenever the plants needed irrigation, Pal would follow my dad to a wooden water tower atop a hill adjacent to the house. My father would then turn a valve to release the water. Pal proved to be a good insurance policy for any rattlesnakes they might meet along the way, for he barked at everything that moved.

Not long after, my dad acquired an additional follower: an actual native California kingsnake. The reptile for some reason decided that Herbert was his best friend, and it slithered behind the man everywhere he went, even up to the water tower. That dissuaded any rattlesnakes from bothering him for certain because the kingsnake species was well-known for attacking and swallowing rattlesnakes whole.

The creature's infatuation with my father was fine until one day it followed him right into our house. I thought the snake would make a beautiful pet, with its brown coloration and yellow stripes.

"Not a great idea," cautioned my mother. So out the kingsnake went.

One of the highlights of my life was the day that my mom came home with a beautiful, six-week-old silver tabby kitten. She named it "Whiskers", but it soon became *my* cat. He sat in my lap while I stroked his ears, and whenever my mother spanked me for misbehaving and I cried, Whiskers appeared out of nowhere to give me comfort. Whiskers was soon joined by two other kittens: a semi-feral, long-haired orange cat named Tomi, and Hyrem, a lovable, short-haired feline.

Once my father discovered a functional old chicken coop down the trail from our house, he decided to buy fifty little chicks. We kept them inside the house for the first few weeks, and my parents carefully checked on them at nighttime to make sure they stayed warm until their feathers grew out properly. After they were big enough to survive life in the coop, my father put them all in one crate and carried them out of the house. On his way down the trail, however, he tripped, and the crate shattered. The little pullets scattered into the brush. My little sister and I went searching for the chicks, listening carefully for chirps and peeps until every last one had been caught and placed within the coop. *Success!*

The adventure proved unlucky for me, however. I came down with an awful case of poison oak. The rashes covered me from head to toe, and I was miserable. My mom did everything she could to make the episode bearable for me. I sat for hours in the washtub we used as a bathtub, soaking my skin in cold water to ease the itchiness.

When my mother became pregnant with her third child, my parents decided the farmhouse was too isolated. It was more important to have medical assistance closer at hand, so we moved into a new house on a rise overlooking Calistoga and its eight hundred residents. Pal came with us, as he remained my father's faithful companion, as did Whiskers. However, my mom decided that Tomi and Hyrem would be better off living on another ranch in the Franz Valley, helping our old neighbors control their rat population. Annie and I cried for days.

Another sad consequence of our move was that our dad had to slaughter the chickens. No one was moving into the farmhouse immediately who could continue to care for them. Also, the flock had a high proportion of roosters, and nobody on the nearby ranches wanted to add a bunch of belligerent roosters to their own flocks of hens. I was an impressionable child, and the sight of all our poultry being slaughtered affected me to the point where I couldn't stand to be in the same room when someone was cooking eggs for breakfast. The smell reminded me too much of dead and dying chickens.

We rented a freezer locker in Calistoga to store the meat, and my mom planted a fresh garden next to the new house. She nurtured it carefully until little Billy was born. My dad was ecstatic to finally have a son. He named him Herbert William Fredlund Junior, but we always called him Billy, and Annie and I took special care looking after our newborn baby brother.

Our family seemed to be prospering, and our new residence was quite the happy home. My mother would always sing as she did chores around the house. My favorite song of hers was a parody of a song from the opera Carmen:

*Toreador-a,*
*Don't spit on the floor-a,*
*Use the Cuspador-a,*
*That is what it's for-a.*

That always made me laugh.

After coming home from work each day, my father still spent hours practicing or fiddling with one instrument or another. He could play piano and saxophone with ease, though the clarinet had to be his favorite.

He never spoke of his time fighting the Japanese during World War II. In fact, my parents seldom liked speaking about their private lives. There was only one story I remember my dad relating to me. In between battles, my father was once in charge of guarding a Japanese prisoner, and they eventually became quite friendly. The POW taught Herbert how to do origami - the art of folding paper to create elegant, three-dimensional shapes, like flowers, cranes and other creatures. In turn, my dad taught these patterns to his children, including my favorite: a bird that flapped its wings when you pulled its tail.

Herbert was a popular man in Calistoga. His job was to teach music for both elementary and high school students. His predecessor had formed a dance band, but when my father took over, he decided to steer things in a more traditional direction. He worked toward developing a concert band, hoping to expand it into something orchestral in size by using as many students as possible. However, because his teaching salary was so low, my dad had to supplement his income by getting a chauffeur's license and driving a school bus in the morning and afternoons.

Every Friday night, the town put on a talent show where local performers could showcase their skills in front of their fellow citizens. It was held in an open field next to the Calistoga airport. A bonfire helped to keep the audience warm while a covered bandstand served as the primary stage. Dad played the piano, accompanying a succession of comedians and singers, some with rather dubious vocal talents.

One night, I was sitting with my mom and sister in the Buick parked behind the bandstand - a common arrangement that allowed us to hear the entertainment while allowing my mother to relax and not have to keep an eye on her two wandering children. On stage, a drunken woman bellowed a tortured tune while my father gamely tried to match her tempo. When the song was over, she ran over to the piano and gave my dad a big, sloppy kiss. Annie and I thought our mother was going to choke with laughter. She didn't stop good-naturedly teasing my father about it for years.

When I was five years old, a terrible illness overcame my father. It happened so quickly. His joints became inflamed to the extent that he was unable to walk. Upon examination by a doctor, my dad was diagnosed with rheumatic fever. It can be caused by an untreated strep throat or a similar bacteriological infection. The body's own T-cells start attacking healthy organs, including the heart. Recovery was possible, but only after a long, painful journey.

Dad was placed on a new drug developed by a doctor in San Francisco called ACTH - a new type of medicine derived from the adrenaline glands of cattle. He was confined to his bed while ACTH poured into his bloodstream intravenously. The drug could cause several side effects, including moon face, manic depression and other erratic behaviors. But in my father's case, it seemed to be effective, and the doctor was pleased with the results.

One day, however, my father's heart began to beat slowly and erratically. His pulse slowed down to twenty beats per minute. We rushed him back to the hospital, and he was not expected to last the night. Many of his friends in the community came to sit by his side and pray for him. Fortunately, mom took a moment to look at the label on the side of the ACTH medicine bottle and noted that the chemicals within depleted the amount of potassium in the body. She immediately called the doctor, who gave my dad a massive injection of potassium. By the next morning, my father was much, much better, apart from the continuing effects of the rheumatic fever, and the doctor was genuinely sorry that he had not read the label closely enough.

My father's illness and the period of enforced bed rest that followed lasted for almost a year. That meant that no income was coming in, apart from the seventy-two dollars that the state welfare department sent us once a month. My mother did her absolute best to make that money last. We also had to depend upon the kindness of the community. One day, I came home from school and was not able to even walk into the house because the floor was covered in donated canned goods. The citizens of Calistoga really missed my dad.

My mother tried to maintain her participation in several social groups in town, but she was overwhelmed sometimes, having to take care of my father *and* three children. She wept a lot, but at the same time, I remember her being really strong. Little Billy didn't help matters, though. By the time he was six months old, my mom had to put a lid on his crib to keep him from climbing out. At seven months old, he was up and walking about. Soon he was engaged in his favorite sport: running away from her. One of his favorite places of refuge was underneath the dining room table.

As if those trials weren't stressful enough, Annie and I came down with the measles. The disease can cause blindness, and the treatment at the time was to confine the sick in bed within a darkened room because the sunlight could be too bright at times. We felt wretched. We whined and cried, and our mom would nurture us with soup and water. She brought in a doctor to check on us along with her ailing husband. Our fevers rose to 104 degrees, so we mostly slept to make the time more bearable.

My sister and I recovered. Then slowly, over the course of many months, my father did as well. He lay in bed most days and did oil painting as a hobby, but eventually, he was able to start tutoring mathematics to pupils in our home. Regaining the ability to walk took longer. While he rehabilitated, his mother, Bessie, moved up from Los Angeles to come live with us in Calistoga. Her husband had passed away several years earlier, and Bessie herself was a musician in her own right, playing the piano in theaters as an accompaniment to silent movies.

I loved having a grandmother again, and it certainly took pressure off my mom. However, friction soon developed between the adults in the house. After a lot of arguments and tears, my grandma decided to move to a neighborhood called the "Little Village" in the middle of downtown Calistoga. She started working for a tobacco store in Calistoga, fell in love with her boss and was soon remarried.

My father resumed work. He was exceedingly lucky that the rheumatic fever hadn't affected his heart, but a different tragedy struck one day when Pal was hit by a car and paralyzed. The little fox terrier had been a scrapper, getting into fights with a lot of the neighborhood dogs, but this accident proved too much for him. We took him to the vet and had to say goodbye before he was put to sleep. The pained look on his face, begging for help, burned itself into my memory. I cried so hard, I was inconsolable.

The loss took a toll on my father as well. Not long after, he came into the house after work and announced that we were leaving Calistoga. His long illness had left the family in debt up to their ears. He'd tried getting more loans at the banks to no avail, so he'd started to apply for teaching jobs in Southern California, where he believed he could earn a higher salary. Today, he'd finally received an answer to one of his applications: the San Bernardino school district had hired him to teach at Lake Arrowhead High School for the upcoming school year. The pay was much better than Calistoga, and they would be a lot closer to Santa Barbara, the town that my dad *really* wanted to end up in.

After shedding more tears at the thought of having to leave behind friends, a garden and a cherished house on a hill, my mom began to pack up our belongings. The exhausting task of rehoming ourselves in a new town was about to begin once more.

∾

WE RENTED A HOUSE IN DEL ROSA, A FEW MILES OUTSIDE OF SAN Bernardino, but when my father checked in with his new boss, he was informed that his job had already been given to another person. Rather than having to commute every school day up the mountains to Lake Arrowhead, my father was assigned to teach Music Appreciation at Highland Junior High School, on the northeast side of San Bernardino. Even though he was able to lead the girls' chorus, he still hated his job. I hated the area too. My school was dismal, and it took me forever to make new friends.

After a year had passed, my dad received a call from the superintendent of the Barstow Unified School District. He wanted Herbert to apply for the job of Band Director at their Junior High. My father was ecstatic. On a hot Sunday in late summer, the family drove up Interstate 15 to take a tour of our potential new home in the high desert.

We had scarcely entered the city of Barstow when my mother burst into tears. "You're not going to make me move to this god-forsaken place, are you?"

"Yes, I am," my father replied.

Barstow sits in the middle of the Mojave Desert at about 2,000 feet above sea level. Temperatures could reach 120 degrees in the summertime and well below freezing in winter, with a rare blizzard blanketing the landscape every few years. Most of the year's sparse rainfall fell during the winter months, though the summer skies conjured up the occasional monsoon thunderstorm. The prospect of facing these extremes of nature may have intimidated my mother, but the first time I witnessed a summer lightning show with cascading tendrils of electricity arcing across the wide open sky, I felt similarly electrified.

The city also lay at the crossroads of Interstates 15 and 40, making it the perfect stopover for anyone traveling from Bakersfield and Los Angeles to Las Vegas or points further east. Its strategic location also convinced the military to build one of the largest marine supply depots there: Camp Irwin. The base was established at the beginning of World War II when a training camp was needed for tank warfare. In time, my father became the organist at the church on the base. My siblings and I would be dragged along to the services and forced to attend Sunday School afterward... probably so my mother could have a short, weekly break away from her demanding kids. Church bored me to tears; the only thrill I felt was during the drive to the base and back when Daddy drove fast across the dips in the road that had been designed for flood control. Billy, Annie and I would giggle and laugh in the back seat, daring him to go faster.

Despite my mother's reservations, my parents decided to purchase their first house together. They located a duplex on Elizabeth Street on the east side of town that was affordable on a band director's income. Shortly thereafter, the new Barstow High School music teacher serendipitously moved across the road from us. Far from being rivals, Daniel Heistand and my father quickly became fast friends. And because my mother was a staunch Christian Scientist, when she found out that Mr. Heistand and his wife shared her religion, her attitude toward living in Barstow changed dramatically.

The two band leaders were a credit to their respective schools. My father's junior high band made him proud, winning every contest that they appeared in. At the Los Angeles Coliseum, Mt. Heistand's high schoolers competed against bands from all over the Western United States and placed first in the marching competitions.

With our new house came a new baby sister. Meredith was named after Meredith Simpson, the composer of the Broadway musical "The Music Man", which was very popular at the time. She was born at Barstow Hospital a full month early, but she was still a strong baby, squalling at the top of her lungs on day one. Annie and I had great fun with her antics. As soon as Meredith learned to walk and run, she would pull off all her clothes, slip out of her diaper and bolt out the front door. We would have to chase our naked little sister down the street, though we laughed the entire way.

I was enrolled in Tene C. Cameron Elementary - a tough school where children had to learn how to survive schoolyard fights at an early age. At least the teachers were exceptional. Our fifth-grade teacher, Mr. Smith, was a fine man who knew how to handle our class clown, even when the student faked a sob and loudly blew his nose during sad stories, setting off a fit of giggles. Mr. Smith took us on field trips into the desert so we could pretend to be pioneers crossing the barren stretches in search of fertile land. He even had us make period-authentic hats and aprons out of cardboard and cotton so that we could fully immerse ourselves in the setting.

Our sixth-grade teacher, Mr. Ribbicoff, was a lot less fun. He would put our names up on the chalkboard for acting out in class. Then if we continued to do mischief, he would draw an 'X' next to our names. After school, the trouble-makers would receive one spanking for each X, delivered by way of a paddle that Mr. Ribbicoff kept by his desk. My fellow students and I would linger outside the classroom window, peeking in to watch the spectacle. The victims would always yelp and jump into the air to make a show of it, but no one cried; among us kids, we considered the spankings to be a badge of honor. Some of us would even act out in class on purpose, just to show the other students how tough we were.

Barstow was fun for me because for the first time, I had a best friend. Doris was blond and freckled, just like me, though she had a strong southern accent. We were both tomboys, too. We'd play cowboys and indians, where I rode around the backyard on a toy stick-horse - a black stallion named King. During other war games, we'd pick teams among the neighborhood kids, gather dirt clods and hurl them at the opposing side. It was good training for real life; because many tough kids went to our school, Doris and I would sometimes have to fight our way out of a circle of bullies during recess.

One of our favorite pastimes was to walk out into the desert on a windy day. Wind gusts sometimes developed into full sandstorms, and we loved facing downwind while the sand pelted the skin on our backsides. What a massage that was. We'd also spend time collecting desert creatures, like horny toads and alligator lizards, before placing them in a zoo in one of our backyards. Neighborhood children would have to pay us a nickel to come see our wild menagerie. Once, we even had a bobcat for a few hours. She'd been trapped by some friends of our family, and I remember the poor, frightened animal hissing at me through the bars of her cage. It was a relief when she was released back out into the desert, as we tried to do with all our zoo specimens.

Doris and I also got in trouble together. She got me to try cigarettes and she also convinced me to shoplift one day. Of course, we were caught. I tried to smuggle a book of matches in my armpit, and Doris tried to sneak out of the store with an individually-wrapped ice cream. We put the items back and received a strong lecture from the store owner. The man happened to know my dad, and I'm not sure if that was a good or a bad thing. He told us to go home, tell our parents and have them call him.

Later, Doris told me that her punishment was that she was not allowed to see the movie "Old Yeller". My penance was to sit at the dining room table and write a letter of apology to the owner. I never stole again.

Music might have also kept me from getting into too much trouble. I started playing the clarinet soon after we arrived in Barstow when I was eight years old. *If the instrument brought my father so much joy*, I thought, *it must be worth a try*. In time, I became proficient enough that my teacher entered me into a competition at a local music festival. The judges awarded me a blue ribbon - one of my proudest moments. My younger sister Annie picked up the flute, but I stayed with the clarinet and sang in the elementary school choir for the rest of the time that we remained in Barstow.

Unfortunately, our stay wasn't nearly as long as I or my family had hoped. After three years in Barstow, a new superintendent took over the schools. His priorities were political survival and landing cushy jobs for his friends. Daniel Heistand, the high school band leader, saw the writing on the wall, so he applied and was hired for a state college position. Daddy would have liked to have done the same, but no opportunities presented themselves. When the superintendent announced his intentions to cut the middle school band, my father started laying the groundwork to take over Mr. Heistand's position at the high school. To my dad's dismay, however, the superintendent gave the job to a friend of his from Arizona. By then it was too late in the summer for my father to try and land a school position elsewhere. He was furious.

I couldn't remember seeing my father so mad. He walked off his job and vowed never to return. When the principal of the junior high school phoned him at home and said that he couldn't just refuse to show up at work, my dad called the superintendent a "son-of-a-bitch" and said that the only way he'd go back is if the junior high band was restored.

Somehow, my father's audacity paid off. The superintendent gave in and actually apologized to him, so my dad agreed to continue teaching the junior high school band for another year.

He went back to work. However, rumors accumulated over the course of the year, exposing the superintendent's plans to eliminate the music department from the entire city school system. Music and the arts are always the first subjects to get cut when administrative staff members want to give themselves raises. Math and science are important, but music is the education of the soul, and its imminent loss from the curriculum saddened my father. He knew this would be his last year in Barstow, so he started thinking hard about how he could finally secure a job within the Santa Barbara School District.

A few years earlier, he'd been offered a position by his friend Henry Brubeck - older brother of the famous jazz musician, David Brubeck. At the time, my dad had been experiencing enough success and fulfillment in Barstow that he turned Henry down. But now that the music department in Barstow was folding, my father decided that he should rekindle that opportunity, and to convince Henry that he was serious, he chose to seek out the Santa Barbara teacher in person.

A parade was taking place in Long Beach, south of Los Angeles, and my dad knew that Henry's band would be performing. He arrived early and was wandering along the band entries on the side streets, looking for his old friend, when he felt a jab in the center of his back. When he spun around, there was Henry Brubeck, holding the far end of a long ceremonial spear with a flag on it.

"You old son-of-a-bitch," Henry said with a grin. "What are you doing here?"

"I'm just casing out the parade," Herbert replied half-truthfully.

Henry gave him a hard look before asking, "How would you like to come to Santa Barbara and teach with us next year?"

It turned out that there was an opening at La Cumbre Junior High School. After nine years away, our family was finally going back home.

## ❧ 2 ❧

# A DREAM OF GLORY AND GRANDEUR

As much as it thrilled my parents to return to the Pacific Ocean, leaving Barstow after four years felt devastating to me. I screamed and cried for days. I didn't want to leave the desert... the open landscape that stretched for miles and miles. I didn't want to leave my best friend Doris behind. But my father had to go back to Santa Barbara. I don't think he was truly happy anywhere else.

Henry Brubeck helped him secure a position teaching music at La Cumbre Junior High on Modoc Road. Herbert loved teaching secondary school, so this was his dream job. By now, I was thirteen years old, so I was enrolled in the same school as my father. That meant that my own father was in charge of my clarinet lessons. I didn't mind that situation at all; he was a good teacher, and I think my parents were grooming me to follow in his footsteps.

Making friends proved to be difficult, so music was one of my few comforts during eighth grade. Unfortunately, right when I started to get socially comfortable, our family moved to a new school district. We'd been renting a duplex from the city mayor on Barranca Avenue above City College on the Mesa, but a housing tract was being laid out on the north side of Goleta, just west of Santa Barbara, and my dad found a plot of land that became the site of our new home. The house was built for $13,800, which gave us a low mortgage of $72 a month.

I loved our new residence, but after three months, I was required to transfer to a closer middle school. La Colina Junior High had just been built along Foothill Road to service the burgeoning population, and once again, I was forced to scramble to find new friends. I finished eighth grade there and all of ninth grade. Mostly, I kept to myself, spending hours tucked away in the band room practicing clarinet or sitting alone on the school grounds at lunchtime, reading my favorite books of the era.

Once I graduated from middle school, I moved into another new building - San Marcos High on Hollister Avenue. The students of Santa Barbara High School were our chief rivals, and the battles between our two sports teams were legendary.

During my first year, I was studying in one of the classrooms when a fellow student shouted and pointed out the window. Snowflakes were actually falling onto the pavement outside. We were absolutely amazed. Snow would fall occasionally on the 4,000-foot mountains that loomed above Santa Barbara and Goleta, but almost never that close to sea level. The principal got on the intercom and bellowed, *"Classes are dismissed!"* We were allowed to spend the rest of the school day having snowball fights and making snowmen. Even the principal took part in the snowball battle, challenging all the children to defeat him. Four inches fell during that one event, and a storm of that magnitude has not occurred in our area in all the decades since.

Also during tenth grade, my new baby brother was born. With James Brewster Fredlund joining us, we were now a family of seven. Brewster was a family name, as my mother was a direct descendant of William Brewster, who served as the chaplain aboard the Mayflower that sailed from England in 1620.

Whenever I was home from school, I spent time tending to the new baby, treating him as if he were my very own offspring. My mother appreciated the assistance; she had no time for her own recovery as she quickly found herself pregnant again with a sixth child. This time, it did not go well. In her second trimester, she began to bleed regularly, and the doctor put her on bed rest so she could try to hold onto the new life she and my dad had created.

It didn't help. She had a miscarriage and nearly bled to death. The rest of us children were both scared and saddened, for we almost lost our mother. After coming home from the hospital, she entered a phase of severe depression. She refused to get out of bed, and she even started smoking cigarettes, which she had previously been adamant against. Her grief over her lost child took a long time to pass, and it was nearly a full year before she got out of bed and resumed a normal life again.

To help spur her healing, my father drove her one day to the animal shelter to choose a puppy. My mother selected a mixed breed with a heavy dose of collie genes, giving her the rather unoriginal name of Lassie. Despite my father's original intention, Lassie became my dog. I taught her to sit, lay down, stay, roll over and shake hands. She could even climb up the stairs of the metal slide in our neighborhood playground and thought it was a gas to slide down into my arms. Lassie and I went everywhere together, as did our cat Whiskers. The old feline would come along on our walks, trotting alongside Lassie and me just like any other dog.

Since there were no leash laws at that time, many of the other neighborhood canines liked to pay me visits as well. There was a Borzoi that grew lonely and would come sniffing around the house when her parents were at work. An overgrown boxer puppy named Thumper was another frequent visitor who loved to play with us. Whiskers loved to tease that dog. The cat would walk nonchalantly to the top of the street without looking back. Thumper couldn't help himself; he would rush up to chase the kitty, but Whiskers would wait to turn around until the boxer was almost upon him. Then the cat would launch himself at Thumper's face, grabbing it with all four paws and riding the panicked dog all the way back down the street. Thumper would yelp pitifully the entire distance, but he never learned. It might not have been the puppy's favorite game, but it was definitely Whiskers'.

One year, I was gifted an English budgie from a boy that was moving out of the neighborhood. Petey fell in love with me, as most parrots do with their owners. He was adorable, with black-and-white striped wings, cobalt blue breast feathers and a white forehead. Petey was also smart as a whip and rather fond of sitting on my shoulder and screeching "pretty birdie" into my ear. His favorite toy was a silver quarter, especially when I rolled it across the bedroom floor. Petey would leave his perch atop a curtain rod and dive-bomb the coin, grabbing it in his talons and then tossing it with his beak around the room. Finally, he would carry it back to me, place it in my hand and lean back to ask me to roll it for him again. He never grew tired of chasing it, even when I brought company to watch his antics.

One unfortunate day, when I was stroking the budgie's chest, I felt a small bump that hadn't been there before. When the vet told me that Petey had tumors and would not live much longer, I was a mess. I think he knew his time was short as well, for he would wait for me to come home from school and then scream to be let out of his cage so that he could be with me.

The day finally arrived when I opened the front door of my house and heard no screeches coming from the bedroom. Petey was clinging to the bars of his cage, hanging on with his beak with his last reserves of energy. I took him out, held him close and he chirped a few times. Then all of a sudden, he flew a loop around the room, landed in my hands and passed away. I was devastated.

Soon after, my father built an aviary for me in the backyard. He knew that I had a desire to breed and sell parakeets, and the enclosure was big enough for me to follow through on that dream. Eventually, I had twenty of them - all different colors - and I managed to sell quite a few for ten dollars apiece.

Word spread through the neighborhood that I was good with animals. A woman across the street ran up to me one evening and asked me to pull a dove out of the grill of her car. She had struck the bird while driving and only realized it was still alive once she'd reached home. Luckily, I was able to extract the dove and tend to her injuries. The first thing I learned was that she was a female because I could see her ovaries through a cut in her breast. I gave her water at first, then foods such as wild bird seed, fruits and vegetables. Until she grew stronger, I kept her in a cage and monitored her health. One month later, I released her into the garage and left the door open. She flew off to join her flock once more, and I felt happy, knowing that I had helped save a life.

Animals continued to be one of my passions through high school because, although I made friends, I wasn't that interested in spending my time socializing. I worked hard on my studies and found I had a talent for languages, excelling in English, Latin and Spanish. But music felt like my greatest calling. I spent a lot of time working on my clarinet technique in the band practice rooms or under the tutelage of my dad's friend Henry Brubeck. Mr. Brubeck was a great musician in his own right, and as a band leader, he knew how to bring out the best in all of us. I loved the performance aspect of music and never shrunk in front of an audience, so in my senior year, Mr. Brubeck chose me to play most of the solo parts. He thought I could coax one of the best tones out of a clarinet that he had ever heard, which was quite a compliment.

I finally graduated from San Marcos High in 1963 with grades good enough to secure me a place at Santa Barbara City College, provided I could afford the tuition. Many of my friends would be there, and I wanted to study music and psychology. With an Associate of Arts degree under my belt, I could transfer to UCSB if I desired. But none of this would be cheap.

I decided to continue living with my parents for the time being so I could save money. They didn't mind; they had just purchased a 28-foot Coronado sailboat that they named The Selina, and I became their go-to babysitter whenever they wanted to sail from the harbor to Goleta Beach. They'd anchor the boat offshore and spend hours alone, enjoying each other's company away from all the children.

Sometimes my dad would lend me his Renault Dauphin to get to City College. Otherwise, I'd take the bus. Part of the campus was situated atop a gorgeous mesa overlooking the Pacific Ocean. La Playa Stadium, with its track and field, lay at the foot of the mesa across from the harbor and Leadbetter Beach.

On the whole, college life was just plain fun. The music department was headed by Dr. Harold Dunn, another talented musician. I took classes in music theory, music history and piano, but I also joined

Dr. Dunn's two-hundred-voice choir because I loved to sing. I even set aside my clarinet for a time so that I could focus on my vocal talents. The choir was an amazing group of singers, and I helped Dr. Dunn by transposing many pieces of music. We undertook tours of Northern California, performing at music festivals, churches and even the Grace Cathedral in San Francisco. The forty-minute cantata Catulli Carmina was one of our more ambitious productions.

One day, all the students were told to gather in the Student Union cafeteria. The terrible news was that our beloved president, John Fitzgerald Kennedy, had been shot. My friends and I were emotional wrecks as we waited to hear if he would survive his wounds. He did not. It was a sad, sad day for our country, especially for us college students who had heavily supported his candidacy.

I suffered a personal loss that year as well. My wonderful cat Whiskers had lost the use of his kidneys. At the age of 13, he was worn out and had to be put to sleep. He had been the best companion, surviving all the moves across California as well as countless skirmishes with local felines. As an uncut tomcat, he had a bit of a wild streak, but he was also so loyal and loving to our family. I remembered him sitting by the hallway door, waiting for my mother to get distracted so that he could slip down to my bedroom for a nap. Whiskers would hide beneath the blankets on my bed, but my mom would get suspicious after not seeing him for a while. She didn't allow animals in the bedrooms, so she'd track him down, grab him by the scruff of his neck and haul him to the front door, spanking his bottom and shouting, "Bad kitty!" the whole time. Whiskers would lose house privileges for the rest of the day. Such a good friend... I would miss him dearly.

One of my pastimes at college was to sit with my friends Cathy and Virginia in the stadium bleachers and watch the football players practice for their upcoming games. Eventually, we decided it would be more fun to run around the track that circled the field, so that's what we did. The football team teased us mercilessly, but that didn't deter us. Running made us feel good.

We inquired with the athletics department about joining a women's track team, only to find there was none. So we started one up ourselves. Virginia trained in the hopes of racing in the Olympics someday, even though her buxom figure put her at a disadvantage. The pixieish girl Cathy practiced throwing her javelin on the football field, for that was her passion. She proudly carried her javelin everywhere. As for myself, I discovered I was a really fast sprinter, so I focused my training on the 100-yard dash.

There were also no shower facilities for women at that time, so we used the men's showers to rinse off before going to class. Their locker room always stank to high heaven, and one day, Virginia and I decided to make a cheeky statement on the matter. We bought a can of deodorant, gift-wrapped it and placed it in the quarterback's helmet. The next day, we went to take our showers and were stunned to see, taped to the chalkboard, a picture of a naked woman wearing nothing but a pair of track shoes. They'd done us one better!

Virginia wrote a poem to help push us toward our goals. The words I can remember are:

*Our lives are governed by a special dream*
*A dream only a few possess*
*It is a dream of glory and grandeur*
*A dream of ultimate success.*

*You see our dream is centered around*
*A medal shiny and gold*
*A medal with many memories*
*We can cherish as we grow old.*

*Our dream is to run for the Nation*
*Which we so dearly love*
*And to stand tall with pride under our flag*
*And the symbol of the dove.*

Eventually, our efforts caught the attention of the football and track coach. Opportunities blossomed outward from there. We were invited to several meets in Southern California, and the coach ordered us sets of beautiful track outfits so we could better represent City College. We felt so proud to wear them. During our second spring season, I won a bronze medal in the 100-yard dash and a gold medal in the 440-yard dash.

Our successes encouraged more women to join us, and soon our track team became an official part of the athletics department. Now, it's easy to see how Women's Track at City College would have been established sooner or later, but it's pleasant to think that three girls with dreams of the Olympics were the ones who got it started.

~

WHEN SUMMER CAME AROUND AFTER MY SECOND YEAR OF schooling, I went looking for a job to help my parents with their mortgage payments. Little did I know the extent that this detour would impose on my education.

In the back of the Jolly Tiger Restaurant on Chapala Street was a car wash, and I was assigned to scrub car windows. A woman named Penny and her husband Duane also worked there, and Penny and I became good friends, swapping stories while we washed windows inside and out. I loved the more tangible benefits of employment, like the steady wages and steady hours, so when the fall semester arrived, even though I only needed three credits to earn my associate's degree, I decided to keep working at the car wash. I intended to return to school at some point in the future, but life somehow caught up with me.

After a full year working at the downtown location, the owner, Al Vido, decided that I had a good mind for management and transferred me to the Goleta Car Wash to become their assistant manager. He bought me a fancy uniform, and I cashiered and kept charge of the books for quite a while, helping with window washing whenever the regular crew got too busy. In the course of my employment, I became close with his family, serving as a babysitter whenever Al and his wife wanted to leave town.

My life changed again when Al hired two girls from England to work on the line washing windows. They hailed from Reading, a large town west of London. Anna, a stoic, capable woman of Polish descent, had been sponsored by a family who needed nanny services for a year.

Linda was a short brunette who looked like she could be Ringo Starr's sister. She'd been sponsored by her sister and her sister's American husband, who sheltered her until she became eligible for a permanent visa. The three of us window-washers quickly became fast friends, and the energy of the car wash shifted dramatically in a positive direction. I felt a little separated from them because I was the assistant manager, so one day I made a bold choice: I quit my position and went back to working the car wash line with them. That decision brought us even closer.

We sang, danced and laughed while cleaning windows. Their favorite was to dance the jitterbug to a cheerleading ditty I'd learned in high school:

*Cuma walla, cuma walla, cuma walla viste*
*Cuma walla, cuma walla, cuma walla viste*
*Oh, no no no not the viste*
*Oh, no no no not the viste*
*Eenie meenie desi meeni ooh walla walla meenie*
*Hex a meeni, salla meenie ooh walla walla*
*Hex a meeni, salla meenie ooh walla wall*
*A bee billy otin dotin bo bo a ditten dottin*
*Shhhhhhhhhh!*
*A bee billy otin dotin bo bo a ditten dottin*
*Shhhhhhhhhh!*

Before long, Linda and Anna asked me to move into a two-bedroom apartment with them. It had just become available in the Westside neighborhood of Santa Barbara, and the apartment complex featured its own swimming pool. The idea sounded grand to me. I was twenty-one years old, in possession of a car for the first time - a used Austin Cambridge sedan - and starting to become jaded about living at home in Goleta with my parents. When I approached my mom and dad, they were thankfully supportive of the idea. Mom knew it was time for me to get on with my life, and my dad agreed to take care of the parakeets for me.

I was lucky to claim one of the bedrooms for myself; Anna and

Linda shared the other. My roommates and I shared many adventures together. We would run up to Cold Springs Tavern on the weekends and party all night with the owners. One of our frequent pastimes was to hang out in one of the restaurant bars on Fairview Avenue. Gentlemen looking for a quick score would buy us drinks in the hope of loosening our inhibitions, but it only served to loosen our tongues. The only score they'd receive was our stories, but those tales fascinated them enough that they kept the drinks flowing. My favorites were the elaborate fictions we concocted about being from the planet Mars. The three of us also frequented the local barber shop next to the car wash, and the gossip and anecdotes that we overheard there could have filled the pages of a second book.

Partly to help us stay out of trouble, we also took continuing adult education classes and joined their choir. I was thrilled to have another opportunity to perform for people. During one performance, I was chosen to sing one-half of a duet from the opera Hansel and Gretel, and my sister Meredith said it made her want to become a singer as well. The adult education choir was once chosen to help a traveling opera group put on a production of Madame Butterfly, and that was a great experience. The three-act opera was staged at the Granada Theatre, and our chorus received glowing reviews by the critics.

～

ONE DAY, KIP, THE CAR WASH MANAGER, ASKED ME IF I WANTED TO buy a horse. The fact was, I'd wanted a horse my entire life.

The animal in question was stabled close to the butterfly preserve in Ellwood. He was a beautiful thoroughbred chestnut with a flaxen mane who went by the name Viking - an appropriate moniker for the steed of a woman with Swedish ancestors. Kip told me I could make payments over the coming months, and we settled on a price of two hundred dollars. Little did I know that I was in for a real ride with this creature.

Viking was the Tasmanian devil of the horse world. Cinch-bound and barn sour, he knew every trick in the book on how to unseat an inexperienced rider.

The first day after we signed the paperwork, Kip took me for a ride on the beach. He had recently purchased an elegant saddlebred horse for his own usage, so Viking and I would have some equine companionship. I had no horse tack yet, so we searched around the tack room for a used bridle, and in the absence of a saddle, we found a blanket to lay across Viking's spine so I could ride bareback.

Being a complete novice, I thought everything was okay at first once we hit the beach. After a time, Kip suggested that I take Viking back to the stables so that I wouldn't get too sore from riding without a saddle. Then he rode off, leaving me alone with this giant, unpredictable animal that I knew nothing about.

No sooner had I attempted to turn Viking's head around than he threw his head back, striking me in the face and knocking off my glasses. I tried to grab them, and Viking's chin strap snapped. The horse sensed his opportunity immediately. He took the bit in his teeth and bolted down the beach.

At that point in my life, I had never ridden a horse apart from a few trail rides and never a horse anywhere as fast as that beautiful thoroughbred could run. This was an uncontrolled gallop, and if I fell off of him, I probably would not have survived the fall. I tucked my toes under his belly, trying to slow him down, but to no avail. The sand and the surf flew past me, and I screamed out to beachgoers for help. They could do nothing, but at least they scattered appropriately before they could be trampled.

Once I managed to control my fear, I finally was able to pull on the reins and turn Viking's head toward the deep sands of the upper beach. His hooves sank down, which slowed him to a walk. I got him to stop, and then I slid off his back. That was the wrong thing to do. Viking refused to let me mount him again. Kip was nowhere in sight, and since I wasn't sure of what else to do, I decided to walk Viking across the freeway to my parents' house so I could introduce them to my new pet.

That *also* turned out to be the wrong thing to do. I tied Viking to a tree in the front yard and excitedly called for my mother to come out and see who I'd brought. As soon as mom stepped out of the front door, my horse slipped out of his bridle and took off running down the street toward the freeway. Frantically, I ran into the house, grabbed an apple from the kitchen and a clothesline rope from the garage, then sprinted after him. Thank the lord that a fence had been erected along the freeway. I found Viking running back and forth along the fence-line, looking for a break in the barrier so that he could return to the stables.

I tried tempting my horse with the apple, but he wouldn't pause long enough for me to throw the clothesline around him. Finally, a man got out of his car to come help. He ran up to Viking as he galloped past, threw his arms around the horse's neck and slowed him to a walk. I gave Viking the apple to calm him down and fashioned a makeshift halter out of the thin rope. Using that, I was able to walk him across the Glen Annie overpass and back to the stables. A couple of flakes of hay, and Viking was mellow enough to allow me to kiss him goodbye.

His temper had soured again by the time I tried putting a real saddle on him, several days later. Someone must have worked the horse over at one time because whenever I attempted to reach underneath him to grab the cinch, he would freak out. A horse of Viking's size was dangerous to be around when he was being temperamental, and I was lucky to have help getting him ready for riding. After I finally managed to climb into the saddle, Viking promptly threw me into a fence. That hurt. I felt my torso carefully for broken ribs, but all I had sustained were some extensive bruises. I forced myself to scramble onto Viking's back once more, but my steed refused to leave the stable. A different tactic would have to be considered.

My parents couldn't offer much guidance. My mother, in particular, was afraid of horses. Viking somehow sensed this, and he would creep up behind her, lay his chin on her shoulder and blow a hard nicker. She'd scream, to my horse's delight, and then he'd walk away, snickering evilly to himself.

It became evident that I needed professional assistance. A friend of mine had a sister who owned a horse and boarded it on an eighty-acre spread at the top of Fairview Avenue in Goleta. After receiving the phone number, I dialed up George Stiny, the insurance broker who boarded horses to help him pay the ranch bills. Thankfully, Viking was accepted to join the resident herd. For sixty dollars a month, my steed would have his own stall, all the hay and grain he needed and eighty acres of grassy acreage to graze upon. It was a horse's paradise.

George offered to drive to Ellwood to pick up Viking in his trailer, but of course, the horse was afraid of trailers as well. He fought us on every attempt to drive him inside. We finally had to blindfold him to get him to step into the trailer. It was already dusk before we were able to release him into the herd of horses to get acquainted... too dark to see how his presence would be received. I'd have to wait until morning to learn the outcome.

I needn't have worried. Viking and the others seemed to get along fine. But because I was the new boarder, I was assigned the task of bringing the horses into the barn at the end of the day. When the time came, not a horse was in sight. I sighed, filled my pockets with carrots and started hiking up the hill. Hopefully, the carrots would be tempting enough to draw Viking in.

After cresting a rise, I spotted the herd, heads down, munching on the lush grass. They saw me coming. Viking, however, chose to walk up to be to receive the treats I carried. Before he could change his mind, I managed to do justice to the many hours of practice I'd undertaken, grabbing his mane and launching myself onto his back like a Native American from the Great Plains. The rest of the herd followed us back to the barn without protest.

George Stiny was a fine horseman himself. He noticed my difficulty in saddling Viking, as well as Viking's tendency to throw his head back and strike me in the face, and he told me that if I couldn't control my horse's behavior, I wasn't going to have any fun at all. To help me out, he and his ranch hands helped saddle Viking for me one day. Then George walked into the tack room and brought back a short whip called a quirt. "Next time that horse throws his head back, you bust him right between the ears with this, as hard as you can."

I looked at the quirt. The handle was very tough. I didn't want to hurt my horse, so I felt very squeamish. With great reluctance, I took George's advice. I mounted my horse and gave him a cue to start moving. Viking threw his head back, right on schedule. I immediately hammered Viking right between the ears with the handle. After that, I never had to hit my horse again. If he ever hesitated, all I had to do was lift my arm, and he thought better of it.

For the first time, Viking and I started to have fun together. He lost his "barn sour" personality where he was often reluctant to leave his stall, and we went on numerous adventures through the orchards surrounding Goleta. Anna and Linda came to the ranch sometimes to ride him. On rainy days when the carwash was closed, I would go to the ranch and hang out with Viking in his barn. Once, we even went riding in the rain. On one ambitious day, we rode all the way to the drive-through window of Durbiano Dairy on Hollister Avenue so I could buy myself an ice cream cone.

Viking always looked forward to his bucket of oats after a long ride. I made it a point to instruct him to get into his stall first, however. After taking off his tack, I'd say, "Get in your stall." He would shake his head, turn around, trot over to his corner of the barn and neigh excitedly. Only then would he receive his munchies.

Eventually, it became obvious that Viking was costing me money that I did not have. His veterinary bills outgrew my ability to afford him. Sadly, after one year, I put an ad in the paper and sold him to a young girl who lived in Hope Ranch. My horse lived out his days in a large, fenced corral, and I was still able to visit occasionally, pet him and feed him carrots. Despite missing the thrill of riding, I never owned another horse after that. Viking had been enough to satisfy my curiosity and needs. If I ever became wealthy enough to own a large property, I thought I might acquire some horses again. But my life and my fortunes never drifted in that direction.

Quite the opposite, in fact.

## ❧ 3 ❧

## THE STALKER

A t age twenty, I was still somewhat naive about the country at
large, but I was tremendously enjoying the possibilities of life,
and I couldn't wait to see what else fate had in store for me.
In time, however, the dark reality of being an attractive young female
in a male-dominated world made itself glaringly known.

It began when I acquired my first stalker.

Back when I worked at the Santa Barbara car wash location, the
crew boss was a handsome man by the name of Ken. He looked like
the Marlboro Man that appeared on billboards across town, except
that in person he came across as a little desperate rather than suave.
The few times I interacted with him, I went away feeling uneasy.
When Al Vido decided to close the Santa Barbara location and just
retain the Goleta property, Ken showed up at my workplace looking
for a job. Times were slow, so Al couldn't hire him. Unfortunately, I
caught Ken's eye again, and before long, I became the man's new
obsession.

Ken had been married to a woman named Donna, but something
had gone wrong with their relationship, and she was now out of the
picture. An all-too-familiar story. The stalking began once Ken discov-

ered where Linda, Anna and I lived at our Westside apartment. He started stopping by every day to hang out. In the beginning, it was just on the weekends when my roommates and I liked to rest up for the coming work week. He had a bad habit of pushing his way into our home without calling first to warn us he was going to show up.

Anna and Linda were very protective of me at those times. They knew I wasn't interested in getting tied down in a relationship. We quickly grew tired of him and sought out alternative places to relax without male company. Ken was forced to change his game; he'd sit in the parking lot of our apartment building in his Nash Rambler and wait for us to drive off so that he could follow. We had to get more creative and sneaky each time we left home, just to elude him.

Then Ken landed a job delivering newspapers in the early morning hours, which enabled him to continue stalking me in the daytime. He started sleeping in his car, maintaining a near-constant presence outside the apartment. And his wife was still nowhere to be seen.

At least the Goleta car wash was a safe space where I had supportive male allies. One day, I was called into the office and introduced to a man named Paul - a family friend of the owner. He was a middle-aged businessman, overweight and amiable, and he had the idea of selling car wash ticket booklets to our customers. The scheme would guarantee return business from our patrons, which made sense. The manager wanted to run the idea by me first, but I had no objections. In fact, I started pushing the coupon books at the cashier's counter, and I even approached customers who were waiting for their cars to be finished.

Paul and I became great friends over time. He was kind and gentle, and we talked for hours about life. Eventually, he trusted me enough to tell me his real name: Vic Tanny, the owner of the Vic Tanny Gym franchise.

Vic was a bodybuilder who opened his first gymnasium in New York in 1935. He sold it four years later and moved to Santa Monica, California, which became the hub of an exercise gym empire. Each of the gyms under his name were modern and inviting, and they were also among the first to allow women through their doors. His businesses flourished in the 1950s and early 1960s, but an aggressive expansion strategy, along with poor franchise management, forced Vic to declare bankruptcy. That was why he'd been available to help Al Vido.

I also learned that my boss was the son of a prominent Italian businessman. Al preferred to keep his professional and family lives separate, but when his car washes had begun to struggle financially, forcing the closure of the Santa Barbara location, his father sent Vic to help turn things around. And it worked; the coupon books were a hit, and they helped bring in more repeat customers.

I was never one to become enamored by celebrities, so discovering Vic's true identity didn't affect our friendship at all. We even exercised together. I had started jogging at the track at San Marcos High School on weekends since I was no longer a City College student. Vic had gained a lot of weight, and I think being out-of-shape was a little embarrassing for the former Mr. America, so eventually, he asked if he could come to the track and work out with me. We jogged together until he found enough motivation to run on his own. When he managed to jog his first 440-yard lap without stopping, the man was ecstatic.

During this time, I also met a young Japanese man named Tommy who had emigrated from Okinawa and was hired to work at the car wash. We all loved the heck out of him, for he was a true gentleman. The two of us went for long walks on the beach together. He was handsome and kind, and I loved him dearly. I also knew that he wanted to marry me, but that didn't sit well with my father. Dad became very upset that I was running around with a person from Japan - his World War II enemy - and he concocted a plan to get me out of Santa Barbara for a time.

My dad asked me if I would help him drive to Connecticut to pick up my mother, who had recently flown to Bristol to visit her family. I agreed to help him, and I told Tommy that I would be back in a couple of weeks. When I finally returned, however, my boyfriend was gone. He had left Santa Barbara to join the Marines. I was upset at first, though I eventually understood Tommy's reasoning. My father would never have given his blessing, and because I'd kept Tommy waiting for a while, it made sense for him to cut his losses and get on with his life. Sad, but understandable.

Soon afterward, Al Vido's father showed up at the car wash in a limousine to retrieve Vic Tanny and take him back to Florida. I didn't even have a chance to say goodbye. Vic spent his remaining years in Tampa with the rest of the Vido clan and passed away from a heart attack at age 73.

It was hard to lose all these positive male figures from my life, especially when Ken was still lurking in the shadows, waiting for his chance to slip in. The stress felt overwhelming at times. Fortunately for my mental health, while I'd been traveling to Connecticut, Anna and Linda came across the recreational drug known as "Mary Jane". They introduced it to me, perhaps as a means to distract me from my broken heart, but I was frightened and alarmed and did not want it in our apartment. At that time, you could be sent to the State Penitentiary for an automatic seven years for the possession of just one joint. "Bury it in the backyard," I told them. That remained my position until I was finally convinced to try it.

I had always been plagued by stress, and marijuana proved to be the best medicine for me. I hated alcohol and didn't like what it did to my friends. Whenever we'd host a party at the apartment, I would just sip on a soda. But this drug was different. The smoke soothed me, although I remained paranoid about being discovered by the authorities. We only smoked indoors, behind closed curtains and only with trusted acquaintances.

I loved my friends deeply, but after a full year spent living and working together, fate began to pull us apart. A surfer named Jay stole Anna's heart, and she moved into a trailer on the Eastside so she could better take care of him. Linda and I found a small cottage on Victoria Street next to the freeway that we could better afford. It cost seventy-five dollars a month and was furnished with an antique refrigerator, an equally-ancient couch and one bed. I took the surprisingly-comfortable couch and let Linda have the bed.

The best part was that Ken didn't know about the cottage at first, so we enjoyed a few days of peace. It didn't last. He soon found us again, and the stalking continued. He'd be leaning against his car, smoking a cigarette when I walked outside to go to work in the morning, and then usually when I came home at the end of the day. To stay on friendly terms, I would engage Ken in minimal conversation, but whenever I asked him to leave, he simply ignored me. I was 21 years old at the time and had never had a physical relationship before. I'd had plenty of crushes over the years, but the thought of being tied down to a steady boyfriend was not what I thought I needed.

The one crucial night when I really could have used his company, however, Ken was nowhere to be found.

That evening, Linda and I were relaxing at the Victoria cottage, smoking a joint and giggling about life's experiences when our front door was kicked in. A co-worker from the Santa Barbara car wash who I hadn't seen in nine months barged into our apartment, drunk, belligerent and unintelligible. He ran over to the cupboards and started pulling out dishes, pots and pans and smashing them against the walls and furniture. The two of us crouched into the corner, absolutely petrified.

His name was Duane - the husband of my good friend Penny. The two of them had always made an unlikely pair; he was a thin, wiry man with a Southern accent, while she was a fun-loving brunette of Chumash descent. I loved Penny and tolerated her husband for her benefit. However, after the Santa Barbara car wash location closed, Penny traveled north to San Luis Obispo to visit her parents and she never returned. That's probably when things started to go terribly wrong with Duane, and tonight felt like the culmination of the man's emotional breakdown.

After the smashing paused and Duane's anger settled momentarily, I was able to ask him what was wrong and why he was doing this to us. I knew he was upset that Penny had left him, but I didn't know why he was here in our house, right now. Duane wasn't able to give us a logical answer; instead, he demanded that I go outside with him or else he would continue to destroy our cottage, piece by piece. He even threatened to hurt us if we tried to call the police.

Thinking that Duane just wanted to talk, I told him I would go with him. I was always ready to help a friend, or in this case, a friend's husband, but I should have known better. I thought I could somehow trust him, but I still had a lot to learn.

He took me to the beach and held me down while he had his way with me. I cried and cried, telling him to stop, but he ignored me and kept on.

Afterward, he walked a very depressed and shocked woman home and left me there. Linda had left to visit Anna, so I had no one to talk to. I swept up the shattered pieces of crockery, smoked six joints and drank copious amounts of wine until I threw up. *How could I have made the mistake of going outside with him?* Just like any other woman, I blamed myself for what had happened. I had no idea how to fix myself or to achieve justice. My one solace was that over the long term, I had Anna and Linda to help me through any repercussions. But the anger... that never faded.

I saw Duane only one other time after the incident. He came by the car wash and asked me to drive with him to San Luis Obispo to pick up Penny. I knew that if my friend had wanted to be with Duane, she would have returned to Santa Barbara a long time ago. Regardless, I told him in no uncertain terms that I wouldn't be going with him anywhere ever again. He left, but I was still shaken and afraid for my own safety.

Meanwhile, Linda was reaching the end of her rope with my stalker, Ken. She told me that he had to go, and I agreed. However, when I informed Ken that he could not visit us any longer, he simply started sleeping in his car outside of the cottage.

Linda lasted a few more months, but she finally decided she'd had enough. She found her own trailer to rent on the Eastside, closer to Anna. I was both saddened and a little frightened for the future. Being raped had affected me deeply. Though I was strong for my size, I was still thin and unable to fight off a man like Duane on my own. All of a sudden, it felt safer having Ken close at hand and on my side than to be constantly pushing him away.

Ken's stubborn persistence also wore me down. I accepted an offer to join him on his nighttime route as he delivered newspapers for the Santa Barbara News-Press. Riding around in the Nash Rambler and leaning out of the window to hurl papers into driveways was a fairly good time. I invited him inside once or twice to use the shower after I came home from the car wash. Eventually, I gave in and let Ken crash for the night. He promptly moved his belongings inside and made himself right at home.

Since the cottage was just a studio apartment, I moved back to the couch and let Ken take the bed. The couch was a lot more comfortable anyways. After a month's time, we progressed from an unsteady friendship into an actual relationship.

Ken wanted to take things in a physical direction, but when I told him about Duane and the depression that I had suffered from that experience, he backed off. It angered him that I had been subjected to such trauma, and he waited for me to settle and become comfortable before we started having sex.

It proved to be a terrible decision, but I quit my job at the car wash. Ken said he would take care of me, and in the 1960s, men were supposed to be the breadwinners of every household. Women were meant to be housewives. Like my mother, I thought this was my proper role in our relationship. When Ken invited his boss over to visit, my job was to serve coffee and food and keep them happy.

The first of many negative incidents occurred when I started itching. I couldn't understand why I wasn't getting any relief when I took a shower. Finally, Ken looked up at me one night and said that he had crabs. "What the heck are crabs?" I asked him. Crabs, it turns out, were a type of pubic lice, and I was just covered with them. Either Ken had acquired them from some other sexual partner, or they had come with the furniture when Linda and I moved in - one of the wonderful experiences that can occur with pre-furnished, low-income housing.

I took charge of the situation immediately. Instead of going to the doctors and taking medication to get rid of them, which could have cost more money than we had, I took us to the store to buy a bottle of rubbing alcohol and some shavers. I knew we had to destroy the environment that the crabs thrived in, so I shaved both of us below the waist and cleaned us off with the alcohol. Ken balked at shaving off his chest hair, which infuriated me to no end. His masculine self-image seemed more important than getting rid of all possible nesting grounds for the little pests. Thankfully, the treatment, plus multiple rounds of laundry, proved effective in eradicating the infestation.

The twisted personality that had led Ken to become a stalker began to emerge in other aspects of our relationship. He threw temper tantrums when he couldn't get his way. He'd kick my puppy and stick my parakeet Amos' head in a glass of gin to see if he could get the bird drunk. When I finally spoke to Ken about marriage, I learned that he was still legally married to Donna. I wanted to ask him if he intended to get divorced, but the look in his eyes convinced me to drop the subject.

Next, Ken began to separate me from my family and friends. He went ballistic whenever I wanted to go anywhere without him, and eventually, he took away my means of doing so. After the brakes on his Nash Rambler failed, Ken claimed my Austin Cambridge as his method of work transportation. It didn't take long for my dear car to be ruined, for he took his frustrations out on the vehicle with regularity.

Eventually, Ken quit his job because he couldn't stand to let me out of his sight. I felt isolated and so terribly alone. I knew that I needed to figure out how to get rid of the man, but at the same time, I feared his temper. I tried to keep him happy at all costs, but slowly and surely, things became worse. *Was this what a relationship is supposed to be like?* I asked myself late at night, staring at the ceiling.

I needed my mom and dad, but once my mother learned I was living with a man out of wedlock, she wanted nothing more to do with her daughter. Anna and Linda were still out there, though, and I missed them tremendously. So one afternoon, I waited for Ken to take a nap, and then I snuck out of the house, caught a bus and jumped out at the Goleta car wash. Anna and Linda were thrilled to see me. We were chatting and laughing up a storm when Ken pulled up in his Nash Rambler. It was in bad shape, and he shouldn't have been driving it because the emergency brake was broken and only the drum brakes were functional. He jumped out of the car, grabbed me and called me a bitch and a whore, screaming at the top of his lungs at my friends and everyone else at the car wash who dared to speak to him. "If you ever leave like that again," he told me, "it will be the end of you!" Scared and mortified, I allowed Ken to drag me into the vehicle, and the tires squealed as we tore away from the car wash.

Considering the condition of the brakes, the speed at which Ken took us down the freeway was suicidal. I curled up into a ball on the floorboards in a desperate act of preservation. That was enough to snap Ken out of his haze of fear and anger. He slowed the car down to a reasonable speed, but I still knew the man was out of control. Something had to change.

Soon, we ran out of money, as well. We were eating egg sandwiches three times a day and had no funds to pay the rent, so one morning I dressed in my best clothes and told Ken that I was going out to look for a job. I asked him to watch the pets while I was gone. Normally, Ken would have thrown a fit about me leaving without him, but I suspect his hunger finally convinced him to hold his tongue. I think he also knew that I had reached my breaking point.

I found a job in Goleta at a processing plant called Mission Country Photo. They developed negatives and made prints from rolls of film sent from drug stores and photo shops all over the county. One problem though: I didn't have a car to get to work. Ken had destroyed my Austin Cambridge out of anger and sheer possessiveness, and I had to show up at 11 p.m. each night to operate the black-and-white printing machine so that the prints could be packaged and shipped out in the morning. Buses weren't running at that late hour, so my options were limited.

At first, I walked to the processing plant, even though the trip took me three hours. I didn't mind traveling at night, but my boss worried about me. He set me up with a car salesman friend of his, and even though I couldn't afford a down payment, we worked out a deal that allowed me to start driving to work in a used AMC Rambler.

I was free... or so I thought. Right away, Ken decided to take me to work, sleeping in the Rambler overnight just so he could control my comings and goings. My boss found it strange, but as long as it didn't affect my work, he let it slide.

Receiving my first paycheck was a big moment. I was so tired of starving. I cashed the check and immediately went shopping for groceries - steaks, salad, rice, beans, potatoes and just about everything

I had craved for so long. There was enough left over to pay for a month's rent at the cottage, too. I cooked up a feast that night, although all Ken could do was whine that I hadn't bought him a fishing pole so that he could go fishing. The lack of gratitude was stunning.

I loved my job and I excelled at printing operations, so they decided to move me to the more-complicated color printer. Then my boss asked me if I had any friends who could work for the company. I happily gave Anna a call. She couldn't stand the car wash anymore, so she hustled over to sign up. When I learned that Mission Country Photo needed a delivery person, I reached out to Linda, and soon our womanly trio was reunited.

I did not extend the employment invitation to Ken, as much as we could have used the income. I was actively trying to get rid of him at this point, and his constant presence outside the building was bad enough. Also, my boss was unnerved by the man and probably wouldn't have hired him anyway due to his unmistakably obsessive behavior.

Ken was depressed, psychotic and acting out with increasing regularity. My feelings for him had never evolved into anything deeper than friendship, and even *that* was stretching the definition of the term. If I was going to be able to unload this man, a constructive first step would be to find him a job so he could start taking care of himself.

One day, I sat Ken down and asked what he would like to do for a profession. He had no idea, so I set up a test for him to take at the Unemployment Office in order to learn what he was best qualified for. The fact that he agreed to take the test was an encouraging sign.

The results pointed toward some kind of outdoor job. I scanned through a list of positions that might cater to his strengths until I found one that felt promising. "What about a Forest Ranger?" I asked him. "There are schools that can teach you how to become one."

For the first time, Ken started to get excited about the process, especially once I said I would love to be the wife of a Forest Ranger. We found a school in Susanville, tucked into the woods in the remote, northeastern corner of the state. "A beautiful place," I told him. I said he could start his classes up there, while I'd save up for a truck. Then I'd load up my things and join him in Susanville for a change of scenery.

I was truly shocked that he trusted me this way, but also scared that he might guess my true intentions.

As fate would have it, the day Ken left on a bus for Northern California was the day I realized I was pregnant. I knew immediately because I became terribly sick. The pregnancy itself wasn't surprising, since my doctor had refused to prescribe birth control pills to unmarried women. It was bound to happen at some point, and now that it had, I was more or less on my own. Access to safe abortions performed by real doctors was unheard of among my friends.

I was still twenty-one years old, frightened and unsure of my next steps. The one thing I knew, at least, was that I needed to hide the fact of my pregnancy from Ken. There was no way I could stand being paired with that psychopath for the rest of my life.

Ken's Easter vacation was swiftly approaching, however. I knew that because I had failed to come to Susanville, Ken would travel all the way down to Santa Barbara to look for me. It was time for hard decisions. I gave my parakeet Amos to my sister Meredith and a newly-adopted puppy named Princess to another friend. Then I called up my girlfriend Penny, who had moved up to San Luis Obispo after her breakup with her husband, Duane. I told her my situation, and to her credit, she immediately drove down to Santa Barbara to help me pack. She offered to let me stay with her and her parents, and I gratefully accepted.

After a week of settling into the new town, I got a job at a laundromat. It was hard work for a pregnant woman, but I had told Penny's mother that I'd pay the rent on their apartment. One of the rules she laid down, however, was that I had to call my parents and tell them what had happened. I'd been reluctant to do so, particularly because my mother held deeply-set moralistic attitudes about life. To my surprise, however, my mom showed a great deal of compassion. She'd been awfully worried about me after I'd dropped out of contact.

Unfortunately, I lost the AMC Rambler. Amid the move, I'd been unable to make payments, and the car loan issuer came to the house and reclaimed it. At least the laundromat was within walking distance, so in the short term, I wasn't too inconvenienced.

During this time, I also chose to give the baby up for adoption. It was a heart-wrenching decision, but I was only twenty-two years old and unprepared to raise a child all by myself. I applied for welfare and medical assistance, but there was an awkward moment when the application required me to include the whereabouts of the father. Uncertain, I wrote down the address for the Forest Service school in Susanville, even though I cringed at doing so. It had taken me so long to shake Ken, and I didn't want to risk bringing him back into my life. Unfortunately, I needed government help to deliver the baby, and this application was the only way I could get it.

The welfare department had a legal obligation to contact the father, and Ken promptly wrote them a letter in response that cast him in the role of the ideal parent. It detailed how much he wanted to take care of me and the baby and was stuffed with all kinds of juicy garbage that he had made up in his mind. When the welfare worker read the letter to me, it sent chills up the back of my neck. I told the representative about everything that Ken had put me through… how Ken's psychopathic personality could appear rational at times, at least until his temper blew, and then he became a different person entirely. "Do you really want me to live with a man like that? Why do you think I am alone?" I asked the worker. The idea of being reunited with Ken was way too frightening to contemplate.

Thankfully, the social worker recognized how scared I was, and he opened up a new case for my benefit. He agreed that putting the baby up for adoption was the right choice. It seemed like the only way I could keep myself from getting saddled with Ken again or stuck in a family situation with him. It was the right decision for the baby, too; I didn't want my son or daughter to develop psychopathic tendencies as a result of growing up around their birth father.

Life in San Luis Obispo went well for a while, but instinctively, I knew I was not safe from Ken or his highly-refined stalking abilities. If my ex-boyfriend came to Santa Barbara, he'd eventually learn that I'd moved up north. I confided in Penny's mother about my fears, and the woman said that whatever happened, she'd be there to protect me.

Unfortunately, Penny herself would not be there. After I'd lived in the house for a few months, my good friend moved out of her parents' place and back in with her husband Duane, who had returned to town in order to pursue his wife once more. It shocked me; I had no idea they were even in contact with each other. I couldn't understand why she did it. I still hated Duane with a purple passion, and the fact that I felt unable to tell Penny about the rape also drove an emotional wedge between us.

I felt sad and a little betrayed. The idea of seeing Duane again seemed utterly repulsive, so I called my parents and told them that I had no reason to continue living in San Luis Obispo. I gave the laundromat two weeks' notice, then rode the bus back to Santa Barbara and stayed with my parents.

Penny's mother gave me a call a few weeks later. Ken had shown up on her doorstep, asking for me. Thankfully, she'd refused to tell him where I'd gone.

Somehow, I managed never to encounter that man again. The plan had worked. There's a chance I actually helped Ken find his purpose in life. I would like to think that he ended up in a better place, but considering how hard it had been to get rid of the guy, there's no way I would ever risk contacting him to find out.

～

LIVING BACK HOME AGAIN FELT STRANGE, BUT NECESSARY, considering my circumstances. Apart from my twelve-year-old sister Meredith and six-year-old brother Jimmy, my other brother Billy was sharing the house as well, having been released from the military on a medical discharge. He'd become addicted to PCP while in the service, and it had messed up his brain, causing him to appear catatonic at times, though he would laugh maniacally at other moments. Billy had already suffered through chemical withdrawal at the Navy hospital, but his other symptoms took many months to subside. I sat with my brother whenever he lay unresponsive on the couch and spoke gently to him, reassuring him of our love and support.

After two months, my parents decided that I needed my own place to live. The house was feeling a bit crowded, but I suspect that my mother didn't want the neighborhood to discover that her daughter was pregnant out of wedlock. That wouldn't have been easily accepted in the 1960s.

They found me a one-bedroom apartment in Isla Vista, which welfare helped me pay for. It was a lonely existence, living there. I felt like I was under a kind of moral quarantine. For companionship, I had only the remnants of the flock of parakeets that my father had taken care of for the last few years. Only two birds had remained in the aviary, and their presence was a poor substitute for my family and former pets.

To alleviate my isolation, I wandered into the pound one day and rescued a small black kitten with a white patch of fur on his chest. He was fond of climbing atop the parakeet cage and staring down at the birds. I'd have to chastise him and tell him that scaring the parakeets was taboo... and that became his name: Taboo.

Taboo was an exceptionally-smart kitten, and he learned a lot of tricks just as a puppy would. He knew the commands for *up* and *down,* as well as how to sit and shake paws. While I sat knitting a sweater for the baby, I would throw balls of yarn across the room. Taboo would trot over, pick them up in his mouth and deliver them to me. I loved him immensely.

Still, it was easy to become bored. I was six months along in my pregnancy with little to do. My mother would come to visit occasionally, but otherwise, I found myself walking along the streets of Isla Vista to pass the time.

Another visitor was Ross - Ken's old supervisor from the Santa Barbara News-Press who had come over for coffee and dinner sometimes when Linda and I lived on Victoria Street. He seemed like a good man, just four years older than me, but he always wore the same jacket and tended to avoid baths, so he was usually a little stinky. I'd tease him about it, but it seemed like a hard habit for him to break.

During one visit, I asked him if I could deliver newspapers for a couple of months. He managed to find me a route in Isla Vista, and he also lent me a red and white Chevy truck to use for the duration. That was truly kind of him. I enjoyed my mobility and was able to add to my monthly welfare check.

As the due date grew near, I gave up the route and returned the vehicle so I could prepare for the baby's arrival. When I went into labor, I immediately called my mother so she could drive me to the hospital, but no one picked up the phone. It was a frightening moment. I found myself second-guessing my decision to give the baby up for adoption. If I'd kept the father around, I would have had some measure of support at this critical time. But ditching Ken was the right thing to do for both me and the child. I just needed to take a deep breath and think of who else to call.

I was finally able to get in touch with my brother, who took our father's Peugeot sedan over to see me. Billy's brain was still getting over the effects of PCP, but his presence at my side helped to ease my panic. Although I was in active labor, I was still not close to giving birth, so we chose to wait in my apartment for a bit. After an hour, my mother came home from shopping, saw the message Billy had left for her, and drove immediately to Isla Vista to take me to the Goleta Valley Hospital.

Baby Fredlund came into the world on October 28th, 1968, that same evening. She looked just like her father. Even her screams sounded the same to my ears. I was overcome by an instinctual need to keep my baby. I cried out to the nurses that I wanted to stop the adoption. That scared the adoption agency, who had come to the hospital to ensure that the baby was healthy and a good candidate for the family they'd chosen for her.

As I held my baby girl, they sat beside my bed and told me the child would be going to parents who were unable to have kids of their own. They had already adopted a boy, so Fredlund would have a brother for companionship. Her new mother played the organ in a church, so if Fredlund had acquired a genetic disposition toward music from her birth mother, she would have an opportunity to shine in that field. I began to feel better about releasing her to this new family.

Then my mother came into the room and said that *she* wanted to adopt the baby. "No!" I told her. I had to put my foot down. I could not envision a life where my daughter grew up to become my sister, even if that would give me the opportunity to keep Fredlund close.

The next day, I watched through the window of my hospital room as my little girl was placed into a car and driven away. I knew that I would never see her again, for in those days, closed adoptions were the law of the land. She was going to be a beautiful woman someday, for her father was very handsome. I would think about her for the rest of my life, and every October 28th, I would quietly celebrate my child's birthday. Sometimes, my thoughts would be regretful, but mostly I just hoped she was leading a good life, full of health and vitality. And some-times I would grin, wondering if she was occasionally giving her parents a hard time like I had.

## ❧ 4 ❧

## A MARRIAGE OF INCONVENIENCE

On the third day after giving birth, I sat in my mother's living room and sobbed with grief. I missed my baby so, so much. Thankfully, my mom was there to comfort me. I also took to heart the words of my father: "No matter what your station is in life, you hold your head up high and go ever forward." It was hard to summon the strength to pull back from this overwhelming sense of loss, but I wiped away my tears, looked up at my mother and told her that I needed to find a job. A new life had to begin, and I had to get my independence back.

Searching the newspapers, I found an ad that would soon launch my career in the book industry. The family-owned Osborne's Book Store on State Street was looking for help with their financials, so I worked in the office with the Osborne patriarch for a while, learning their accounting system. The work grew tedious rather quickly, and after a month, I asked if I could work the floor and deal with customers instead. Graciously, they allowed me to switch to a role that better suited my talents. I was quite good at selling books and cashiering, for I excelled at talking and listening to people.

The minimum wage job allowed me to rent a small studio at the back of the Westside apartment complex where I'd lived with Anna and Linda. At the time, very few people needed to pay more than a third of their salary to be able to live in Santa Barbara. By the twenty-first century, no one in the city could afford to rent a studio on a minimum wage income, let alone a place that came with a swimming pool, like the Westside apartments. But in 1968, I only had to pay eighty dollars a month to stay there.

Since I was doing so well, I decided I would return to City College to finish up my Associate of Arts degree. I only needed a few last science credits, so I registered for night school, penciling in three evenings a week so I could finally earn my diploma.

One day, Ross, the man who had given me the newspaper route while I was pregnant, walked into Osborne's Book Store and asked me if I could help him with his newspaper delivery business. I told him it would have to wait at least a month so my body could recover from the physical exertion of having a baby. Mainly, I wanted to continue my life as an independent woman, and I suspected that Ross might have romantic intentions toward me. Although I appreciated his friendship, I wasn't ready to get bogged down in another relationship.

Ross persisted, however. He came by the bookstore every once in a while, bringing me beautiful gifts like watches or lockets, which led to embarrassing moments and a fair amount of teasing by my co-workers.

After a few weeks, I relented and started working for Ross again. I helped him deliver copies of the Los Angeles Times in the early morning hours using the same Chevy truck as I did previously. Then I did my shift at the bookstore. I had a short amount of time to eat dinner and read my college textbooks before my night classes began. After a few hours of sleep, I'd wake up at 2:30 a.m. to begin the workday again. Suffice it to say, I was beginning to run myself ragged, which wasn't good for a woman recovering from pregnancy.

Then one evening, I came home from work and was shocked to discover that Ross had moved himself into my studio apartment. I had no idea how he had gotten the keys to my place, but there he was, sitting in my chair, watching the television that he'd brought with him. His clothes were already arranged in my closet. I couldn't take it. I walked out of the house and hid among the sandstone boulders of

Mission Creek where no one would be able to find me. I needed a few moments to consider what to do about this strange wrinkle that felt disturbingly similar to my early situation with Ken.

I didn't want to live with anyone, and I'd had no clue this was going to happen. But I was also too exhausted to have a fight about it right then and there. I crashed on the couch, just like I had when Ken moved in with me, and I remained there until it was time to go to work at 2:30 a.m. again.

The following day, I assessed the recent developments and decided I was okay seeing where things would lead. Ross and I were working together anyway, and it would help to have another roommate contributing to the rent. I didn't have sex with him or engage with him romantically for a long time, however. It wasn't that I wished to remain celibate; I just wanted a better idea of how a relationship with the man would pan out first.

My stress levels made it difficult to make rational decisions, however. I was eating only one meal a day and drinking immense amounts of coffee just to remain functional. One afternoon, I was sitting at home, trying to study for a biology exam. My mind was so exhausted that I couldn't concentrate. The fact that my brain was unable to process the words on the page actually scared me. I stood up and threw my biology book clear across the room. It bounced off the wall, and by the time the textbook hit the floor, I knew that something had to give.

I had already quit jogging because I lacked the time. Night school was just too much to manage with my work schedule, so I withdrew from City College. Maybe down the road I could reapply once I saved up and didn't have to work two jobs to be able to afford tuition.

One evening not long after, I was sitting at the counter of the Jolly Tiger Restaurant next to Ross when I blacked out. My body fell to the floor. As I climbed back into consciousness, Ross helped me to my feet, but my limbs were shaking and shivering uncontrollably. We went straight to the emergency room, and after a couple of tests, I was diagnosed as suffering from simple stress and exhaustion.

Once I was told what was wrong with me, the fear dissipated. The doctor wrote me a prescription for Valium, but after he handed it to me, I promptly tore up the paper and threw the pieces at his feet. Doctors in the Sixties were prescribing "Mother's Little Helper" to nearly every housewife in America, but there was no way I was going to allow myself to become addicted to another chemical. As it was, I was already smoking a pack of cigarettes a day. I didn't need another crutch... I just needed a vacation.

First, I went home and arranged to take the next day off from the bookstore. Then I spent twenty-four hours in bed, with limited trips to the bathroom and kitchen. It did me a world of good.

To further my recovery, I took a full week off from work and went to visit my old childhood friend Doris in Barstow. We'd kept in touch over the phone all this time, and she was very excited to see me, especially because her husband had been called up by the military and she was feeling quite lonely. It was great to relax and feel like a human again, and the week flew by far too quickly.

After my vacation was over, the Greyhound bus dropped me off in downtown Santa Barbara. I walked the block-and-a-half to the Jolly Tiger, figuring that Ross would stop by before long and take me home. By now, Ross and I had become romantically intertwined. I had given in to his advances, having grown to like his company over the last few weeks. I even developed a bit of a crush on him, despite having to still harass him to take a shower once in a while. He wore his hair in the slicked, "jelly roll" style that was popular at the time and always wore his jacket and flip-flops, even in winter. The man suffered from a lot of tooth infections, though... probably because of all the soda bottles he went through. He'd also drink half-and-half straight out of the carton. But despite his flaws, Ross was a good worker. He showed up to facilitate his newspaper contract jobs every day, and I never had to fear that he would stop working like Ken had.

When Ross came into the Jolly Tiger and sat down at my table, I could already tell something was up. He was acting a little strange, so I asked him what was wrong. That's when he told me his ex-wife was coming into town.

*That's weird,* I thought. But then my mind flashed back to one afternoon, weeks ago, when Ross had told me of his dream of living with two women. He had it all figured out. One would live in each of two bedrooms, and he would hop back and forth, giving each woman a little rugrat to raise. The idea went over as well as one could imagine. I wished him well in his fantasy, but I said he was insane if he thought I would want to take part in it.

Ross had dropped the subject, but now I realized that, weeks later, he was still trying to manipulate me into agreeing to his plans.

I glared at him from across the restaurant table. "So, where is Linda going to stay?" His ex had the same name as my British friend.

"I'll get her a motel room," he promised.

That sounded fine. But when the day of Linda's arrival from New Mexico came and Ross told me he had to pick her up at the Greyhound station, I knew that he had not made any provisions for her.

"Just bring her to the apartment," I said. Whatever my feelings were on the matter, I didn't want the young woman sleeping out on the streets somewhere.

When the two of them walked through the front door a short time later, I got my first glimpse of this other woman. Linda was a petite, blue-eyed blond... pretty enough, but she wore a look of extreme confusion on her face. It was time for me to head to work delivering the Los Angeles Times, so I gave her my apologies, told her to make herself at home, and left for the night.

When my route was over, I returned home to change and get ready for my shift at the bookstore. Linda had slept on the couch, and she still seemed as confused as before about the situation. I suspected that Ross had lured her here under false pretenses, and I felt bad for her. The two of them had gotten married in Mexico a few years earlier, but during an extended honeymoon in Portland, Ross purchased a trailer and abandoned her to go off on solo adventures too many times. Linda's father rescued her and bribed some Mexican officials to get the marriage annulled. That should have been the end of it, but it seemed that Ross still had his hooks in the young lady somehow.

After a few days of Linda's uncomfortable presence, I took my blankets and pillow out to my work truck and slept on the front seat. Ross was angry, but I couldn't take the stress of my two jobs and Linda too. I needed peace and privacy, which were sorely lacking in our tiny studio.

One morning a couple of days later, I twisted my back during my newspaper route and tweaked a nerve that caused excruciating pain. I tried to work my shift at Osborne's bookstore, but by the middle of the day, I had to admit to my boss that I was hurting too much to continue. I staggered painfully to the Jolly Tiger where Ross was holding court with his cronies, and I begged him to drive me home. He seemed rather frustrated by my request, though I didn't discover the reason until later.

Ross dropped me off at the studio and left again. Linda was there, but I ignored her and curled up on a chair in a fetal position and just cried. My strained back muscle felt agonizing.

Linda knelt beside the chair. "Nancy, we have to talk."

"About what?" I whimpered.

"Well, about this snow job that Ross is trying to pull on the both of us."

The truth finally came out. Ross had claimed that Linda had reached out to him, but it was the other way around. He had called and invited her to stay in Santa Barbara with him, describing his apartment and other incentives to get her to come. He hadn't mentioned me at all. And today, Ross had requested that Linda meet him at the studio while I was at work. Linda suspected that my boyfriend wanted to bed her and that my bad back had ruined his plans... that was why he'd been barely able to hide his anger.

After we'd sufficiently compared notes, I decided to strike up a friendship with Linda... a unique friendship that would last for decades. We both knew that we had to get back at that man. Linda had even more reason than I to be outraged, for she had uprooted herself from her home to come to Santa Barbara under false pretenses. The nerve in my back had settled by now, and the two of us came up with a devious plan to strike at Ross where he was most vulnerable - his libido. He was so self-deluded that I knew he'd never suspect a thing.

In the evening when Ross came home, he found us lounging on the bed in our nighties, well-groomed and smiling seductively. Ross jumped onto the bed between us, purring, "Let's have an orgy, you lovelies."

I immediately sat up and told him, "You can get out of this apartment and find yourself a girlfriend if you want sex."

"But why should I do that when I have you two beauties here?" he moaned.

I gave Linda a look and picked up a quarter that I'd placed conveniently nearby. "Shall we toss for this guy?" I asked her. "The winner gets to go out for a cup of coffee. The loser has to stay here with Ross." She nodded in agreement.

I flipped the coin, won the toss and quickly put on some street clothes. As I was walking out the door, Linda screeched, "Wait for me, Nancy!" She grabbed her clothes and flew outside with me before Ross could say a thing. We drove to the Jolly Tiger and laughed uproariously for the next two hours. *That should take care of Ross' ridiculous ego for a while,* we decided. And if for some reason it reared its ugly head again, we came up with a few additional strategies to bring the man back down to size.

~

My new friend Linda continued to stay with us while she looked for work in Santa Barbara, and I put my relationship with Ross on hold for the time being. I continued to sleep out in the truck, mainly to drive home the point with Ross that his dream of living with two women was not going to happen.

After a month or two of this unconventional living arrangement, my landlady called me into her office to complain. She said it was hard on the eyes of everyone at the apartment complex to see three unmarried people living together, and even if their assumptions were wrong, I still needed to rectify the situation. So that night, I announced in front of Linda and Ross that we were going to have to move. Either that, or one of us needed to move out, and that person *wasn't* going to be me.

By now, Linda had taken a job waitressing at the Jolly Tiger and she had found some friends who were more compatible with her lifestyle than Ross and I, including the cook, Joe, who was destined to become her future husband. Linda hated the newspaper business as well, so she decided to move into a townhouse with her new colleagues.

Ross and I repaired our relationship, but we didn't end up staying in the Westside studio for much longer. He had a good friend named Phil who worked for the Hi Time liquor store chain, and when the bottom half of the duplex Phil was renting in Montecito became available, we decided a change of scenery would be good for us. This place in the back of Jameson Lane had a country feel to it, with a beautiful creek in the backyard, but the house was also conveniently close to the grocery store and laundromat on Coast Village Road. I loved the brick walls in the kitchen, and I was able to sleep in a real bedroom for the first time in what felt like ages. Things were finally looking up again.

One morning, Ross took me out to the Santa Barbara airport, and to my great surprise, he informed me that was an actual pilot. He had a multi-engine rating and had been flying since he was young. When I asked why he'd never told me, Ross said he'd kept that part of his life secret because he didn't want me to stay with him due to some shallow, romantic fascination with pilots.

There was a rented Cessna 172 waiting for us in the hangar, and Ross took us out that day on a flight above the Channel Islands. It was my first flight in any kind of aircraft. Our path encircled Santa Rosa where I could look down on a shipwrecked barge that had crashed on the backside of the island three years earlier. I was hooked. During my time with Ross, I learned the basics of flight navigation and even got to sit behind the wheel on a few occasions. I never went to pilot school or got a license, but I was able to watch the altimeter and keep the plane flying straight and level.

There were aspects of Ross' history that I was only just learning about. Ross was an adopted child, born in Boston and brought home from the hospital by his first father, Andrew Ross McCradie, a heart and lung surgeon. His mother Jane was also a pilot - a woman who counted Amelia Earhart and Howard Hughes among her friends. Andrew died of Hodgkin's Disease when Ross was just twelve years old. Jane remarried, but her second husband, an airline pilot, lost his life in a tragic accident when Ross was eighteen.

On October 4th, 1960, Captain Curtis Fitts took off out of Boston Airport with a Lockheed Electra four-engine plane, bound for Philadelphia. Twenty-seven seconds after it began its takeoff and just seven seconds into its flight, the aircraft struck a flock of starlings that numbered between ten and twenty thousand. The birds were sucked into the propellor engines, disabling three of them. Two engines partially recovered, but the plane began to stall and dip sharply to the left. The nose pitched up as it rolled counter-clockwise and plunged almost vertically into Boston Harbor, fragmenting into pieces. The whole event had happened so quickly that the only words captured from Captain Fitts on the flight recorder were "Fuck it!" Out of the seventy-two people on board the plane, only ten survived. It was the worst bird strike in American history.

Fitts and his co-pilot were pulled from the cockpit alive and taken to the hospital, but they died en route. Grieving mightily for her husband, Jane was unable to travel to Boston Memorial to identify the body. Ross was brought in to identify his stepfather's body instead, and until the end of his life, Ross carried around the waterlogged money that his stepdad had in his wallet when he died.

~

BECAUSE MY CAT TABOO AND MY PARAKEETS HAD BEEN ADOPTED BY my parents again, I decided to answer an ad in the paper that advertised German shepherd puppies. When I drove over to Ashley Road to have a peek, it didn't take long for me to fall in love with a little cutie named Tina. She threw up in my car on the ride home, but despite that initial anxiety, we managed to bond right away. The pup couldn't bear to be apart from me; even when I went to the bathroom, she would sit and cry just outside the door. Eventually, Tina became a good and obedient dog. Ross even took the time to teach her how to "army crawl" whenever he gave the command to grovel. He thought it was hilarious.

Although Tina grew up to be an obvious German Shepherd mix, rather than the purebred I'd been promised, I didn't mind. She was my faithful companion for all my newspaper routes over the next four years.

Our time in Montecito didn't last as long as I'd hoped, however. Ross and Phil argued about rent, and after one particularly big fight,

Ross resolved to move out. We found a fourplex apartment on Lillie Avenue in Summerland - a town further down the coast that many Santa Barbara families fled to for its beach access and affordable housing.

In those days, Summerland had a real hippie vibe. There were few community rules, like leash laws, so roaming packs of dogs patrolled the streets. That wouldn't have been a problem except that my puppy Tina reached six months of age and went into heat right on schedule. I tied her to the leg of our kitchen table one afternoon, gave her a blanket and a bowl of water and left with Ross to socialize for a few hours at the Jolly Tiger Restaurant. When we returned home, there were twenty dogs in our apartment.

The hounds growled and snarled at us. It was a scary sight. Somehow, they had found an open window and broke through the screen. We yelled and chased them out the door, then went to comfort Tina. The poor girl looked terrorized from the sexual pressure that had been placed on her.

While we attempted to clean up the damage caused by those four-legged vandals, a man up the street offered to help by shooting the dogs in the butt with his BB gun to hold them off. Tina's pheromones were still potent, but we had to keep the windows open to air the place out. It stank of urine because most of the dog pack had taken turns marking their territory on our furniture.

After several days of cleaning, we were able to get our apartment back to normal. I took Tina to the vet so she could get a shot that prevented her from becoming pregnant. She was just a baby herself... far too young to be raising her own litter of puppies. I never spayed her, but from that point on, my dog was never left alone at home again.

~

ONE DAY, MY MOTHER LOWERED THE BOOM ON ME. SHE ASKED ME TO get married to Ross. My grandmother was traveling to the West Coast for a visit, and my mom didn't want her to find out that I was unmarried. According to my mother, I was living in sin; she could tolerate it, but my grandmother's sensibilities derived from the Victorian Age.

I thought the potential for drama was exaggerated, but I agreed to go home and propose to Ross. The man still had an aversion to baths and he exerted too much control over my paychecks, but nevertheless, I liked him. He showed up for his contract jobs with the Santa Barbara News-Press on time and seldom, if ever, missed a shift. I had come to consider Ross a good friend, and I enjoyed our long talks over cups of coffee. Whenever he felt guilty about something, he would buy me a twelve-string guitar or some token to show how much he appreciated me. Because we were unmarried, however, I didn't have much of a hold on him, and his reputation for being a womanizer stood out from time to time. Perhaps if we were married, the man could finally convince himself to stay loyal to me.

Ross was never the type to take the initiative in such matters, so it was up to me to propose to him. It took a small amount of persuasion, but Ross agreed, and my family made plans quickly before my boyfriend could change his mind.

We first asked the presiding municipal judge, Judge Kearny, to marry us, but the man politely declined. Over the years, the official had witnessed Ross' misbehavior on numerous occasions. Ross had failed to appear in court several times, and Kearny told me that he had to personally work hard to keep my boyfriend out of jail. These episodes usually had to do with traffic tickets, but regardless, the judge couldn't believe that anyone in their right mind would want to marry Ross. Some trickery had to be at play.

Thankfully, the next judge I approached, Judge Patillo, agreed to administer our vows. We wrote him a check for the marriage license then and there.

The wedding was held in the backyard of my parents' home in Goleta. My British friend Linda Strong from the car wash stood as my witness, and Phil, who had repaired his friendship with Ross, served as his best man. Apart from Judge Patillo, only my mom and dad, along with various dogs, cats and parakeets, observed the ceremony. The judge refused to take additional payment from us. He merely shook our hands and wished us well before leaving. The rest of us devoured cake and broke open a bottle of champagne that my parents had purchased for the occasion.

The party went on until after dark, and then my new husband and I climbed into Ross' Pontiac Delta 88 convertible and Phil got into his Dodge Desoto. Unfortunately, the two of them decided to race down Highway 101 to the Jolly Tiger. I braced myself as Ross took the Pontiac up to 130 miles per hour. He was determined not to lose on his wedding day.

When we approached the exit for Patterson Avenue, Ross noticed Phil was no longer in sight, and he allowed himself to slow down. All of a sudden, lights appeared behind us, and Ross instinctively floored the gas pedal. He was convinced Phil had snuck up behind us. I shouted to Ross that it wasn't Phil, it was the cops, but he couldn't hear me. The speedometer went back up to 130mph.

I looked up the highway and saw two more squad cars enter the freeway from the Turnpike on-ramp. They switched on their beacon lights and moved side-by-side to slow us down. Ross finally understood the situation. He pulled the Pontiac over, and the police had him step out of the vehicle.

*Great,* I thought. *I'm going to go to jail on the night of my wedding.* Somehow, however, Ross managed to talk the officers into writing him and Phil a 79-mile-per-hour ticket instead, perhaps due to the unique celebratory circumstances. If they'd wanted to nail us for 80mph or higher, we would have been arrested and thrown into prison.

Neither Phil nor Ross was the most disciplined of men. I don't think either of them understood the relationship between cause and effect. But the episode finally humiliated them enough that they never raced down the highway again.

∼

ONLY ONE WEEK OF MARRIAGE PASSED BEFORE ROSS BEGAN sneaking off to see other women. He was so insecure about his manhood that he needed to prove that marriage was really no commitment at all. I was both devastated and lonely, spending my time waiting for him at home, alone. Marrying that man had been a terrible mistake.

To make the best of a poor situation, I started hanging out at a new restaurant on Carrillo Street called Carrows. Like the Jolly Tiger, I appreciated the camaraderie of the place. I'd sit at the counter, drink coffee and chat with other locals. The new friends I made there helped me deal with the situation happening back home, and I would go there every free moment that I had. The only bad experience I had there was the night I arrived to find Ross hanging out with another woman. As insecure as I was at my young age, his transgressions hurt me to my core.

Time passed, and we moved from Summerland back to Danielson Road in Montecito. The Osbornes' bookstore had closed by then, and I was growing tired of working solely for Ross. For a salary, he was tossing me only two dollars a day - enough just to buy a cup of coffee and a pack of cigarettes. He paid the rent and the bills, and he brought home the food I needed to cook for him, but I longed for independence.

One morning, after finishing my newspaper route, I walked into the office of Mr. Monson, Ross' boss at the L.A. Times, and I asked him for my own route and paycheck, independent of Ross' control. I was sick of living underneath my husband's shadow. He warmly agreed, but Ross became extremely upset when he found out what I'd done. He'd be making much less money off the hard work his wife was doing. Thankfully, Mr. Monson became my advocate, telling Ross that it was unhealthy for me to completely depend on him for everything. Ross was forced to accept the new arrangement.

I was given one of the better delivery routes to do - four hundred homes in Montecito. I faithfully drove that route for four years, driving a small Datsun truck and pitching rolled newspapers into driveways with my dog Tina at my side. I made a lot of people happy, as evidenced by the two thousand dollars I made in tips every holiday season after putting homemade Christmas cards into the mailboxes of my customers. Of course, I never saw a penny of their generous donations. Ross confiscated the tips, then bragged to his friends about how much money his wife was making for him.

～

ONE SHOULD NEVER DISCOUNT THE CREATIVITY OF A GROUP OF bored men. On a whim, Ross and Phil decided to purchase an Austin-Healey Bugeye Sprite from my friend Linda Strong for one hundred dollars. The toy-sized yellow convertible was in poor shape. The drive shaft was about to fall off the U-joints, and it severely needed a paint job and a tune-up. Nevertheless, the two men decided to put the vehicle in motion one Sunday afternoon.

They planned out the scenario. I squeezed into the middle seat in between Ross, who was driving, and Phil, who was outfitted with a felt hillbilly hat, a rawhide bullwhip, sunglasses and a cigar. First, we drove to the main four-way intersection in Montecito. After pausing at the stop sign, our little car chugged into the middle of the road, where Ross feigned an automotive breakdown.

In front of all the impatient drivers, Phil jumped out of the little car. He took his bullwhip to the backside of the Sprite and lashed it like a bad donkey. Only then did Ross let the vehicle putter its way out of the intersection. I giggled so hard that I nearly peed myself. The onlookers laughed hysterically as well. And of course, we had to go around the block and do the performance all over again. It was a great way to spend a Sunday afternoon, and one of the most fun times I had in my deteriorating marriage.

~

ONE EVENING, ROSS AND I WALKED INTO HI TIME LIQUOR ON Milpas Street to visit Phil, and in a box, standing up with her paws clutching the sides was an adorable six-week-old puppy named Tawny. The clerks said her husky mother had been impregnated by a coyote, which raised some suspicions, but I became enamored and had to have her as a companion for Tina.

We took her home, and Tawny grew up to be an unusual canine. She hid from us, and it would take both Ross and I working as a team to corral and catch her. Then one day, I found chicken feathers in the front yard. That was not a good sign. When Tina had a litter of puppies, their Aunt Tawny carried a rabbit's head into the house and placed it in the box with the newborn pups. *How thoughtful.*

However, we had to start tying her up whenever we left her outside in the yard.

As Tawny grew older, she finally calmed down and became a great dog. Getting her spayed probably helped to control her hormones, too. She and Tina would ride in the back of the pickup truck or the Bugeye Sprite as I delivered papers around Montecito, happy as two dogs could be.

~

EVENTUALLY, ROSS AND PHIL DECIDED THEY WANTED TO MOVE BACK in together. They found us a place on La Paz Avenue that doubled as the gatehouse to Westmont College. It came with orange trees, a large backyard barbecue and a beautiful stream that ran behind the property. I loved the space and its gardening potential, although Phil made me uneasy sometimes. He was a fairly nice man, and small enough that I never felt threatened by him, but he also had a crush on me. Every time Ross would leave for a while, Phil would start flirting and going on about how the two of us would make a much better team than me and my husband.

We got wind that the dealer for the L.A. Herald Examiner newspaper wanted to retire, and he recommended that Ross take over his job. Ross was excited. He aced the interview, and soon we were delivering Herald Examiners in the afternoon and L.A. Times papers for Mr. Monson at night. I handled the motor routes. Ross filled the newspaper racks, and he hired a group of News-Press paperboys to assemble the papers on the weekends. The work was endless - seven days a week, beginning at 2:30 in the morning. One had to be committed, because taking a day off was virtually impossible.

Eventually, the teenage paperboys began crashing at our place instead of in their own homes. They were all between twelve and thirteen years old and had previously been running wild on the streets of Santa Barbara, getting into mischief. Alcohol was a problem in most of their home environments, so Ross got permission from their parents to have the boys stay with us on the weekends when the newspapers needed assembling. They slept on floor mattresses, couches or wherever they could find space. Apparently, it was preferable to living at home, because they ended up staying over longer and longer until the kids moved in with us full-time. Somehow, their parents didn't seem to care one way or another.

I always had a nurturing soul, and I came to love the boys. They were fed well, kept clothed nicely and received a lot of attention. We even looked into becoming official foster parents, but the state rules and regulations were not to our liking.

Ross used the kids for both work and play. They became the tools that my husband used to perpetuate his many pranks. For example, when my friend Anna needed a temporary place to live, I rented out a bedroom in our duplex. Ross convinced the boys to go streaking through her room, repeatedly, jumping up and down before running back out again. It made Anna so mad that she moved back out again.

Sometimes Phil would be taking a shower and Ross would have the kids help him fill a gallon container with ice water so he could dump it on his friend. Phil would always give Ross the reaction that he craved. In Ross' mind, his prankster tendencies were an endearing part of his personality. Ultimately, however, Ross was an insecure man and simply desired the attention. He also needed to put others down to make himself feel better. I felt the brunt of his belittling comments on many occasions, although I would usually just stand up and leave the area when it occurred. However, if Ross ever sent the teenagers to torment me, I would pick up a two-by-four that I kept by the front door and brandish it. The boys wisely fled from my wrath.

I began spending more time with Anna and Linda, just to maintain my sanity around all the rambunctious male energy. Also, I started smoking joints again to help me cope with the dysfunction. That helped, until one day when the possession of a few marijuana plants nearly got me thrown into jail.

Our property had started to collect too many broken-down vehicles as a result of Ross' refusal to do any automotive maintenance. Whenever a car stopped functioning, Ross would simply park it in the front yard and go out looking for another deal. The wrecks began to pile up, so we called a tow company one afternoon to see if they'd help us get rid of the excess. When they arrived to take the cars to the junkyard, Ross, Phil and I were hanging out in the backyard. Tina suddenly began to snarl. I looked up and saw a young deputy approaching the three of us. Tawny maintained her composure, but Tina lowered her frame into a crouching position and was about to spring forward, so I screamed at the dog to break her focus, then told the deputy that I'd meet him on the front lawn once I put Tina in the house.

The man obliged. Once Tina was safely inside, I headed out to speak with him. It turned out that a neighbor had been alarmed to see our vehicles being towed away, and he called the sheriff's department out of concern. The deputy merely wanted to make sure that no one was being robbed.

I promised him that everything was going as planned, and I felt a huge sense of relief when he walked back to his police vehicle and drove off. On the back porch, there had been seven marijuana plants. If the young man had seen them, we all might have been carted off to jail that day.

*Good dog, Tina.*

～

ONE DAY, ROSS MADE A DEAL WITH A BUSINESS TO PURCHASE A SILLY-looking, jeep-like car called the Austin Mini Moke. It had no doors, but it had a windshield and the option to secure a fabric over the top to give it a roof. Ross got it for the low price of four hundred dollars because he promised not to paint over the business slogan written on the side: "Lonely? Joe Rents TVs". With its pink paint job, the vehicle barely looked street legal, and police officers would pull me over from time to time to check its registration.

I had great fun driving the Mini Moke around, and I used it to deliver the L.A. Times because it got great gas mileage. Tina and Tawny went with me on every route, and Ross started calling the vehicle "The Puppyship". At one time, Mini Mokes were used by tourists to drive around Catalina Island, and if Ross or I had held onto the Puppyship for a few decades, one of us could have sold it for a hundred thousand dollars.

When Tina turned four years of age, I decided she needed to get spayed. It had been an easier decision to spay Tawny, because the first time the coyote-husky hybrid went into heat, she tore up the drapes and ate part of the carpet. I'd waited longer to spay Tina, but she'd just produced a litter of eight pups and it had been hard to find homes for them all. I didn't want either Tina or I to have to suffer through that experience again.

I took Tina to the Montecito Pet Hospital to drop her off for the procedure. She looked at me one last time with a smile before she was led into the back rooms for her surgery. Alas, my dog never came back. The surgery was botched and Tina died from internal bleeding.

I was devastated when I heard the news. I stormed out of the veterinary office after the attendant demanded payment for killing my dog, and I cried for days. For four years, Tina had barely ever left my side. Poor Tawny had to grow up fast. Her best pal was gone, and she had to step up and become my new number one companion.

Of course, my credit rating fell because I refused to pay the vet. As a result, whenever I went to the bank to ask a loan officer for a line of credit, I was turned down. Stubbornness has a price, but there was no way I was going to submit to such an unjust demand.

$\sim$

FROM TIME TO TIME, ROSS KEPT HIS PILOTING SKILLS HONED BY renting a four-seater Cessna plane and cruising around Santa Barbara and the surrounding mountains. One windy evening, we drove out to the Santa Barbara airport with a more direct purpose in mind. Phil's artistic girlfriend Susan needed to deliver a painting to a client in Burbank as payment for a yearling Morgan colt that lived in her back-yard. The Cessna rental company warned us about the potential for 35-knot crosswinds, but Ross reassured them that he knew how to pilot an aircraft safely through such obstacles.

Phil, Susan, and my husband and I climbed into the small plane and secured Susan's painting for takeoff. The first few minutes were turbu-lent, so Ross took the Cessna up to the aircraft's height limit of 11,000 feet to escape the buffeting. The air currents were much smoother up there, and as we passed over Ventura, Ross radioed the tower in Santa

Barbara to report on the calmer conditions. However, as soon as we reached the skies above Oxnard, we hit 100 mph up-and-down drafts.

The plane suddenly nose-dived 8,000 feet toward the earth. At 3,000 feet of elevation, we were suddenly shoved back up to 6,000 feet. Nothing had prepared us for the roller coaster ride we'd found ourselves in. Winds rocked us sideways, backward and forward. Susan panicked. Thank god our seatbelts were on, and I was able to keep her from unbuckling hers. Her acrylic fingernails tore gashes in my arm, but all I could do was tell her to stay calm. I had faith in my husband's skills and know he would get us all out of this.

Ross, meanwhile, was feverishly busy up in the cockpit. He'd had to slam his fist into Phil's jaw to knock him out because his friend kept trying to grab the control stick. In situations like this, a little rudder action could help to guide a plane out of severe drafts, but you never wanted to forcibly steer the aircraft. It was far better to let it go wherever the wind wanted to take it. If you fought the winds too much, like Phil wanted to do, a small plane like this one would have broken into a thousand pieces.

Ross managed to guide the Cessna out of the windstorm and take us back toward the Santa Barbara airport. When the runway lights came into view, I breathed a huge sigh of relief. Susan was crying and Phil was vomiting into a sick bag, having just returned to consciousness after Ross' knockout punch.

"Are we close to Burbank?" Phil asked.

Ross informed him that the painting would not be reaching its intended destination that evening. Ignoring any further arguments from Phil, he fought the crosswinds above the runway and managed to land the plane in one piece. We staggered back into the rental office, where Ross slammed the keys onto the counter and told the clerk, "In all my hours of piloting aircraft, I have *never* seen anything like what we just experienced." He also mentioned that the struts on the aircraft would need to be thoroughly checked for weaknesses after the stresses we'd put on them.

That night's experience was seared into my memory, but it wouldn't keep me from getting into a plane again. I still loved to fly. After all, I was related to Charles Lindbergh on my father's side. On other trips,

Ross flew us to the San Diego Zoo and once took us underneath the Cold Springs Bridge. But the Cessna that we'd tried to fly to Burbank... one day it crashed, killing its two passengers. I couldn't help but wonder if the struts hadn't fractured after all.

The skies above Southern California could be both dangerous to pilots and full of mystery. One evening, I needed to drive to Goleta to pick up a check from a Herald Examiner subscriber. I climbed into the Austin Mini Moke, whistled for Tawny to jump in, and drove down Cold Springs Road into the city. When we reached the neighborhood of my old high school, I spied a bright light in the corner of my peripheral vision. Looking to the northwest, I saw a celestial object that looked like Venus. However, I knew that Venus was currently rising before dawn and was not visible after sunset as it was during other times of the year. *What could that light be, then?*

I pulled over to the side of the road to take a longer look, just as two smaller lights moved quickly to the bigger one. Then within seconds, the three lights shot off like meteorites to the north, up and over the Santa Ynez Mountains. Their speed was completely inexplicable.

When I arrived back home, Ross and Phil were hanging out in the living room. Unable to control my excitement, I jumped around the room and screamed as I described my UFO encounter. The two of them, of course, laughed their fool heads off. However, the next morning, the News-Press ran a story about an airplane pilot who had reported seeing a UFO fly over Carrillo Street in downtown Santa Barbara. Phil and Ross didn't laugh at me after that, and the written confirmation made me a staunch believer in unexplained aerial phenomena.

~

I BEGAN TO NOTICE THAT PHIL AND ROSS WERE DRINKING BEER more and more often. The problem crept up slowly. We used to hang out at the Jolly Tiger because they served coffee twenty-four hours a day, and because none of us drank alcohol at the time, the restaurant matched our needs perfectly. But now, the two men began guzzling

Colt 45s every afternoon after they came home from work. They were never without a beer in their hands. Before long, they were also never without a beer tucked into their back pockets for when the beer in their hand went empty.

Their behavior became a little bizarre, and they started to torment the environment around them, committing small cruelties like hooking up cats to electrical wires. I was unaware of their activities at first. But the two of them hung out together more and more often, leaving me to fend for myself for long periods of time. I tended to my garden and played with the animals, but it was a lonely existence. My relationship with Ross became shallow. He only seemed interested in deepening his relationship with Phil, even if they were just arguing over who knew more about orbital mechanics in outer space.

The situation grew more and more difficult, for I realized that under the influence of alcohol, their personalities were gradually changing, and not for the better. I still had to pretend that everything was okay, even though I felt confused, angry and very sad. That's the nature of the co-dependent relationship. I was too invested to think that I could leave Ross, and although I hoped that things would improve, they never did. If I ever tried to set boundaries or push back against the mental abuse they were throwing at me, it was always two-against-one. They made me think that *I* was the crazy one, not them.

Soon, keeping up with rent payments on the Westmont College gatehouse became too much for Ross and Phil. Most of their money was going into cases of Colt 45 and other toys rather than essentials like food and rent. I hated saying goodbye to my garden again, but Ross found us a smaller and cheaper apartment near Oak Park in Santa Barbara. Because six of our foster children moved in with us as well, the space was excessively crowded. At least Phil eventually found his own accommodations, moving in with his long-term hairdresser girl-friend, Susie.

The adopted paperboys were hard to handle at times. I took care of them like they were family, but whenever I had enough of their antics, I would turn to the 2x4 I kept by the back door and brandish it threateningly. The boys would fly out of whatever window or door they were closest to, and the house would gain some semblance of peace and order... at least for a few hours.

One night, Ross and I were woken by a knock on the front door. It was the police. They had caught our foster sons driving around in one of our delivery trucks. Being that the kids were only thirteen years old, the cops had noticed the impropriety right away. When questioned why he'd left the keys in the ignition, Ross told the police that the teens would have simply hot-wired the truck if they'd wanted to take it for a spin. Leaving the keys saved him from having to fix the wires every time.

In a later era, our foster kids would have been carted off to Juvenile Hall. But in this case, the cops let us put the kids to bed without further repercussions. At least the boys never repeated the same infraction... they learned *some* lessons. Unfortunately, there were always new infractions to be discovered in the city of Santa Barbara.

~

I MISSED MY GERMAN SHEPHERD TINA FROM TIME TO TIME, BUT ONE of her puppies came back to live with us. I had given him to one of the paperboys to take home to his family, but his aunt kicked the dog across the room. The incident explained why that particular kid had so many problems; he had seen a lot of violence.

Thankfully, the boy was smart enough to bring Tina's offspring back to me, which meant that Tawny had a new, twelve-week-old friend. I named him Proton after the many arguments that Ross and Phil had over astrophysics. Proton, or "Proto" for short, was a shepherd-beagle mutt and grew to become the sweetest canine. One of my favorite pastimes was to take him to Oak Park so he could play with his Auntie Tawny.

We weren't able to enjoy our local park for too long before we moved again - this time, to a three-bedroom condo on North San Marcos Road. The foster kids came too, and I finally taught them how to drive the Mini Moke. They took trips around the neighborhood, which occupied them for a time. Then things started to vanish around the house. Meaningful mementos like my silver coin collection disappeared. And every time I looked for my stash of weed, it was gone. It didn't matter where I hid it; the boys found it. At ten dollars a quarter-ounce, it was an expensive thing to have to continuously replace.

One day, I looked around the living room and realized that if I hid the marijuana in plain sight, they would never find it. I tucked it into my choir music folder and set it back down on the coffee table. They looked high and low, and I overheard them discussing possible hiding spots, but they never found it.

I knew it was time to have a conference about the weed, so I sat them down on the couch and told them that I was sick and tired of them stealing from me. I was putting my foot down. I explained that Ross and I would go to jail for a long, long time if they were caught in possession of my marijuana. Now, I knew that if I grounded them for smoking, it would steer them in a more rebellious direction. So instead, I offered them a deal. If they wanted to smoke, they would have to do it openly, on that very couch, under my supervision. They couldn't take it outside, nor could they watch television or read books while doing it.

Surprised by my attitude and maybe a little desperate, they agreed, and I gave them a joint or two to share. It didn't take very long for them to grow bored, just sitting there on the couch, smoking. My scheme had taken all the fun out of it. When I sensed the teenagers were at their weakest, I presented an alternative. I asked them if they had combed the neighborhood for girls to hang out with. It certainly would be more fun than what they were currently doing.

They looked at each other for confirmation and agreed. It worked. The boys headed outside, and soon they were bringing girls around the house for me to meet. They quit smoking, too.

I felt grateful that the crisis was over. Girls could also be trouble, I knew, but at least I didn't have to keep worrying about losing my possessions.

~

ONE OF THE UPSIDES TO THE PRESENCE OF THESE NEW TEENAGE girls is that they had access to horses. Horse-wrangling kept the boys busy, and the girls didn't mind me riding their horses either because the creatures always needed attention and exercise. It felt great to sit in a saddle again, and far more exciting than watching Ross guzzle cans of Colt 45 all day long.

One afternoon, I asked Ross if he would like to take a ride down one of the neighborhood trails. He was drunk as usual, but to my surprise, he said yes. I took a chestnut gelding that looked a lot like Viking, and the girls helped Ross get on the back of a beautiful black quarter horse that was well-behaved and could stop on a dime.

We started down the trail at a gentle walk. I looked back at Ross, and he seemed to be enjoying himself. "Are you ready for a canter?" I asked. Ross gave me a thumbs up, so I gave the gelding his head and we pushed forward at a slightly faster gait.

Within seconds, a scream erupted behind me. I pulled hard on the reins and got the chestnut to stop. Then I glanced back again. Ross was laying on the ground being sniffed by the black mare. I laughed my head off. When I finally regained my composure, I dismounted and said that the best thing to do is to get right back up on her so that the horse doesn't learn that she can shed a rider that easily. When I boosted him back up onto the saddle, however, I must have given him too hard a shove, because the result was straight out of a Laurel and Hardy movie. Ross' center of gravity shifted too far to the other side and he slid straight back down to the ground. This time, even the black mare started to snicker.

I laughed so hard that I started crying. The girls rushed up to us, and that was the end of our ride. They walked the horses back to the corral while I escorted my bruised-up husband back to our apartment.

Not that I myself was immune from embarrassment. One morning, the boys were helping me bundle the unsold newspapers from the Herald Examiner. Periodically, we'd toss them into the back of the truck and take them to the recycling center so we could earn a little extra cash. In the midst of our labors that day, I suddenly felt something crawling up the front of my shirt. When I looked down, there was a potato bug staring me in the face. Those six-legged critters absolutely petrified me. Though cricket-like in appearance, they looked to me like underdeveloped fetuses.

I began screaming, which then scared the insect. It turned around and darted straight down my pants. My cries intensified as I danced across the front yard, desperately shaking the fabric before finally pulling down my pants to rid myself of the creature. Half-naked, I looked up to see the boys running to my rescue. That poor potato bug... it didn't stand a chance. The teenagers stomped it into oblivion. I was somewhat grateful, but when the boys described the scene of me hopping with my pants down in front of our house to my husband, Ross laughed just as hard as I did when he fell off the black horse.

⁓

EVENTUALLY, SUSAN HAD ENOUGH OF HER BOYFRIEND PHIL, SO SHE broke up with him and threw him out. Of course, Ross invited his best friend to come live with us. I wasn't thrilled to have their hypermasculine dynamic start up again. The two of them were bad influences on each other whenever they were in close proximity.

At first, however, Phil was in no mood for mischief. For days on end, he wallowed in depression, whining and crying over his fate. The man needed to take responsibility for his own role in the breakup and stand on his own two feet again. Unfortunately, self-realization wasn't in his nature. Phil's constant moping started to bring the whole household down with him, and after a week or two I decided I couldn't handle it anymore. "Snap out of it!" I told him. "If you really want to do something to make your grief go away, why don't you send her a pig's head or something? That'll make you feel better."

I was joking, of course. I never thought he would actually do it. However, not long afterward, on Susan's birthday, Phil and Ross went to a butcher shop and brought home a frozen pig's head. They pried open the pig's mouth with a crowbar and stuck an apple in it. Then they boxed it up and mailed it to the beauty parlor where Susie worked, gift-wrapped and everything. I decided then and there that I would never joke around Phil and Ross in that fashion ever again. They were simply too crazy to be trusted.

A few days later, an article appeared in the Santa Barbara News-Press that a hairdresser received a freshly-killed pig's head as some kind of sick birthday present. Police officers had to pick up the parcel for disposal. The whole situation was insane, but it did the trick; Phil had his "revenge" and was cured of his depression. He felt like he was in control of his own destiny again.

I often wondered what it would have been like to be in that beauty shop when the present was opened. The police officers probably laughed their asses off as they drove away to dispose of the evidence.

## ❦ 5 ❧

# THE PILOT HOUSE MOTEL

In the summer of 1974, I unexpectedly passed a clot of unidentified matter into the toilet while going to the bathroom. *What is that?* I wondered in a bit of panic. *Was it a miscarriage?* There was a lot of blood, but I didn't think I could have been pregnant since I was on the pill. *Maybe the birth control had led to a buildup of estrogen in my body?* The episode scared me enough that I went to a clinic, but there wasn't much my obstetrician could tell me. So out of concern for my well-being, I quit taking the pill.

Naturally, a few months later, I discovered I was pregnant. Ross was furious at me, though it was just as much his fault as mine. "You know I didn't want any rugrats!" he yelled. I could never understand why it was always the woman's fault for getting 'knocked up'.

Days went by with Ross continuing to fume silently. But I refused to get an abortion. After my husband came to terms with my decision, I overheard him tell Phil that becoming a mother just might make a better woman out of me, and I had to choke back my tears. I consoled myself by imagining what it would be like to take care of my own child. This one would never be given up for adoption.

Around this time, a young woman of seventeen came by named Charisse - the older sister of one of the fifteen-year-old girls who had latched onto our pack of paperboys. She was adorable and sweet, with curly brown hair and hazel eyes, and Phil quickly became smitten with her. Charisse felt absolutely the same way about him, despite their questionable age difference, with Phil on his way to turning thirty-four. Less than two months later, as soon as Charisse turned eighteen, they got married.

Our apartment was not big enough for two married couples and a gaggle of teenagers, so we moved across Highway 101 to a large house at the bottom of a cul-de-sac called Kodiak Way. It came with an expansive, fenced-in yard, so Tawny and Proto could dash about and chase each other to their hearts' content.

The fence was six feet high, but I discovered that it could not contain Tawny for very long. Her coyote genes gave her the drive and the ability to scrabble up and over the fence like it wasn't even there. Every night, she would slip out and explore the neighborhood. She'd scratch on people's doors, and when they would answer, the dog would look up at them with a sad smile that said, "Feed me. I am cute, but poor and very hungry." Their generosity only further encouraged her bad behavior. Whenever I heard her nails on the wooden fence outside my bedroom window, I would wait until she dropped down to the other side before shouting, "Tawny! You get back in this yard right now!" Again, I would hear the scraping of claws on wood as she swiftly returned to our side of the fence. *Busted!*

Within a month of marriage, Charisse was pregnant with her first child. Two women, knocked up at the same time. We stayed at the house on Kodiak Way for the duration of our pregnancies, but it wasn't entirely pleasant. Ross and Phil were drinking more and more alcohol. Eventually, they determined that the grocery budget was getting too expensive, so they took the job of purchasing food away from us; that way, they could minimize expenses and still have enough for a steady stream of Colt 45s. One meal a day was good enough for us, they determined. So we got by on a package of drumsticks and a can of pork-and-beans every night. The men supplemented their calories with the cases of beer that they drank, but Charisse and I had to suffer through the day without breakfast or lunch. More often than not, Ross and Phil burned the chicken on the barbecue because they refused to let us help and they were too tipsy to be mindful about it. They didn't care, so long as they had enough beer that they could still sit out back and get drunk around the fire.

Managing a household with six teenage boys, two alcoholic men and my own pregnancy was grueling. On top of it all, I had to do it while hungry. Charisse and I grew angrier and angrier. To try and make a joke out of the situation and get our husbands' attention, we walked around the house, clucking and flapping our arms in imitation of all the chicken we'd been forced to eat week after week. Finally, I just snapped. I screamed at Ross, telling him that we were starving for nutrition and could not eat burnt chicken and baked beans every night. Then I broke down and began to sob.

Ross sat down beside me and put his arm around my shoulders. *Woah*, I thought. *Is he finally ready to show me a little compassion?* I reminded him that I was carrying his child and that it was using up all the nutrients I was putting into my body, leaving nothing for me. I needed substantial food like salad, red meat and fresh vegetables to stay healthy enough to keep the baby. Charisse and I couldn't go through another week like this... we were desperate.

We held a family conference soon thereafter that finally produced results. Our husbands relented, and Charisse and I were given forty dollars a week to buy food for four adults and our teenage wards. The first meal was a revelation. Veggies... how I had missed my veggies.

～

ALCOHOL REMAINED A CONSTANT PRESENCE, TURNING OUR LIVES upside down in so many ways. When I was eight months pregnant, lying in bed, asleep, Charisse came into my bedroom and woke me up. Ross and Phil were drunk and tormenting my poor pup Proto, striking his paws with a whip to try and make him mean enough to become an attack dog. I could hear his yelps of pain from inside the house. They were such pitiful men, they had to constantly do things like this to feed their egos.

I grabbed a broom on my way out to the backyard and let them have it, slamming the end into their faces hard enough to knock their inebriated asses completely over. All the abuse that Charisse and I suffered... all the neglect and the sheer cruelty came rushing out of me, fueling my righteous anger as I swatted them again and again. Then I called Proto and ushered him into my car. It was time to get out of there, at least for a few hours.

As I was looking over my shoulder and backing out of the driveway, Ross ran up and grabbed the driver's side door, attempting to open it. Not seeing him, I kept the vehicle moving, and somehow, Ross' fingers got caught in the handle. He fell, and I unwittingly dragged the man several yards before he managed to free himself.

Once I had fully backed into the street, I looked toward the house and noticed Ross lying in the driveway. *Had I run him over?* I jumped out to check if he was okay, and he got up and started screaming at me. We started a back-and-forth argument that got so heated that the neighbors ended up calling the cops. Ross tried to play the victim, claiming that he'd been assaulted, but as I explained to the police officers, "No one gets away with hurting my animals. No one!"

The cops expressed concern over my well-being, seeing that I was so far along in my pregnancy, so they stuck around our house until Ross quieted down. I still drove off to Carrows and sat quietly at the counter for a while. The hormones that went along with that kind of stress and turmoil were probably not good for a developing child.

A few weeks later, I was overcome with a fit of nighttime restlessness, so I got in the Austin Mini Moke and decided I would collect all the money from the newspaper racks between Camarillo and Buellton. At each stop, I would pull out my log book and write down the location and the number of quarters I'd taken. Women, I've found, can become especially obsessive at the onset of labor. I wasn't aware I had started labor at the time; I simply left the money on the dining room table when I got home the next morning and went to bed.

Still restless, I slept fitfully until around noon. When I got up to use the bathroom, I was surprised to see I was discharging blood. In my state of alarm, I called my doctor, who told me to get to the emergency room immediately. If my body wasn't ready to start hard labor, he said he would induce it. Apparently, my baby was going to be born two weeks early. Anxious, I asked him if going to see the movie "Jaws" two days ago could have caused this premature delivery. That movie had induced so much adrenaline... it was *terrifying*. "Definitely not," the doctor reassured me. More likely, the umbilical cord had wrapped itself around my baby's neck and it was uncomfortable. That image didn't make me feel any better.

I got off the phone, still in a panic because I did not have a driver to get me to the hospital. Ross and Phil were awake, but only conscious in a technical sense; the two of them were chugging beers around the backyard campfire, soused to the gills. I had to turn to Charisse for help. Even though Phil's wife didn't have a driver's license, at least she knew how to keep a car on the road.

We climbed into the car, and I told her to drive to Carrows first. Charisse gave me a strange look, and I explained that I needed a bowl of ice cream... badly. Women are not supposed to eat anything during labor, but I couldn't suppress my compulsion.

Dutifully, she took me to Carrows. We sat down, and I told the waitress that I was in the throes of labor and on my way to the hospital, so *could she please hurry with our order?* The poor woman freaked out and scurried to the kitchen. After that wonderful treat, I felt energized and ready to continue. We made one more stop, though. I walked into the Vons grocery store and dropped a dime into the pay phone so I could call my mom. I needed her to be with me today, too.

At last, we made it to the Goleta Valley Hospital. The nurses produced a wheelchair for me, but I rejected it. My labor pains were getting heavier, and I needed to walk off the cramps. They finally made me lie down, and since I had chosen a natural childbirth, I was in agony. When Fredlund was being born, I'd been given an epidural, but it caused me to suffer from dizziness and headaches for a long time afterward. This time, I refused the procedure, but at a heavy cost. Charisse stayed at my side as the nurses placed a monitor on me. Immediately, they noticed that I had dilated enough for the baby to start pushing its head through the cervical walls, so they swiftly wheeled me into the delivery room and summoned the doctor.

My obstetrician walked through the doors soon afterward and announced he was glad I was ready to deliver now... it meant he'd be able to return home in time to catch the evening basketball game. As he was putting on his gown, I felt my baby's head pop out. I breathed a sigh of relief; the worst was over. I had to call to the doctor to hurry up and come catch the baby, for it wasn't going to wait for him. He guided the newborn the rest of the way out of the birth canal. Pleased with how smooth the delivery had gone, he cracked a joke about how much women stink when they're giving birth. It was crude, but he knew how to make me laugh.

Little Sean Ross McCradie was born at 6:20 p.m. on June 30th, 1975. His umbilical cord was wrapped twice around his neck, and the doctor quickly cut it away so that he could breathe. The women in our family are genetically disposed to have long umbilical cords. My sister Annie, in fact, lost her child after nine months of gestation because of that problem. The doctor carried my six-pound, one-ounce son back to me, and when I saw him kicking his feet and holding his fists up to the sky, I lost it. I wept and wept. This time, I was going to be able to keep my child.

After Charisse stepped over to stroke the baby's brow, I thanked her and told her she could go home. I needed some rest and would see her as soon as I got out of the hospital. After listening to Seanie coo for a time, I held him to my breast so that he could have sustenance. Then I passed out. It had been a wild ride.

The next morning, my doctor showed up in the hospital room wearing a Panama hat with purple balls hanging off the rim. Grinning at each other, we joked for a while until he was confident that I felt strong enough to leave the premises. Happy to be leaving, I called up Ross and asked him to come get me. He said he'd be right over. I slowly got dressed and wrapped Seanie up in blankets for the journey. But Ross never showed up. Two hours later, I gave up on him and called my parents. They drove me home.

After thanking my mom and dad, I walked through the front door with Sean and peeked out the back door. Ross and Phil were back there, throwing rocks and arguing drunkenly as usual. I could have said something then and there, but I was learning that it wasn't worth it to talk with Ross about anything negative. I didn't bother asking him for an apology or excuse, for I knew there wouldn't be any. Instead, I turned to poor Charisse, who looked exhausted from having to deal with them, and I asked her if she wanted to go to Carrows. She nodded gratefully.

We returned to the restaurant. I placed Sean's baby seat in the booth and waited for service. When the waitress appeared, she was surprised to see me so soon and she remarked, "Oh! Must have been a false alarm, huh?"

I smiled and said, "Here he is," revealing the baby. The little guy was softly snoring away. *So darn cute.*

⁓

FOR A COUPLE OF MONTHS, WE STAYED AT THE HOUSE AT KODIAK Way while Ross and Phil slowly drank up our profits, leaving nothing for rent and utilities. First, the electrical was cut off. The gas for hot water and the stove came next. The downward spiral continued until we were finally evicted from the premises. Phil and Charisse moved in with Phil's mother, who lived in a cabin off Paradise Road in the Santa Ynez Valley, while Ross, Seanie and I took a room at the Pilot House Motel.

The Pilot House was the last resort for housing for many people in Santa Barbara. It served as a stayover motel for pilots flying into Santa Barbara but was also affordable for lower-income residents. The rooms were in fairly good shape, and each had a porch where one could sit and watch the traffic on Fairview Avenue go by. Behind the building were tiedowns for private aircraft and a taxiway that led to the main airport runway.

The place was owned by Richard and Vivian Cho - two immigrants from Taiwan, which was technically part of the Republic of China. They had fled with several relatives when they feared that mainland China was about to invade their island and take away their family's teak wood farm. Richard was a balding, hard-working, boisterous man who strode around the property like a king in his castle. Vivian, in comparison, was a sweet and shy lady. Richard treated her more like a slave than a wife, I thought, but she only complained about not being allowed to drive a vehicle. For extra income, Vivian would cook up shrimp and pasta dinners on some nights for boarders who requested them.

They had four daughters, although they'd tried several times for a son. Vivian's third pregnancy resulted in twins, so they gave up after that. Consequently, my baby Sean became the son their family never had. The Taiwanese-American children loved playing with Seanie. He became something of an adopted brother, and they helped me rest from time to time by babysitting him.

Our room had a bed, a dresser, a full bathroom and a counter upon which we put an electric hot plate. I became quite efficient at cooking our dinners with it. Ross refused to shell out money to buy Seanie a crib, so I removed a drawer from the dresser, set it down on the side of the room and arranged some blankets to create a makeshift mattress for the little guy.

It was truly difficult living with Ross in that space. Every time the baby cried, Ross told me that I had to take him outside, whether it was freezing out there or not. I thought the father was being a bigger baby than his son. Ross's behavior upset me regularly, and Sean, who could sense my stress, would cry even louder as a result. I would have to sit in the car and rock him and myself to sleep.

Though it was hard getting through this period of adjustment, I did my best to focus on the good aspects of life at the Pilot House. Tawny and Proton loved the motel. They ran around, greeting the residents and playing on the grass. There was a swimming pool on-site, and starting at the age of six weeks, I began teaching Seanie how to swim. He was a natural.

One day, about six months into our stay, I was sitting on the front steps of our motel room when Ross and Phil approached me. Ross had decided that life at the Pilot House wasn't agreeing with him, and he was going to move in with Phil at the cabin.

The news came without warning, for we hadn't been fighting or anything. "What about me and Seanie?" I asked. Ross informed me that I could go on welfare. The news was utterly disheartening. I asked if I could keep the Pontiac for transportation to appointments, and he told me no.

I was stunned by the injustice of it all. A sense of fear and a need for survival took over. Without even thinking, I walked over to the white Pontiac, lifted the hood and started pulling wires off the plugs and the distributor cap. I tucked the distributor wires into my pocket and walked off.

They left the car. It was a piece of shit anyway, but I needed it to get by.

One of my first trips in the Pontiac was to the welfare office so I could apply for financial aid. Then Seanie and I learned to make do with government assistance. Richard and Vivian were immensely supportive; they hired me to teach their girls the piano. I let them and their daughters play with Sean as much as they wanted.

Life in the absence of Ross' cumbersome presence became easy. I was able to pay rent, put gas in the car, buy food and have enough left over to buy Sean a shiny, red wagon. It's remarkable how far one's budget can stretch when half isn't being spent on alcohol. Whenever Seanie needed a nap, I would set him in the wagon and pull him around the neighborhood. Motion always lulled him into slumber.

Seanie learned to walk about the same time that Richard's mom and dad moved into the motel. They started teaching Sean Chinese phrases, and he would run to fetch their slippers when asked in that language. My little son became part of the extended family, and despite our humble means, I felt proud to be able to raise Sean in a loving environment.

~

SEAN AND I CAME BACK FROM CARROWS ONE AFTERNOON TO FIND Ross waiting for us on our front porch. I hadn't seen him in three months. He looked defeated, like a shell of the man I once knew.

I sat down next to him and listened to his story. Our boss Rollin Monson had let him go; his alcohol addiction had become too much of a liability. Ross was devastated. He knew he would have a hard time finding another job because of all his missing teeth. It embarrassed him. His gums were perpetually bleeding and swollen, and his breath smelled foul. No one would hire him in that condition. And on top of all that, the infections in his mouth were making him sick as well.

He and Phil must have had another falling out because Ross asked if he could move back in with me. He also wanted to get added to my welfare case so he could get some dentures, clean himself up and go back to work. I thought long and hard about it. Ross was never going to be husband material again, but I still considered him a friend. We simply had a barrier between us - alcoholism - and I would have to remain on my guard for as long as I agreed to have him around.

I told him I would go to the welfare department and see what they had to say. In the meantime, I allowed Ross to come live with us again. We shared a bed out of necessity, but there was no physical relationship. Alcoholism and erectile dysfunction go hand-in-hand, so it wasn't likely we could have enjoyed any intimacy even if I'd wanted to.

Social services agreed to add Ross to my case, and he immediately went to the dentist and applied to Medi-Cal for a set of dentures. I hoped that the dental work would help curb Ross' need to numb the pain with alcohol. That didn't happen. He just hung around the pool, drinking his Colt 45s like usual. Then Peter came into his life.

Peter was a large, bearded trust fund baby from a wealthy oil family in Louisiana. He went to a private school in Monterey but had come back south on his summer break. Despite having a credit card that covered just about everything he needed or wanted, he chose to spend his sabbatical at the low-rent Pilot House Motel. The kid was intelligent, but he was already an alcoholic at the age of 18, and somehow, he convinced Ross that drinking Colt 45s was a waste of money. Peter gave Ross his first taste of Southern Comfort whiskey and orange juice. That one event made my husband's life so much worse, setting him down the path toward non-stop hard alcohol consumption.

The characters that came and went from the Pilot House could populate a year's worth of Hollywood movies. In one of the rooms lived a boy with his long-haired, mentally-ill father, who was a strict vegetarian. The only protein that he would allow his son to eat was peanut butter. From time to time, the boy would smell hamburgers being grilled outside and I'd hear him beg his dad for one. The answer was always a loudly-shouted, "No!"

The father had multiple obsessions. He always wore white clothes, and whenever he opened a can of food, he would shave an inch off the top and toss it into the trash, just in case aluminum shavings might have sprinkled down from the blade of the can opener. He also claimed to be his son's sworn protector because the boy was being groomed to become the next king of the Korkaraline Galaxy. That was why the child had to be kept in a state of optimum health. The father was on the board of directors for the galaxy and was able to contact the other members by holding a beryllium ball bearing up to the heavens. They would transport him to the other side of the universe if the Korkaraline citizens needed him. Of course, whenever Ross and his cronies asked for a demonstration, the boy's father would bring out the beryllium ball and nothing would happen. "They must not need me at the moment," he'd explain to them.

One day, Ross came up with an idea for employment that, to me, didn't seem much less crazy than Korkaraline politics. He'd failed to find work, despite his dentures, but he and his stocky friend Brian got wind of a job opportunity distributing softcore porn newspapers in the greater Los Angeles region. They were hired by some shady-sounding entities to deposit them into newspaper racks just like Ross and I had done for years with legit publications. *What could go wrong?*

I didn't consider myself a prude, even then. In fact, it was good to see Ross take some initiative again. But the project required purchasing a small aircraft to fly the newspapers in from Whiteman's Field Airport, northwest of Los Angeles. Brian fronted the startup money. He was a fastidious popinjay who liked dressing up in pinstripe suits from time to time, and he worked for the Santa Barbara News-Press as a paper delivery contractor, as I had. His wife was furious at him for getting involved in the porno business, but Ross agreed to pilot the plane and slowly repay Brian for the cost of the aircraft until he gained full ownership.

The two of them searched around and found a twin-engine Apache for ten thousand dollars. Although old, it had been retrofitted with new engines and was sufficient for the task. The Pilot House Motel had tie-downs out back, so they were able to park the plane for free and taxi it to the main airport runway when it was time for pickups. For my part, I detailed the paint on the outside, cleaned the interior and reupholstered the seats so the plane would shine once again, regardless of what kind of cargo it was carrying.

With their method of transport secured, Ross recruited his alcoholic friend Peter and the two of them began installing newspaper racks throughout Santa Barbara and Ventura Counties. Brian didn't want to be seen doing this kind of work; his wife was the daughter of a famous environmentalist, and to avoid antagonizing the woman any further, Ross agreed to be the front man for the business. As far as the City was concerned, Ross, not Brian, was the sole business owner.

Soon, Ross was bragging about how much money he was making to anyone who would listen. Perhaps it was to deflect attention from Brian, but I began to believe it myself. I called my social worker and shut down our welfare case because I didn't want to get in trouble with the authorities. Soon after, I discovered that all the profits were flowing in Brian's direction to pay off the airplane and their startup costs. Ross wasn't really making anything. But by then, it was too late to get back on welfare.

I went to Mr. Monson of the L.A. Times and asked him to give me a job as soon as he had an opening for a local driver. It didn't take long. A week later, I found a note on my door telling me to report to work.

So I returned to the newspaper business. I still liked the job, especially on days when the rich kid Peter offered to let me drive his Porsche 911S. I would back that silver beauty up to the loading dock at the Santa Barbara News-Press building, then step out of the vehicle and look around at all the jealous faces. "I'm going to beat all of you back here, you know," I'd tell the other drivers. Best delivery car I ever had.

Complaints started to pour in at City Hall about the smut that was being delivered weekly to Ross' newspaper racks throughout town. There was The Advocate - a publication in support of gay rights - along with Screw West and other choice titles. Ross and Brian had to hire an attorney from the ACLU to fight for their "free speech" rights to display and sell these papers. And to make himself appear like a strong and successful businessman in front of City Hall, Ross continued to brag about his profits, even though I was still the main income provider for our household.

They decided to expand into the Santa Ynez Valley, choosing the sidewalk outside the famous Andersen's Pea Soup Restaurant as their first location for the new racks. The idle college student, Peter, agreed to help Ross with this mission so that Brian could maintain his professional distance. Not wanting to miss the fun, I tagged along as well. Sean and I sat inside the restaurant, observing the patrons so that we could report back on their reactions to the "filth" being introduced to their community.

The manager soon figured out what was going on. He called the sheriff, who sent a few officers to try and chase Ross and Brian away. The two of them knew their rights, however. They had the freedom of the press on their side, and because the vending machines were placed in a public area, there was technically nothing the police could do about it. Still, those facts wouldn't stop the officers from trying.

Ross and his partner had a plan to counter them... one involving Korkaraline technology. They stole the idea from our crazy neighbor at the Pilot House. Taking a handful of washers, Ross and Peter set the metal disks on the sidewalk, creating a ring around the two racks they were attempting to install. Then they placed a ball bearing within each of the washers' holes. As the police officers approached, the two men started making buzzing sounds with their tongues as if some advanced technology was being brought online. Ross then announced in an ominous voice that a beryllium force field had been erected around the newspaper racks. "And if you step over the line of beryllium balls, we will install *twice* as many newspaper racks!" The officers stopped dead. Quickly, Ross and Peter bolted the racks onto the sidewalk and filled them with Advocate and Screw West papers, then hustled off to their next location.

Though I took no issue with the content of these periodicals, it was still a terrible business to get involved in. I received phone calls from Christian die-hards who were aghast that such thinly-disguised pornography was being placed within public view. Some threatened to kill me. Others vowed to take my son away. We were the very spawn of Satan, we were told.

Despite the backlash, our business continued to grow. We started selling hard-core magazines like Hustler in liquor stores along the

Central Coast, and the profits from that enterprise were even greater than the newspaper initiative. Santa Barbara's city government continued to rail against us, even though one of the City Council members was one of our best customers.

Perhaps the success went to Ross' head. One day I received a phone call from his mother. She was moving from Santa Ynez to Santa Barbara, and Ross claimed to be too busy to help her pack, so I agreed to lend a hand. I left Sean with Richard and Vivian and told them I'd return around 5:00 p.m. to pick him up. Then I drove to her place on Quail Valley Road.

Ross's mother was not an easy woman to work for because she was obsessively careful about her possessions. She was always looking over my shoulder and second-guessing every single packing decision. Around 4:00 p.m., Ross gave us a call to confirm when I'd be home. I told him it would still be another hour.

When I got back to the Pilot House, Ross was nowhere to be found. I searched the premises, and as soon as I walked into the bathroom I knew where he had gone. There was a very black ring around the inside of the bathtub, indicating that my husband had taken a bath. Ross *never* took baths unless he had a special reason... or a special *lady*, to be precise.

Sean and I jumped into the car and drove across the freeway to a house where my British friend Anna's younger sister Genowefa lived. I'd catch them flirting with each other on too many occasions. The front door was wide open, so there was no way to miss the sight of the two of them on the couch, kissing.

I was furious. I stormed up to them, pulled Ross away from her, then slapped and pushed the man clear across the room. "After slaving away for your mother all day," I bellowed, *"this* is how you're repaying me?" I turned my back to that imbecile, walked up to his new girlfriend and told her Ross was all hers. Then I left the house. Before driving away, however, I walked over to this motorcycle and pocketed his keys out of sheer spite. I didn't want to see Ross again that night, or *ever*.

Three days later, Genowefa showed up at my door, begging me to let Ross come home. *Not a chance.* She wanted him when my husband was unobtainable, but now that she'd caught him, she'd discovered what a wretch he was. If only she'd had the brains to realize that sooner. Still, it wasn't my problem anymore. There was no way I was going to live with that man ever again.

~

THOUGH I'D HOPED ROSS WOULD FIND ACCOMMODATIONS elsewhere, Santa Barbara had few affordable housing options like the Pilot House Motel. Ross went to Richard Cho, who gave him his own room in the motel complex. He could now afford it with the money he was making off porno magazines, and I could support myself and Seanie with my income from my route with the L.A. Times. Eventually, the two of us rekindled a friendship of sorts and drank coffee together on occasion, but it took a while to reach even that minimal level of trust. In the meantime, I focused on raising my son and hanging out with a more reliable set of friends.

One morning, we woke to find that half of the Pilot House Motel had been taken over by Saudi Arabians. I soon learned that the Crown Princess of that country had a child with special needs named Aziz, and they needed a place to stay while they checked out the nearby Devereux School to see if was suitable for the prince. The Chos gave the Princess and Aziz one room, while her entourage of armed guards took several others.

For the first few days, the guardsmen mostly stood around the swimming pool, flashing paranoid looks at all the other tenants, while the fourteen-year-old Aziz ran around the premises in his grey pajamas. He came off as a complete brat, but when I was told that the Princess wanted him to learn English, I decided I would make friends with him.

I sat the boy down and began teaching him the ABCs. For hours, we worked on this basic concept. He seemed insistent on writing everything sideways. One time, he grew bored and snatched my purse, then ran around the swimming pool, threatening to throw it into the water. I screamed and ran after him, which caused the guards to bolt out of their rooms and reach us within seconds. Realizing the situation, they quickly relaxed and laughed at my predicament. At least their reaction told me that Aziz was only teasing. I threw up my hands and walked back to the table.

After a few weeks, Peter and Ross decided they wanted to give the guards a good scare. The two of them brought out their shotguns and disassembled them on the tables out by the swimming pool. After cleaning the components and putting them back together under the suspicious eyes of the Saudis, Richard Cho came out of his office with a stack of old kitchen plates. He then threw them into the air and let Ross and Peter shoot at them for target practice. If the guards were freaked out by this, they quickly recovered. Soon, the guards joined in on the fun, laughing as they competed to see who could land the quickest shot. The paranoia that existed between the Saudis and the Americans was finally gone.

In modern times, the police would have swarmed the motel if they'd heard gunshots going off so close to an airport runway. Somehow, the men got away with their mischief. The atmosphere at the Pilot House improved significantly, and before long, the guards were accompanying us on trips to Carrows to hang out and drink coffee. We had a ball together.

On Sean's second birthday, my family came over to celebrate. They joined the residents around the swimming pool, who were all treating my little boy like a king. The long-haired Princess doted over my son, giving him a stuffed Oscar the Grouch as a present. She was a beautiful woman, and I was so sad when after three months she came up to me and said that the Devereux School was not going to work out for Aziz. No one there knew how to speak Arabic, and it would have been exceedingly difficult to teach Aziz with that kind of language barrier. Instead, they were going to move up to San Francisco. Returning to Saudi Arabia was not an option; her brother was trying to kill her and the rest of her family. My own problems paled in comparison.

To my surprise, the Princess asked me to go with them... to be her friend and to continue to tutor her teenager. I strongly considered it, but ultimately, I decided that I could not. Saudi culture was far too patriarchal for a free-thinking American woman like myself. Her guards and I would not get along very well. Although the Princess was disappointed, she pulled a ring off her finger - a stunning fire ruby - and slipped it onto mine, thanking me for helping her son. I would miss her for a long time. She was a good soul.

Charisse remained a friend, despite having had to flee Phil's cabin after far too many abusive episodes. Sometimes, Phil would disappear for days, leaving her and their baby Madalyn stranded on Paradise Road. Another time, he kidnapped their daughter and took the baby to his brother's place, claiming Charisse was mistreating her. It took a court order to force him to bring back the baby. Finally, he got drunk and pulled a gun on her after knocking her to the floor. She escaped after that, fleeing to her mother's house, and she never went back.

One day, Charisse came to me with the idea of putting our toddlers in a beauty pageant. She was absolutely certain that her baby girl was going to win, but she hoped we could enter the contest together. I didn't have any inclination towards pageantry, but it seemed important to Charisse, so I agreed. After all, Madalyn and Sean often had play dates together and they got along well.

The competition was held at the Miramar Hotel in Montecito. Pictures of children were hung on the wall to encourage sponsors to donate to the pageant. Then they could vote on the child of their choice. Sean's picture showed him sitting on a toy horse with the happiest look on his face. His shockingly-white hair and beautiful blue eyes touched the hearts of a lot of people, and I wasn't terribly surprised when Seanie won the beauty pageant for his age group and was dubbed the King of Goleta.

Despite Sean's success, I knew I wouldn't enter him into another beauty contest. In the end, such pageants are all about making money for their organizers. I didn't need anyone to tell me that Sean was a genuine cutie pie; I got to see that truth every single day.

~

THE PORNOGRAPHY BUSINESS CONTINUED TO GROW, AND ROSS STILL could not stop bragging about the money it was bringing in. In the media, he promoted himself as a successful businessman, partially to boost his ego and partially because he thought the image of power would keep his detractors at bay. But because of all the startup costs, including the airplane and newspaper boxes, Ross was still barely breaking even. Even so, the attention he drew to himself made him a target. The City Council considered him a public nuisance, though they were unable to take him down on their own. It was the State Welfare Department that finally put Ross in their sights, making me an accomplice in their accusations of welfare fraud.

Investigators honed in on the months before I ended our welfare case when Brian purchased the Apache twin-engine plane and Ross began making payments. The bureaucrats said that Ross had lied by failing to list the aircraft as an asset, even though it was under the name and ownership of his startup partner. They accused him of illegally collecting welfare checks during the period when he first used the plane.

Because Ross and I were separated, we hired individual lawyers to argue our cases and plead our innocence. The District Attorney tried to get me to agree to a plea deal because they desperately wanted to take down the "Porno King", but I refused. I'd rip up every piece of paper they handed to me, drop it in a trash can and walk away, stating, "Not guilty."

So the case went to trial. I needed someone to take care of Sean during the proceedings, so I called on a new friend who I'd met in the Carrows Restaurant, Clu Carradine. She was a pretty woman in her early twenties of Norwegian and Assyrian descent with long, raven-black hair, and she agreed to watch Sean in her loft apartment while I spent my days in the county courthouse.

It cost the government one million dollars to bring the case to trial, but they ultimately succeeded. After two weeks, the jury came out of deliberations and gave their verdicts. Ross was declared guilty and forced to repay the three thousand dollars that the welfare department said he owed them. It hadn't helped that he had shown up at the courtroom one day drunk as a skunk. The jurors strongly disliked him, and in regard to the claims of airplane ownership, they found him guilty of perjury as well. It was a farce; the attorneys and I knew the timeline and revenue streams, and Ross was innocent of welfare fraud. He'd broken a lot of laws in his life, but this verdict had more to do with the proliferation of newspaper racks featuring bikini-clad women than with any real justice.

On the other hand, I was acquitted of all charges. They thought that I had been manipulated by Ross and Brian into participating in their schemes. One of the jurors found me soon after, in the parking lot behind Carrows, and she explained that they'd come to a "not guilty" verdict because, "Sometimes our husbands make us do things that are beyond our control."

I didn't think that statement applied to my circumstances, but I thanked her regardless. It is remarkable how little autonomy women are thought to have in our culture. To some, a married woman is practically devoid of free will. I was grateful to escape the situation without a criminal record, but the implications of the jury's decision remain unsettling.

~

THE PRESSURES OF THE PORNOGRAPHY BUSINESS CAUSED ROSS TO increase his alcohol uptake to two-fifths of a bottle of Southern Comfort per day. I couldn't help but feel bad for him. Sometimes, he was a friend to me, but the drinking got in the way of any real relationship.

I was sound asleep in my room one night when one of the neighbors banged on my door to wake me up. "It's Ross," they said. "He has Richard and Vivian's kids in his airplane, and they're about to take off, but he's so drunk, he can't even walk in a straight line!"

I jumped out of bed and ran out behind the motel. I had no idea how my estranged husband had talked Richard into letting him take his children on a midnight ride, but the hotel owner was far too tolerant of Ross' bad behavior. The twin engines of the Apache were rumbling as I rounded the corner and spotted the aircraft. Quickly, I got out in front and held my ground. Ross was stumbling through his pre-flight check when he noticed me, and through the noise, I shouted at him to shut the plane down. He began to argue, but I countered, "If you so much as take that plane onto the taxiway, I am calling the tower to have them block you from taking off!" If Ross were heading out alone, good riddance to him. But there were four children inside...

Angry and swearing, Ross turned the engines off. I shooed the kids away, then returned to bed knowing that it was quite possible that I'd saved their lives that night.

Ross continued to use the plane for recreation, occasionally carrying journalists out to the islands and oil rigs. But he began taking chances with his passengers. He would dip one of the wings low enough to send the aircraft into a side dive, frightening the heck out of them. Normally, Ross was skilled enough that he could course-correct and recover from any situation. But the alcohol steadily wore away at his judgment. One day, he decided to dive-bomb a Coast Guard cutter. They took down the Apache's aircraft number and soon Ross was called up in front of the FAA administration. His pilot's license was taken away, and that brought one phase of the porno business to an embarrassing end.

Brian realized that even if Ross were able to earn back his license, the liability of having a drunkard pilot his aircraft was just too much. In addition, a costly major overhaul of the twin engines was coming due. So, Brian made the decision to exit the pornography enterprise. Ross hadn't completely repaid him for the Apache yet, so the plane was put up for sale and with the proceeds, Ross and Brian were able to come to a financial arrangement that allowed Ross to take over the business. Brian's wife was hugely relieved.

The first thing Ross did was to bring in his old friend Phil as a partner. Then, because they didn't have a plane anymore, they hired me to drive to L.A. to pick up the magazines and newspapers and make deliveries on my way back to Santa Barbara. I didn't mind the route, for it was only one day a week and I was paid fifty dollars to do it. But it irked me sometimes to see Ross and Phil sitting around the Pilot House swimming pool, drinking up the business profits.

One day, I was sitting on my front porch watching Sean roam the parking lot, flanked by Tawny and Proto. He had a spray bottle in his hand and was giving all the trees and bushes a drink of water. As he wandered, my attention was drawn to what seemed like a black garbage bag being stirred by the wind in front of the motel. I walked out to the road to investigate, only to find the saddest creature: a tan-and-black-furred doberman, all skin and bones, struggling to make it just a few more yards so it could lay down and die on some green grass.

I scooped the poor thing up and carried him to our room. Then after hustling the other two dogs into my car so that they wouldn't bother my patient, I returned to our unit and started spooning water into the doberman's mouth. He didn't seem likely to recover, but I kept hydrating him over the course of twenty-four hours until he appeared conscious enough to take in some food. I mixed up a batch of oatmeal with some raw eggs and fed it to him slowly. He kept the meal down, and after a crucial week of this regimen, I began adding dog food to his diet.

It worked. The big guy's emaciated frame began to fill out. I already had two dogs to care for, but there was no way I could have turned my back on that poor animal... not on my watch. The doberman finally felt healthy enough to play with us. He didn't like balls, but he enjoyed fetching aluminum cans. It became difficult to keep him out of the pool since he loved swimming so much, as many dobermans do. Thankfully, Richard and Vivian didn't mind. In fact, they adopted him, giving him the name Cho Cho.

I could never understand why people abandon their pets or lose them. From my experience with my own dogs, I've learned that when canines take off on an extended wander and fail to return when you call their names, there are three likely scenarios. First, the animal could have been taken home by a concerned neighbor, in which case, you need to just put the word out. Second, the dog could return to the point where they last saw you, and this can take up to three hours. A lot of owners don't know that they need to be patient, so they don't remain in those locations for long enough. When a dog can't find you, they will sometimes take the third option and try to find their way home by themselves. Perhaps this is what Cho Cho was doing when I found him, though his wretched state made me think that he'd been abandoned far from his original neighborhood.

On one afternoon, Proto hopped out of my truck to relieve himself or investigate a compelling odor. When he disappeared, I searched the area and could not find him, so I continued making my newspaper deliveries. The next day, I found him at nearly the exact place where he'd vanished - beneath a newspaper stand in front of the Greyhound station in Santa Barbara. Nowadays, we have microchips and tracking collars to help us keep tabs on our pups. But regardless of such measures, if one understands the canine mentality, one should have reasonable luck reuniting with a lost dog.

~

THE TIME CAME FOR PHIL'S MOTHER TO MOVE OUT OF HER CABIN ON Paradise Road. Phyllis had retired there with her police officer husband several years ago, and when her spouse passed on, she was left in the woods alone, apart from the short, sporadic times that Phil and Ross would move in. Now Phyllis was succumbing to old age and mental illness, and her son wanted to move her to an apartment on Broadmore Avenue in Santa Barbara where it would be more convenient to look after her.

The first time Ross and Phil took me to meet Phyllis, they warned me on the way up San Marcos Pass that she had schizophrenic personality disorder. She met us at the door of her cabin, took my hand and led me to the couch, giving me a cuddly blanket to keep me warm. I thought she was a wonderful lady, with beautiful Arabic features. An old, red Doberman pinscher followed her throughout the room as she brought tea and scones to the coffee table. Then she sat on her recliner and we got to know each other. We discussed politics, life and ambitions, but then suddenly her eyes changed. "Nancy," she blurted out, "did you know somebody is pulling the hairs out of my dog's vagina?"

I was prepared for the abrupt change, so I asked her what made her think so.

"Because she is peeing ever so much more now," she replied. Then she spoke of the statue of St. Francis of Assisi on her mantle that kept the bees from entering her house. A true delight, this woman was.

After she was relocated to her new apartment, Phil's mother continued to have us over for tea. The curtains were all taped to the wall to keep the Devil out, I noticed. She had her eccentricities, but thanks to this woman, I learned not to be afraid of mental illness.

Not long after, *everyone* at the Pilot House Motel found themselves having to move. The airport had decided that the motel was not a profitable enterprise and they wanted to put a pilot training center in its place. So they shut the business down. Richard and Vivian decided they'd had enough of California for the time being, and they moved down to Texas, bringing Cho Cho and the whole family with them. Phil moved into his mother's recently-emptied cabin and Ross and I decided we would purchase a Dodge window van so we could run newspaper routes and sleep in the back when necessary. It seemed like our best option because most landlords charged new tenants first and last month's rent, plus a pet deposit, and we simply didn't have the money.

We placed a mattress in the back of the van and parked the vehicle behind the Carrows restaurant whenever we weren't doing routes. But Ross only lasted a week. He couldn't abide living in such cramped quarters with Seanie, myself and the two dogs, so he moved into the Paradise Road cabin with Phil. I was more adaptable to the lifestyle change. Thanks to a black market card I purchased from a friend, I was able to sneak in and use the showers at the harbor. Whenever they changed the locks on the building, I would simply buy a new card for twenty-five dollars. That, or pay a dollar and fifty cents to use the Cabrillo Pavilion gym and showers.

The Santa Barbara News-Press hired me to run a street sales route on Upper State, so I put Sean in preschool and managed to scrape by with that job in addition to my work with the L.A. Times. I helped with the pornography business when I could. Ross and Phil continued to supply the newspaper racks with questionable material, working just two days on most weeks. They invited Sean and me to come up to the cabin on weekends and swim in the Santa Ynez River when temperatures were hot.

On a regular basis, we had to deal with vigilante citizens disabling the porno newspaper boxes. Paper clips would be jammed into the coin slots and were a pain to remove, so Ross staked out one of the locations until he discovered who it was... an acquaintance of ours. The vandal would empty the machines of newspapers, then stick paper clips in the slots before going to the dumpster behind the Jolly Tiger

Restaurant to dispose of them. Of course, the man would also flip through the periodicals and masturbate before tossing them in with the garbage. He was just another hypocrite, ashamed of his sexual feelings and trying to feel better about himself by destroying the cause of his temptation.

Ross wasn't about to let the guy get away with it. One night, while the man was inside the Jolly Tiger, Ross and Phil took some stencils and spray painted the male and female sex symbols all over his baby, a classic Mustang. When he discovered what was happened, he was too embarrassed to drive it anywhere; he had it towed to a paint shop. To be fair, the Mustang was in bad need of a paint job anyway. After that, the paper clips stopped being a problem.

Then came the "Permatex Man". Permatex glue started to show up in the coin slots of the machines, so we started a new investigation. This time, my friend Clu Carradine and I discovered the identity of the perpetrator. Ross hired us to serve him court papers and we found his address by visiting the voter registrar's office. Ross and Phil sued the man for damages. Unfortunately, his slick attorney managed to get him acquitted.

Still, despite these setbacks and Ross and Phil's sporadically incompetent behavior, the porno business began to thrive. They were selling Hustler magazines by the hundreds in Ventura, Oxnard and Santa Barbara. A single store on State Street was bringing them over a thousand dollars in profits every week. The City of Santa Barbara continued to push back against their enterprise, and Ross' ACLU attorney had to work even harder to keep the government from ripping the newspaper boxes out of the sidewalks.

At one point, Ross and Phil were asked by their bosses to fly to San Francisco and bump off a contractor who was behind on his bills. They rented a private aircraft for the journey, and I have no idea if they ever intended to do the deed, but instead of killing the man, they took a few days to coach him and help him rebuild his business so that he could start catching up on his payments. I only heard the tale once the two of them returned to Southern California. Perhaps they thought that their bosses would be pleased with their solution. Instead, when the company discovered that their orders had been disobeyed, they sent representatives up from Los Angeles and took Ross and Phil's two most profitable store accounts away.

That was quite a blow. But the two friends went searching for other distributors in Los Angeles and managed to secure another magazine account to add to their deliveries. They needed a place to stash the magazines, so Clu offered her place for a period of time. Hundreds of Hustlers, High Times and other anti-establishment magazines were stacked high across her entrance floor. Some of the foster kids were still hanging around, so they helped recycle the unsold papers after pulling off the front covers for return credit.

Ross and Phil were terrible businessmen, it has to be said. They were constantly facing budget crises, and more often than not, their survival strategies backfired on them. If not for the help of their friends, myself included, their enterprise never would have lasted as long as it did. One of their faults was a failure to be proactive. They preferred to let their cars break down on the highway rather than do simple maintenance ahead of time, like replacing worn-out tires.

I bore the brunt of their negligence on more than one occasion. One evening, while driving back from Ventura after making some porno deliveries, a tire on the driver's side of my Pontiac blew out and forced me to swiftly pull over onto the shoulder of the 101. It was dark, and I was afraid to change the tire so close to the other vehicles whipping past. So, I picked up my son, who'd been sleeping in the front seat, then locked the doors and tried to figure out where I could make a phone call. First, I had to climb over a chain link fence with three-year-old Sean clinging to my back, his arms wrapped around my neck. Then I had to walk across an overpass in order to reach the lobby of the Miramar Hotel. I called up Carrows, and by chance, Ross was there with Phil having coffee. To my dismay, the two of them refused to come help; they just told me to call a tow company.

I was upset and exhausted, but I made the call and persuaded the driver to pick us up at the hotel on his way to the highway. He didn't like where the Pontiac was parked either, so he towed the vehicle to his lot and changed the tire there. I waited inside the office until my car was ready, then drove to Carrows. Ross and Phil were just sitting there at the counter, carefree, so I walked up to Ross and informed him that the route would not be finished. I was furious with them because now I had to go home, put Sean to bed and get some sleep so I could be ready to deliver the L.A. Times four hours later.

Still, the following week I did the porno rounds one more time. In the course of my route, I found several newspaper boxes that needed maintenance. I didn't have the know-how to repair them myself, so I listed the locations on a piece of paper. When I returned to town, I found Ross and his partner at Carrows, handed them the paper and explained what needed fixing.

Ross glowered at me and growled, "What's the matter with you fixing them? Are you stupid?"

I stared at him for a moment, then replied, "Yes, I am, apparently. And by the way, I quit! You can do your own job." With that, I walked away. No amount of money was worth dealing with those idiots.

## 6

# DETOXIFICATION

Sean and I continued to adjust to van life. His preschool building was right next to the L.A. Times warehouse, and there was a bathroom nearby at the McConnell's Ice Cream factory with a sink I could use for Seanie's baths. The van itself was warm and cozy at night, and I was able to stash money away so that someday we could find a new place to live. On most days, after I finished my afternoon route with the News-Press, I would pick up Seanie and drive over to Carrows for dinner. Then we'd return to the warehouse and park across the street in front of McConnell's. A security light shone above the van, allowing me to read my son a bedtime story before tucking him into bed. After he dozed off, I'd do some reading myself, then curl up with Tawny and Proton on the mattress next to him.

This schedule worked for a time. Then after a few weeks, Ross and Phil suddenly showed up in the middle of the night, waking me up. To my disbelief, they were there to kick me, the dogs and the baby out onto the streets so that they could take the van back to the cabin with them. At first, I tried fighting them off, but to no avail. Then I screamed for help. Someone called the police, thankfully, and when the officers arrived, I was able to explain the situation to their satisfaction.

They told Phil and my so-called husband to back off, otherwise they'd be arrested and thrown in jail for causing a disturbance.

The female officer gave me the address of a domestic violence shelter that would keep us from suffering a repeat of tonight's incident. I respectfully declined. I loved my independence too much and didn't want to risk losing it. Also, I believed that Ross and Phil wouldn't have the gumption to try such a heinous act again.

~

ONE DAY, NEW PORNO RACKS STARTED TO APPEAR NEXT TO ROSS'S on every sidewalk location. They contained similar newspapers and magazines, but for a quarter less than what Ross was charging. It was a mystery for a while until I finally learned what was going on. They were Phil's. Phil and Ross had experienced yet another falling out, and now Phil was attempting to undermine his former friend's business. The two of them were constantly vacillating on their friendship... it was hard to keep track of how things stood between them sometimes, rather like my own marriage.

Still, Clu and I thought that Phil's gambit was despicable. He had found a different distributor in Los Angeles and his new racks were deliberately placed to undercut Ross, who was supposed to be his best friend. I wasn't feeling particularly warm toward my husband, but that didn't mean I wanted his business to collapse. Clu and I decided it was time to intervene. It might not change anything, but at least we could have fun while doing it.

First, we went to the office supply store and picked up an ink stamp kit. We created a stamp that read, "If this rack offends you in any way, please feel free to call Swillip W. Stay, a mother-and-son corporation." Next to those words, we included Phil's phone number. This disclaimer was stamped onto Post-It Notes, which were a new product at the time, and placed onto each of Phil's newspaper boxes. Phil might have received some harassment as a result, but the boxes didn't disappear.

Next, Clu and I went to the butcher on Milpas Street and picked up a lamb's head from the meat counter. We asked him to stamp the waxed paper bag with a specific price: $6.66. Thinking it was a joke among friends, the butcher complied. We stuck the bag inside one of Phil's racks in front of a motel on Cabrillo Boulevard. Three days later, you couldn't walk past that motel without gagging. *Mission accomplished.*

But the game wasn't over. Soon afterward, a roadkill skunk appeared in Phil's Advocate rack in front of Carrows. It wasn't one of our sabotage attempts... Ross had done it himself, adopting our tactics of mental and olfactory torture. We decided it was a good time for Clu and I to start minding our own business again. Ross could escalate things if he chose.

And escalate things he did. Sometime later, Sean and I were visiting my husband at his friend Richard's house on Ortega Street, and on our way out the door, Ross asked me to toss something into the trash outside. When I opened the lid of the garbage can, the stench hit me like a fist. Stewing within that receptacle was a revolting mixture of dog feces, fish guts and other decomposing liquified ingredients - an unimaginable soup of stomach-churning filth. Ross realized his mistake and rushed outside, telling me I wasn't supposed to have seen that concoction.

A week later, I spied Phil hosing down the racks and sidewalks in front of the Radio Square liquor store. He surrendered and took his racks down. The war was over.

Phil had other concerns to worry about. He had started to show signs of his mother's schizophrenia disorder. More and more often, his face failed to register any kind of emotional expression, no matter what kind of events were happening around him. Perhaps the stress of being an independent business owner had pushed him over the edge. At any rate, he managed to apply and qualify for Social Security disability payments. It gave him the ability to move into the apartment with his mother, Phyllis. The cabin on Paradise Road was finally sold, and the two of them were able to survive on his disability checks and her widow's pension. They even had enough money to hire a caregiver for Phil's mom.

EVEN AFTER PHIL'S EXIT FROM THE PORNO BUSINESS, ROSS struggled to maintain a profit. He began hanging out around the L.A. Times warehouse, desperately hoping my boss Mr. Monson would give him a shift or two. But despite his improved dental condition, nobody wanted him as an employee. His alcohol addiction was too much of a liability. Instead, Mr. Monson called him into his office one day with a different proposal. My boss had grown tired of seeing me struggle with homelessness, so he offered to help us afford the rent on a new apartment. He would supply the first and last month's rent, plus the deposit. All Ross had to do was find us a place to live.

He chose the Ladera Apartments on the west side of the city. I hated the place. It was a total dive, and the cockroaches were so prevalent that they felt brave enough to scurry about both night and day. They lived in my stereo, in the kitchen and even slept with us in bed. When I sat at the dinner table, the pests would crawl right onto my plate and start snacking. I went crazy trying to keep the population down. None of the cockroach hotels or other commercial products made a dent in their numbers. Even stuffing newspaper into the holes in the walls and spackling them over didn't seem to affect their comings and goings. Clu came over sometimes, and we spent hours swatting cockroaches off the walls while smoking pot to stay sane.

Occasionally, I'd put a wet steak bone in the bathtub. When I came back after a half-hour, the tub would be completely black with their chitinous bodies. I'd turn on the shower head and flush them all down the drain, but just like the Itsy Bitsy Spider, they'd soon crawl up the spout again. *What was I to do?*

Ross was no help. He had purchased a wormwood dining table, two chairs and a desk for himself, but he wouldn't use an ashtray. The cigarette ashes went right onto the floor. He also wouldn't let me clean up the stacked empty bottles of Southern Comfort because he wanted to save them for target practice. That drew even more cockroaches onto the premises because they loved the smell of booze and the scent was ever-present.

Typically, Ross and Phil would stand on the front balcony for hours, drinking and arguing about nothing. Their drunken voices echoed all across the compound. And the abuse I received from Ross began to get even worse. Fear would rush through my system whenever he walked through the front door. I'd try to escape by running into the bathroom and locking the door, but Ross would beat his fist against it and shout, "The white coats are coming for you!" I could cower in a corner and cry my heart out. I never knew if he was going to be nice or nasty, and the anxiety threw me into a deep depression. I resorted to smoking copious amounts of weed just to make it through the day.

One afternoon, I was attempting to make deliveries in a manual Chevy truck with a broken clutch, and I couldn't stop crying over my situation. Just then, the radio announced a class at the Cottage Hospital Detox Center on how to stage an intervention for an alcoholic member of your family. It felt like a guardian angel was reaching out to me in my time of greatest need. I quickly scribbled the number down. Something had to change, and I hoped this program could be the catalyst.

One of the first things we did in the class was watch a movie about the effects of alcohol abuse on the American family. I was stunned - it was like watching my life play out on screen. Afterward, the counselors asked me if I saw anything familiar in the film that I could relate to. "All of it," I answered.

In a co-dependent relationship with an alcoholic, the sober partner gets sucked into thinking that it's their fault that their spouse drinks all the time, and that lie was what I had come to believe with Ross. Co-dependency is its own form of illness... one that can cripple and destroy the enabler. In fact, it was remarkable that I'd lasted as long as I had. My self-worth had become tied to the sacrifices I was willing to make for Ross in order to protect him from the outside world. I had a need to try and save him, so I'd accepted more and more responsibility for our relationship until I was collapsing both mentally and physically from exhaustion. My husband was very willing to accept all of my sacrifices, but ultimately, the co-dependency had to end. I needed to get my life back.

The counselors taught me how to hold an intervention with the goal of convincing Ross to seek treatment, and over the next few weeks, I recruited Mr. Monson, Clu, my father and a number of Ross' friends. Then I managed to convince Ross to come to one of my sessions at the detox center on De La Vina Street. He was very surprised to see the assemblage of familiar faces. Although he felt manipulated into becoming the center of attention and concern, the intervention ceremony provided a loving container where we could all explain our reasons for wanting him to seek help. At the end of the day, however, the decision had to rest with him.

In a moment of rare bravery, Ross agreed that it was time. He checked himself into a room at the rehabilitation center for a two-week detox program.

It was tough; Ross experienced two half-hour seizures while his body adjusted to the lack of alcohol. But it was great to see him eating real food again and making his first steps on the long road to recovery. In the meantime, I vowed to read up on related literature so I could understand my part in our family dynamic.

Sadly, I went to visit Ross one afternoon, only to learn that he'd been kicked out of the program. Phil had shown up the day before with a six-pack of Colt 45s, and the two of them were caught in the act. I was frantic to fix the situation, but it was too late. Ross went back to drinking the bottles of Southern Comfort he was so fond of, and the dysfunction continued.

I was terribly unhappy. The Ladera apartment complex as a whole was dreadful. The neighbors were unfriendly, and domestic violence was exceedingly common. Ross and I were also fighting all the time, and it was taking a toll on our son. Seanie started to make repetitive movements out of stress and anxiety, like opening and closing the refrigerator door over and over again. After I witnessed him banging his head against the living room wall, it truly occurred to me that we needed to get out of there. I couldn't even take care of myself properly, let alone a son and a sick husband.

Clu told me, "You have to get away from all this. You're going to wind up in a loony bin and lose your son." She was right; I could envision the authorities stepping in sooner rather than later, and Sean would be taken away from me. Clu offered to let me live in her tiny loft apartment for a while until I got my life back together. It was tempting. But moving away would mean the end of my marriage to Ross, I knew with certainty.

While I was considering such a major shift, I met a man at work who had a contract to deliver the L.A. Herald Examiner, and sitting on the tailgate of his truck was the most beautiful German shepherd I had ever seen. Stately and proud, with a rich black and tan-colored coat.

"Is she ever going to have puppies?" I asked, excitedly.

He affirmed that was the case. My heart beat quicker, and I told him that I would love to save up for one of them. He named a price of two hundred and fifty dollars, and that was all I needed to hear.

I couldn't wait for my puppy to be born. The afternoon I set out to pick him up, however, Ross put his foot down. "If you buy that dog, our marriage is over."

I looked at my husband in astonishment. *Wasn't it already over?*

Clu picked up the phone when I called. She was happy to come with me to collect the puppy, so I loaded Sean, Tawny and Proto into one of Ross' vans and headed over to her place. I felt a little sick to my stomach, but what kind of marriage did I have, anyway? I was married to a sick man who could not pay the rent, let alone any of the bills... a man who cheated on me and had abandoned our son and I so many times it had rendered our marriage meaningless. I was tired of being a codependent partner, which was a psychological disorder in itself. It was best to cut my losses and get out of there.

So I chose to leave the Ladera Apartments and everything that came with it. Ross and Phil could stay up on the balcony if they wanted, arguing the finer points of orbital mechanics for the entertainment of the apartment complex. I had ceased to care. I prepared myself mentally to spend the night at Clu's place that evening, confident that I had done everything that I could have done to make my marriage work. It was a little heartbreaking, but I kept in mind the words of my father: "No matter what your station is in life, hold your head up high and go ever forward."

MY NEW GERMAN SHEPHERD, WHO I NAMED SCHATZIE, WAS absolutely adorable. The puppy buoyed my spirits as Clu and I drove from the breeder's house back to the Ladera Apartments. Clu offered to stay with me for moral support, which I appreciated, especially when we approached the building and I heard Ross on the balcony above us muttering, "Oh my god, she got the dog."

With Schatzie cradled in my arms, I looked up at him and Phil and announced, "I'm leaving, Ross. If you want anything in the apartment, you'd better get it out of here."

Thankfully, there were no further fights or confrontations. A few hours later, Ross vanished, along with his vehicles and his few possessions. I expected he had gone to live in Phil's apartment in Santa Barbara since there was no chance he could afford to pay rent on his own.

Ross' absence meant I wouldn't have to move into Clu's loft immediately. That made things easier; I could take a few days to pack up the apartment. Clu walked herself home, and that evening, I began the process of putting items into boxes. I did pause to cry for a while when I thought back on the ordeal of the last few months. I never wanted to experience despair like that again.

The next day, we borrowed my father's truck, loaded all the beautiful wormwood furniture into it and drove to a storage facility in Goleta. I paid the first and last month's rent on the storage unit, though in my heart, I said goodbye to all those things. They were too cockroach-infested for me to want to have anything to do with them again.

Back at the Ladera apartment, I continued the nauseating task of going through my clothing, shaking out all the hidden cockroaches, then folding them and placing them in cardboard boxes. I duct-taped every crack, then piled each box next to the door. Once most of my garments and possessions were ready for transport, Clu and I decided to take a break, and we headed to Carrows for a cup of coffee.

Upon our return, I was dismayed to discover that the apartment had been broken into. The thief had gone through a window and taken all the things that meant anything to me - the remnants of my silver coin collection, a pellet gun, my jewelry and my stereo. I was furious. I knew it hadn't been Ross, because he had his own arsenal of guns and wouldn't have bothered taking a puny pellet gun. It had to have been someone from the neighborhood.

Clu and I began roaming the apartment complex, knocking on doors and begging for information. However, the predominantly Latino community was extremely closed-mouth. They didn't want to stir up trouble for themselves. "I'm not going to call the cops," I told them, "I just want to get my stuff back." Still, it took several hours before someone volunteered to identify the perpetrator. It was the apartment manager's son.

I had to make a decision. Most people would have called the police, but I remembered the day when I'd been caught stealing from a store in Barstow. The store owner could have had me taken to the station, but luckily, he knew my dad, and he let my parents dictate my punishment. It meant a great deal to have been given that much discretion, and I hadn't taken it for granted. So I decided to give the boy the opportunity to fix the situation. A little bit of mercy might help him rethink his life choices. At the very least, I knew I had to get the pellet gun back; it could do some damage if it ended up in the wrong hands.

I found the little perpetrator walking around the apartment complex and walked up to him. "I know you broke into my apartment and took my things," I began. "So here's what we're going to do. I'm going to leave and get myself a cup of coffee. When I return in one hour, everything needs to be back where it was. Otherwise, I'm going to go to your dad and charge him for what you've taken. I expect he won't be too happy about that."

The manager's son was only twelve or thirteen years old, and the frightened look on his face assured me that he didn't want word of this getting back to his father. He rallied his friends, and when I returned from Carrows, sure enough, all my stuff was back... except for the silver coins. Turns out, he and his buddies had already spent them. I could have pursued the matter further, but I let it drop. I didn't have the energy, plus, I hoped that giving the boy a second chance would help him turn his life around.

It took a couple of days, but the apartment was finally emptied of everything but the cockroaches. My dad and my brother Bill had helped transport all of my boxes to Clu's patio, where I could unpack my belongings a little at a time. I locked the apartment door, dropped the key off at the manager's office, then walked with Sean and the dogs over to Clu's place on Santa Barbara Street. She lived in a garage that had been converted into a tiny loft apartment. One of her two windows looked out onto Vera Cruz Park, which was nicknamed Needle Park for the amount of drug use that undoubtedly happened there at nighttime. Her kitchen and bathroom were not part of the garage building; they were attached to the main house where the land-lords lived. It was easy to deduce that this disjointed rental arrange-ment had been cobbled together without city permits, but that situation was commonplace among low-income housing units in Santa Barbara.

Sean and I slept that first night downstairs on the front room floor - the same place where, months earlier, we'd stored porno magazines for Ross and Phil's distribution business. We had no mattress; in fact, we hadn't used a mattress in the Ladera apartment either because Ross refused to buy a bed. He had preferred to spend his money on alcohol. So Sean and I bedded down in our usual way, laying a quilt on the bare floor and resting upon that. I didn't mind sleeping on a hard surface; I was used to it, and there were many dogs on the premises to help keep me warm, not just Schatzie, Tawny and Proto. Clu had a pair of Samoyeds named Snake and Sammy who decided to wander downstairs to pay us a visit. Snake formed an instant bond with Seanie and snug-gled in to become a pillow for him. I breathed easy, knowing that Ross was finally gone and unable to torment me any longer. I soon drifted off into a peaceful sleep.

No sooner had I slipped into dreams than I awoke to the sound of Clu grumbling and stomping around the downstairs of her apartment. She was dumping Tide detergent, water and any other liquids she could find into a five-gallon bucket. I asked her what was going on, and she explained that four winos had set up camp in Vera Cruz Park right beneath her window. She'd politely requested that they move on to a different location so their drinking and arguing wouldn't wake up her new housemates, but one of the men looked up at her and told her to

"Fuck off!" Obviously, he was unaware that you should never talk that way to a woman who grew up streetwise in Chicago.

After Clu put the finishing touches on her concoction, she carried the bucket up the stairs, leaned out her window and dumped its contents out onto the heads of the four drunkards. A cacophony of cursing followed, but it did the trick; the winos moved away from her window and they never returned. Everyone needs a little discipline once in a while.

I slept until 2:30 a.m., when I normally would go in to work for Mr. Monson. But instead of extricating myself from the pile of puppies, I decided that I just couldn't do it anymore. I couldn't stomach going to the distribution garages where I knew Ross would be hanging around, looking for work. Mr. Monson still wouldn't hire him because of his drinking problem; it wasn't worth the risk. So I went back to sleep. Perhaps Ross and I could go back to being friends someday, but I couldn't bear to see my ex-husband quite yet.

In the morning, I told Clu of my new plans. I would go on welfare and contribute my food stamps to the household every month in addition to doing all the cooking. She agreed. I loved Clu, for she was one of the bravest and most intelligent people that I knew. My friend was highly social and had a number of boyfriends. She did voiceover work and had even acted in a few commercials for the Nestle chocolate company as a child, though her main source of income came through her job as an answering service operator.

*Clu Carradine and one of her Samoyeds (photo by Robert C. Merritt)*

Being on welfare required periodic trips to the Unemployment office. I was supposed to be looking for work, but I'd already decided on my next career path. I wanted to become a police officer. Some might consider that an odd choice, considering my association with Ross and his frequent run-ins with the law, but my parents had instilled a heavy sense of social responsibility in me. Also, after living in low-income housing for many years, I'd seen plenty of vulnerable people trapped in rough situations, and I wanted to be in a position where I could help them out.

The Unemployment Office helped me take the prerequisite Civil Service exams, and then I applied for an opening at the police department. I aced the written exam, but I failed the physical. They told me to try again next year.

I didn't want to wait that long. I took a Police Science course at City College, then tried for a Custody Officer position at the sheriff's department. If I landed the job, I'd be looking after the safety of prisoners at the county jail. This time, I aced both the written and physical exams but flunked the psychological test because I said I would snitch on a fellow officer if they did something bad. At the time, I wasn't aware that it was considered a cardinal sin to rat on your coworkers in the police department. I had to simply swallow my disappointment and move on.

Soon afterward, I received word that Mr. Monson at the L.A. Times wanted me to come back to work. It seemed like I was destined to work for that man for the rest of my adult life. Despite my reluctance, I was glad to be able to get off welfare, which was due to run out eventually. The food stamps disappeared, but I continued to purchase food and cook for Clu for as long as Sean and I remained as guests in the apartment.

By this point, Seanie was four years old and as precocious as ever. I made him a Superman costume for Halloween, and he couldn't get enough of it. He begged me every day to allow him to wear it, and I would always have to attach his cape around his neck whenever he went outside to play.

Inevitably, Sean would wander across Vera Cruz Park and find himself staring through the fence at the children playing in the adjacent Head Start preschool playground. He attracted the attention of the teachers there, and they managed to contact me and asked if I would like to enroll him. That sounded like a great idea, especially for safety reasons. Even though Sean was an only child, I was still having a difficult time keeping track of him.

Vera Cruz Park had another name: Wino Park. After Clu and I made friends with its homeless residents, we were able to relax and allow ourselves to be entertained. The ringleaders of most festivities were four old men named Winner, Popeye, Joe and Clifford, and they were amiable hosts to any visitors who wandered through their domain from other parts of the city. I started going out to the park every other day to practice my guitar and sing for the often-inebriated crowd. When they asked me why I wanted to hang with them, I answered truthfully that if I were going to learn about the world, I needed to know every aspect of it. I couldn't just ignore the rougher edges of humanity.

One day, the police came to take Winner down to the station. It was part of a familiar cycle. First, tickets for public intoxication were issued, then the outstanding tickets would turn into warrants. Finally, the cops would show up at the park and haul one of the four regulars off to jail. Three days later, the sober individual would walk back to Vera Cruz Park wearing a clean set of clothes and smelling much nicer after having showered. The detoxification process never stuck, however. Within hours, they'd be drinking with their alcoholic buddies once again.

This time, it was Winner's turn to go to the "hotel on the hill". For the police, it was not an enviable chore, so they made the rookies handle the transportation. When Winner was placed in the back of the rookie's patrol car, he promptly pulled down his pants and shit all over the seat. The rest of us could hear the baby cop scream in outrage. He tried to refuse to take Winner to the station, saying he couldn't enter the vehicle without gagging, but his superiors forced him to get behind the wheel and drive downtown. "Atta boy, Winner!" the rest of us shouted enthusiastically.

There was an element of insanity to these scenes in Vera Cruz Park, of course, since no one was trying to find long-term solutions to the crises of alcohol abuse and homelessness. No attempts were ever made to treat the vagrants' alcoholism like the disease it truly was. As a society, we simply accepted that if we paid our taxes, the police would take care of everything, and if the problems weren't addressed to our satisfaction, we would simply pressure the police department to make more arrests.

I suppose I felt sympathy for the winos in the park because my relationship with Ross had taught me how crippling alcoholism could become and how hard it could be to break the addiction, even with community assistance. Thanks to the Cottage Hospital Detox Center, I had learned about codependency and how to keep myself from getting drawn into the manipulative narratives Ross had spun around me. That allowed me to listen to the tales told by the homeless men and women without getting taken advantage of. But even from an objective point of view, it was difficult to keep from getting upset when I learned of the physical and verbal abuse they received at the hands of the police. Likewise, it was frustrating to hear that Santa Barbara had no shelters for homeless people except for an old, rundown mission building that didn't hold nearly enough beds for all of them.

I became a minor celebrity in our corner of Santa Barbara due to my friendliness with the alcoholic community. Every morning, when I drove up and placed the L.A. Times into the racks in front of the

liquor stores on State Street, the winos would all extend warm greet-
ings to the Newspaper Lady. In truth, they were waiting at the store
entrances for the doors to open so that they could purchase alcohol,
but they treated me like royalty all the same.

In the 1970s, drinking on the streets of Santa Barbara was
customary and accepted. People could carry open beer and wine
bottles as they shuffled down sidewalks in various stages of inebriation,
which made it a little unnerving to walk the neighborhoods around
State Street at night. Whenever Clu and I ventured out to Sambo's, we
always carried a cane or walking stick, just in case we needed an impro-
vised weapon. I wasn't irrationally afraid of the drunks in the city; in
fact, sometimes we would invite the park winos onto our patio for a
communal barbecue. It just paid to be prudent.

It paid especially well to be prudent when your ex-husband was an
alcoholic. One afternoon, Clu came running into the house with a
worried look on her face. She said that Ross was outside and wanted to
talk. Reluctantly, I stepped outside, crossed my arms and told him he
had to leave. Our marriage was over.

Ross looked desperate, and so was his story. He pleaded for me to
take him in because he was homeless and had nowhere to live. Phil
must have kicked him out of his apartment. I held my ground and told
him to just sleep in his van until he patched things up with Phil.
Allowing Ross to stay at Clu's house was out of the question, for my
life had improved immeasurably once I no longer had to deal with the
man's boozing on a daily basis. He would have to quit drinking for
good if I were to ever consider getting back together with him.

Ross cursed me as he left the premises. I knew that he and Phil
would bury their differences before too long, however. They were co-
dependent in their own way. Perhaps I should have mandated that
Ross keep his distance, but every once in a while, Clu and I got soft
and invited him and Phil over for a barbecue on the patio. Inevitably, it
led to trouble.

The two men had discovered the hobby of model rockets, which
they built and set off at Vera Cruz Park. Their interactions with
Popeye, Winner and the rest of the wino crew must have gone sour,
because one day, Ross and Phil, drunk off their asses, decided to head

into the park with shovels resting on their shoulders. They walked up to our other friends and asked them where they wanted their graves to be dug.

The old homeless men were frantic. One of them ran to a pay phone, called the police and babbled about rockets and graves. A drove of patrol cars quickly converged on the scene. By this time, however, Ross and Phil had dashed into Clu's house and were rubbing toothpaste against their teeth so that their breath wouldn't smell like booze.

Clu and I leaned up against the park fence so we could observe the cops attempting to interrogate the winos. One officer noticed us and walked over to ask if we knew anything about this model-rocket-and-shovels business.

"Say what?" Clu responded innocently. "You're talking to people who see pink elephants. There's no shovels or rockets here."

Since the police couldn't pull any corroborative information out of us, they left the neighborhood. We went inside the apartment and lectured the troublesome duo before kicking them out. From that point on, Ross and Phil were banned from using the park for their shenanigans.

## ❧ 7 ❧

## WELCOME TO THE JUNGLE

Clu and I spent a lot of our time at a restaurant called Sambo's 101 on Montecito Street, just down from the giant Moreton Bay fig tree. Folks added "101" to its name due to its proximity to the highway. We drank copious amounts of coffee there, smoked innumerable cigarettes and got to know the colorful clientele. It was a great venue for meeting people and we felt well-protected. The regulars kept watch over us, as well as Seanie when he was in our company.

Behind the restaurant was a gay bar called The Pub, and every Friday, the men would all migrate over to Sambo's for Drag Night. They would dress up as waitresses and take over the establishment with hilarious results. Other nights were not as amusing. Things could get out of control, and we witnessed both fistfights and food fights among the patrons. Yet we kept going back because it was always interesting, and our visits yielded Clu a new boyfriend from time to time.

The faces of Clu's partners were mostly a blur to me, for she tired of men quickly and felt no qualms about leaving them by the wayside. I remembered Bart the Fart, who lived up to his nickname. Then there was Kenny, the largest and the most dangerous one of the bunch, especially when he'd been drinking. Clu quickly realized that the man had a sinister side, but by then it was too late - he had latched onto her and would not let her go. I couldn't remember Clu being afraid of anyone, yet Kenny could work her up into a panic.

Normally, Clu was fearless. I recalled one night when a homeless woman was being attacked in Vera Cruz Park by some men who were trying to rob her of her disability money. Clu grabbed a primary chain from an old motorcycle and ran out into the park, whipping the chain around and driving them off long enough so that she could rescue the woman and bring her into the apartment. She let the lady take a shower, then fed her before sending her on her way. That's the Clu I remembered.

But around Ken, Clu was different. One day she saw Kenny approaching from a distance, so she ran inside her apartment and asked if I could get rid of him. I picked up some dirty dishes and walked outside to where the kitchen was attached to the backside of the main house. That way I could intercept Clu's ex-lover before he could reach our apartment door.

Kenny noticed me and asked about Clu's whereabouts. "She's not home," I told him as I began scrubbing plates.

"You're lying," he snarled.

When I glanced over my shoulder at him, I could see his eyes glazing over. "What's wrong?" I asked. "Do you want me to give her a message?"

"Where is Clu?" Ken repeated.

"I think she's gone to her parents' house," I lied. "You know... family time." But I could tell he wasn't buying it.

Ken wanted to go into the house, but I told him I wasn't allowed to let anyone inside without Clu being there. He took off his bandana and began twisting it into what I feared was going to be a weapon. His eyes appeared to look straight through me. That's when I became truly afraid. I put down the sponge and said, "Kenny, start talking. You're scaring me." The fenced-in property didn't give me much of an escape route, but I glanced into the dishwater and saw that I did have a butcher knife down there. I slowly closed my fingers around the handle.

Fortunately, I didn't have to use it. Kenny appeared to come to his senses, shaking his head as if to clear it, then mumbling that he had to go. *Thank god.* I've never had to hurt anyone in my life, but if he had come at me, I would have definitely defended myself.

After that incident, Clu managed to enlist some friends and convince Ken to move to a sober living facility called "The Farm" up in Lompoc. Unlike Ross, Kenny was able to stick with the detox program, sober up and make a better life for himself. Even so, Clu made it clear that Ken's life wouldn't include her anymore.

Ken's exit made room for the bikers. A multitude of motorcyclists made Sambo's their preferred setting for socialization and coffee, and Clu often invited them to sit at our table and share stories about life on the road. She had her own tales to share as well, for she had owned a Harley trike when she lived in Redondo Beach. One cold day, Clu wrapped Crusher, her roommate's pet boa constrictor, around her waist to keep him warm, then put on her leather jacket and took off down the highway on her motorcycle. An officer soon pulled her over because she had a burned-out taillight. He asked her to step away from her bike, and when it appeared that she had some kind of contraband hidden underneath her jacket, the cop asked her to unzip it.

"You're not going to like it," Clu warned him.

Still, the officer insisted. Clu pulled down the zipper, and Crusher, feeling the cold air, poked his head out to see what had disrupted his cozy environment. The snake extended his neck toward the cop, flicking out his tongue, and scared the poor man out of his wits.

One of the bikers who frequented Sambo's was a tall, slender, handsome man named Duffy. When he came to our table to sit with us, I felt a spark inside me that I hadn't felt in a long while. I was hungry for him, for I honestly had not had sex in seven years. If one knows anything about alcoholism, one side effect of the disease is erectile dysfunction, and my husband Ross had been no exception. So my sights were set on Duffy. He seemed nice, even though he claimed to have previously been the vice-president of a notorious motorcycle gang. A lot of women had crushes on him, but I didn't feel particularly worried. Sooner or later, I knew I'd have my chance.

One evening, the biker crew invited Clu and me out to Sambo's for dinner. I put on a nice dress for the occasion, deciding this would be the night when I'd finally claim some romance for myself. After we had our meal, the bikers decided they wanted to go to the San Marcos Bowling Alley to shoot some pool, and they extended the invitation to the cooks and waitresses at the restaurant who were finishing their shifts. Duffy turned toward me and asked if I'd care to ride with him. That was an easy question.

Clu graciously volunteered to head home and relieve one of the foster kids who was babysitting Sean. I gave her a big thank-you, and then Duffy and I set off on foot toward his trailer at the boatyard so that I could borrow a pair of Levi's jeans. It took a few minutes to get there and change out of my dress, but the denim material made the experience of riding on the back of his Yamaha a lot more comfortable.

Clinging to his jacket while zooming down the 101 was a thrilling experience, and a first for me. At the bowling alley, one of the wait-resses from Sambo's who had a crush on Duffy asked him to dance to the music on the jukebox. I just sat back and watched. Dancing was never my thing, and I was confident that the opportunity to spend more time with the man would come soon enough.

Later that evening, the other women in the group glared daggers at me while Duffy and I laughed and played pool. I scarcely paid them any notice, for I was having too much fun. At the end of the night, I had to return Duffy's jeans, which gave us a convenient reason to ride back to his trailer and remove some clothes. I got the romantic engagement I'd been craving, and my life started down an exciting and wild new path.

Duffy was a breath of fresh air, and not just because I spent so much time on the back of his motorcycle. He pulled me into an entirely new community - the biker family. They came to accept me, even though I was more outspoken than most of the women in their group. Thankfully, Duffy was well-liked, so his opinions went a long way toward getting them to accommodate my eccentricities.

Eventually, Duffy told me that I was an independent cuss who deserved to have her own bike. Though I loved being on a motorcycle, I balked at the idea. I was thirty-two years old... too old to start learning how to ride one of those beasts. Still, Duffy was convinced otherwise. He told me he'd already found just the right bike - a Honda 400T that had recently been repossessed for lack of payment. It would be a great form of transportation for myself and five-year-old Seanie, he argued, and he even agreed to co-sign for me, since his credit was excellent. I was reluctant, but I told him that if the bike were blue, I might be interested in taking it on.

Sure enough, it was the right color, so I found myself the new owner of a Honda 400T. That very first afternoon, Duffy took me to the parking lot of the boatyard and taught me how to use the clutch and the brake. I did some circles and straightaways until I had a good feel for the machine, then decided to take off on my own and ride all the way to Foothill Road. Since that trip went well, I followed Foothill to where it crossed Highway 154 and became Cathedral Oaks Road, then continued onward to Glen Annie Road.

After filling up on gas, I headed back the same way I'd traveled, only to get pulled over by a pair of sheriff deputies. They nabbed me because they noticed the bike's registration had expired. After some questioning, they also discovered that I didn't have a motorcycle license. "Oh, boy," joked the female deputy. "Another biker busted on Cathedral Oaks Road!"

We laughed at that, then found ourselves engaged in a friendly conversation. The cops let me go with a fix-it ticket, which allowed me to ride home and get my act together with registration, license and insurance before my court date arrived.

When I showed up at the courthouse, I apologized to the judge and explained that at the time I was pulled over, I hadn't yet learned the rules about owning a bike. "I couldn't help it, your honor," I confessed. "I got on the thing, learned to use the clutch and brakes and just took off." Thankfully, the judge smiled and dismissed my case.

Over the next few months, I became very proficient at riding that bike. Five-year-old Seanie and I had many adventures together, and Duffy was correct - it was a great way for us to get around town.

My new boyfriend was a diesel mechanic and worked for the Radon Boat Works at the bottom of Santa Barbara Street, which was where his trailer was parked. Occasionally, he did maintenance and repairs on boats tied up in the harbor, but work was slow and he needed to find another job. I asked him if he'd like to do a newspaper route, and he jumped at the chance.

Soon, Duffy asked me to move into his trailer with him, pets and all, and I accepted. The boatyard wasn't fenced in, so every so often, my dogs took off together, wandering up Santa Barbara Street so they could visit Clu's apartment and stretch out in front of her living room heater. Schatzie had grown to become a massive animal. She weighed one hundred and twenty pounds as an adult, and none of that was fat. The dog was beautiful, with such large ears that we called her "the Moose".

One day, Proto, my shepherd-beagle mutt, disappeared. He was a friendly animal who paid daily visits to every resident in the boatyard. Unfortunately, one disagreeable man on the premises hated dogs, and he told me numerous times that if Proto came near him, he'd kill him. So when Proto turned up missing, I wept, fearing for the worst. The main suspect admitted nothing, but after he moved away, Duffy and I found a dog skeleton in a nearby ditch. Duffy brought a shovel, and I had to bury my poor dog right where we found him.

Apart from that tragic affair, everything else went well for three or four months, until one day, Duffy suddenly asked me to move back to Clu's place. His explanations were vague and confusing, but I did what he asked. Then just a few weeks later, Duffy said he missed me and asked us to move back in with him again. He also asked me to marry him. At first, I told him yes. After all, Duffy was a nice man at heart. But it wasn't long before he wanted me to move out once more.

I quickly grew tired of this yo-yo game. I went to visit him one morning, but when he came to the door, he told me he had company. In fact, he said he was trying to save a lesbian from her sinful lifestyle. *How noble,* I thought wryly. And this was the man who had asked me to marry him. I went back to Clu and told her that I was through with men for a while. I was better off being alone than dealing with men who could not be loyal to their girlfriends. I'd had plenty of that with Ross and was done wasting time with guys who just didn't get it.

I decided that I needed to get serious about providing for Sean and myself. I couldn't keep depending on other people, even if they were as nice as Clu was. So I called my mother and asked if I could live in my parents' house for a time until I could save up money for the first and last month's rent on an apartment, plus the deposit. She agreed, but the situation was hard on us both. We bickered and fought often, for I was a rebel at heart, and she had a much more rigid sense of morality. I always felt that she was trying to make me feel guilty for the choices I'd made in life.

Despite my best intentions, I struggled to save money. Emergencies kept cropping up with Sean, the dogs and the motorcycle. Also, when I researched potential apartments, I discovered that the rent on any low-income housing in Santa Barbara would still eat up the majority of my paycheck. It was a depressing reality to have to grapple with.

After three months of discomfort and drama, a thought finally occurred to me... *Why don't I find a pickup truck and a camper and try living in that for a while?*

I called a family conference, and my parents agreed to help me track down the right vehicle so I could transition away from living at home. My dad and I looked at several different rigs, but because of the price, I balked at most of them. One day, while scanning the want ads in the Santa Barbara NewsPress, I finally saw her: a green Ford 250 pickup with a brand new, ten-and-a-half-foot El Dorado camper strapped to her bed. I expected the vehicle to be in the five or six-thousand-dollar range, but the owner wanted to sell his rig for just $2,800. *Oh, boy!*

Even though I had ended my relationship with Duffy, I did decide to go to him and ask if he'd take a look at the Ford 250 with me. He wanted to help, so I called the number in the paper and soon Duffy had his head under the hood with the engine running, listening for odd sounds while going over every aspect of the engine and body with a fine-toothed comb. At the end of it all, he turned to me and said, "You'd be a fool not to buy this."

I turned to the owner and told him I was going to round up the money and bring him a check that very afternoon. Then I called my father and informed him that I had found the perfect configuration. He was both shocked and very pleased at the price. He went to the bank, withdrew the money and drove with me to pick up my new rig.

*The pickup and El Dorado camper I purchased with the help of my parents*

I took it to my parents' house in Goleta and told Seanie to come outside and have a look at his new home. The El Dorado camper was brown and white with a tan stripe running along the side - classic 1970s colors. I brought Sean inside and showed him how you could lower the kitchen table and adjust the seats to make a bed for him. There were drawers where I told him he could keep his clothes and toys. Seanie loved it. I appreciated how the camper had its own stove, sink and a small bathroom with a shower. Directly above the truck roof was a queen-sized bunk area that I claimed for my own usage.

I packed up the El Dorado with the essentials we'd need for its maiden voyage, and then my family drove to Hendry's Beach for a cele-bratory picnic. I had a home! We wrote up a contract, and my mortgage was going to be one hundred dollars a month - an interest-free loan, courtesy of my father.

Next, I needed to find a place to park the rig... a place where we'd face the least amount of disturbance from the cops or city employees. The best choice seemed to be an abandoned parking lot outside the Radon Boat Yard on the corner of Santa Barbara Street and Cabrillo Boulevard. Running parallel to this wide expanse of crumbling asphalt was a strip of overgrown shrubs and trees that blocked Cabrillo Boulevard from view. This stretch of overgrown terrain ran all the way to Milpas Street on the Eastside. Homeless people called it "The Jungle", and I could peek through the brush and see the ocean while feeling the fresh, salty breeze on my face. It wasn't paradise, but it also wasn't half-bad.

The dogs appreciated the open space of the parking lot. They could investigate the Jungle at their leisure, but often they were happy to just hang out in the front seat of the truck and nap their lives away. I missed Proto, but Tawny and Schatzie - a.k.a. the "Moose" - did their best to make up for his absence.

Along another edge of the lot was a line of unused Southern Pacific boxcars that ran parallel to the Ice House - an old factory belonging to the Puritan Ice Company that could produce fifty tons of ice in a day. Much of the ice was used to chill the boxcars as they transported Santa Barbara seafood and produce by rail to faraway destinations. The refrigerated truck industry was swiftly making the plant obsolete, but for now, it hung on, its machines humming in the distance. Active trains would also rumble past the parking lot at all hours of the day, but I didn't mind. I'd always loved trains, and the sound of freight cars churning along the tracks, even in the middle of the night, was a comfort to me.

As my venture into this new mobile lifestyle began, I slowly became aware of the shifting face of homelessness in Santa Barbara County. Opportunistic people were shacking up in the disused box cars to get out of the wind and weather, but it wasn't just a bunch of old men in the throes of chemical addiction - the ones you'd see making their own fermented drinks out of discarded fruits and vegetables. There were also young men and women in the boxcars and out on the streets trying to survive on part-time and low-income jobs. From the doorway of my camper, I could observe this younger generation as they went about their hardscrabble lives, and often I would wave and call out to them, inviting them over for a cup of coffee. I always had a pot on. They started to join me in conversation, and if they had a joint to share, even better. They wondered if I knew about their struggles, and of course I did. I was lucky to have been able to secure the El Dorado, but I was still empathetic toward the "Ground Pounders", as they liked to call themselves - the people who had to live on the streets without shelter. The term "Rubber Tramps" was reserved for folks like me who lived in cars and campers.

More and more people seemed to be having trouble coming up with the first and last months' rent, plus deposit, on the apartments in this city. There was a deficit of housing, affordable and otherwise, and competition was driving prices up to obscene levels. Everyone seemed to be affected, Vietnam veterans in particular. PTSD contributed to the domestic problems that led to them being shunted out onto the streets, but addiction and physical disabilities played a part as well, all because of a war that had made little sense to anyone in this country. I listened to countless stories of their time in the service, and I'd like to think that giving them the opportunity to share helped ease the weight of depression that plagued so many of them, at least for a while.

Over time, I got to know so many people: Sniper, Eddie, David, Steve and Mary, a girl who had a job delivering auto parts. Lee and Sandi were of Apache and Arapaho blood, respectively, and they built themselves a hooch - a small shelter made of leaves and branches - down along the railroad tracks. I would walk among the Vietnam vets who resided in the Jungle, but I would have to be wary; they kept the place booby-trapped for a time. The police would sometimes venture into the brush to give them tickets for "camping," so men like Sniper felt motivated to defend their turf. They had all learned how to build traps in the jungles of Vietnam, so they dug holes in the soft ground and filled them with upward-facing punji sticks - sharp, unfolded palm tree leaves that would spear a police officer if he was so unlucky as to fall in. They tied branches back with strings to create spring traps, and

Sniper climbed the trees and stashed coke bottles filled with sand that he could drop on unsuspecting intruders.

*A hooch in the Jungle (photo by Eve Fowler)*

Lee gave me a password that I could use when traveling the Jungle toward their encampment. So many of the veterans were suffering from PTSD that they'd created this password system to help avoid any accidental attacks. It wasn't until a policeman actually got injured that the veterans saw the light and disabled all their booby traps. They finally realized, *What if a child was exploring and got hurt?* The element of danger in the Jungle was fun and invigorating, but I firmly agreed.

Life on that lot was perpetually interesting. Here I was, a woman with a middle-class upbringing, learning to survive while technically homeless in Santa Barbara. Thankfully, if I ever needed anything, I was surrounded by helpful men who were fiercely protective of a mother and her young child, and that made me feel safe and secure, even in my atypical environment.

One day, an eighteen-year-old man named Ed walked up to me and said he'd noticed that the electrical systems on the pickup were not connected to the camper. Whenever I used my brakes or turn signals, the rear camper lights failed to light up, so anyone driving behind me would have a hard time deciphering my intentions on the road. That was dangerous. Ed suggested he could fix the problem for me. I had to tell him that I didn't have the money to pay him, but he asked if I could afford a six-pack of beer since he was underage and couldn't purchase it for himself. Yep! That was something I could do.

Ed slid himself underneath the pickup and got to work. The power system was a mess of wires, and it took him hours to figure out the issue, but he eventually climbed back out and announced that the problem had been fixed. The young man was a genius. I took him to the store and bought him a six-pack like I'd promised, along with a couple of steaks to round out his payment.

When the school year began that autumn, Sean was old enough to attend kindergarten. I took him to the school district office at Santa Barbara Junior High, but because I had no street address, they didn't know where to place my son, or even *how* to place my son, for that matter. I argued the fact that it was against state policy to prevent my son from being admitted and told them they needed to loosen their policy since more and more children were being raised in cars and motorhomes. Thankfully, they found a loophole, placing Sean in the Eastside District because my P.O. Box was at the Milpas Post Office. We registered him at Franklin Elementary School, which pleased me since I had lived on the Eastside since becoming an adult. Also, Franklin had a diverse student body, and I wanted my son to be unafraid of differences in skin color.

Usually every morning, I'd drop Sean off at school and return to the Jungle parking lot. Sometimes, if I needed to catch up on sleep, I'd park outside the school and take a long nap inside the camper. Sean would find me and wake me up when his kindergarten session was over. Both of us were learning to adapt to the new housing situation. Since I didn't have to spend money on rent, I could put my $700 monthly salary toward good food for us and the dogs, plus clothing and truck maintenance.

Of course, I was not the only migratory resident in the city, and those living the vehicular lifestyle tend to flock toward the best places to park. Soon, the abandoned Jungle lot began to attract more people. One afternoon, I was sitting in the doorway of my camper, strumming my guitar, when another small camper vehicle pulled in. A big man with red hair and a beard stepped out and introduced himself. Michael Tice was his name, which confirmed the likelihood of his Irish blood.

He was looking for a good place where he could rebuild his engine undisturbed by the authorities, and though I couldn't promise that the police would stay away forever, I told him to knock himself out.

Michael got busy tearing out his engine, and by the time he was done, we had become fast friends. He was the sweetest, most intelligent man... also a mental patient, but he took his medication regularly and was mostly stable, apart from the occasional anxiety attack. We called him the "Right Reverend" due to his preacher-like presence, and he and I became very close. Because he was gay, there was never any expectation of a physical relationship.

Next came Roy, a friend of Michael's. Roy had a Lance camper on the back of his pickup, and he got by on his disability income, but he was quite the psycho. It would take an entire book to describe the man, but because of his connection to Michael, he was allowed to stay.

Another afternoon, a white Pontiac sedan drove up containing a young couple and a small infant. The baby seemed quite ill to my eyes, like she had pneumonia. The mother was balking at bringing her daughter to the hospital because, at that time, Child Protective Services was taking children away from homeless women and putting them in the foster system. I had to talk the mother into going, convincing her that she could lose the baby if she didn't do something quickly to help her. They took off soon afterward and did not return to the lot, so I could only hope that they made the hard decision and sought help for the little girl.

Clu's newest boyfriend Steve Bagnall moved into the parking lot next with his pickup truck and a dilapidated camper. He was a large, swarthy man who loved his Australian Shepherd dog more than anything else, but he had hurt his back while working for the city as the head of the parking lot department, and subsequently, he lost his apartment due to a lack of income. Because he and Clu were dating, my best friend became a daily visitor to the Jungle lot. Clu had found a cottage nearby on Carrillo Street that allowed her doggies to live with her, and it was great to have her around more often. She and her boyfriend became fast friends with Michael, and our little group quickly grew into a tight-knit community. We shared food and took turns running errands for each other. My friends loved to babysit Sean, taking positions outside my camper so the child could continue sleeping when I took my truck to deliver newspapers. It was wonderful to not have to drag him out of bed in the early hours every morning. In the evening, my makeshift family would come together to play Yahtzee, Spades and other games for entertainment.

Michael had a CB radio hooked up to his truck, and he recommended that I do the same in case my vehicle broke down or I got in trouble somewhere. I took his advice, purchasing a nice Cobra setup, and Michael helped me set it up above my bed in the camper. Besides being important for survival, we used the CB for basic socializing. It opened up a whole new world for Sean and me, and I was amazed at the number of people living in vehicles who were hooked up to the radio. We were no longer isolated from the rest of the van life community. Even Clu was intrigued by the technology and went on to get her certificate as a HAM radio operator.

One day, Duffy showed up at the parking lot for a visit. He sat down with me in my camper and asked why I never came to see him. I told him that if he felt comfortable sneaking out on me right after asking me to marry him, what was the point? If I was just going to be one more person in a string of ladies, it wasn't worth investing time in a relationship. I was sick and tired of men who thought they were God's gift to the opposite sex. I'd had too much of that attitude when I was married to Ross, and I didn't want to continually suffer those emotional wounds. It was too much work. Duffy said that he loved me. I countered, "Yes... but you do not seem to *like* me very much."

He left the parking lot, disappointed. I was sad, too, for I could remember the good times I'd had with Duffy. He did me a huge favor by urging me to buy that motorcycle and teaching me how to ride. But I'd been called in a different direction. At that point, I didn't know where I was headed, but I felt like some kind of motivational energy was starting to build. At least Duffy accepted that I needed to forge my own path. Not all men are able to handle rejection, but Duffy understood the way things needed to be.

For about six months, our little group was able to live peacefully in the Jungle lot and establish a sense of normalcy... although "normal" was a relative term when it came to my eccentric group of friends. One afternoon while Sean and I were sitting in our camper, Michael and Steve came rushing up to the door in a panic. They pointed toward a tan-colored sedan and its owner, a skinny man in his late thirties who sat unmoving behind the wheel. Steve was convinced that the driver was an insurance investigator spying on him to make sure that the injuries he'd reported while working his city government job were legitimate. Michael simply thought the man was an undercover cop. The two of them were beside themselves, but I knew they had a habit of feeding into each others' anxieties. They both suffered from panic attacks on a regular basis.

I took a few steps toward the sedan and decided the guy was completely harmless - just another homeless individual needing a quiet place to rest for a few hours. Still, knowing that I needed to reframe the situation if I was to get my friends to calm down, I told Michael and Steve to get down on their knees and bow three times to the man in the car. Thankfully, they did. When they stood back up again, I asked if they felt a little better. Their answer was an enthusiastic yes. I returned to the camper, laughing as I started dinner for myself and Sean. Perhaps I should have been looking for a job as a psychologist.

The gentleman in the tan-colored sedan ended up becoming a regular at the Jungle lot. We called him New York, simply because he'd moved from there, and once Michael and Steve got over their fear of him, they teased and bullied him a little. New York developed a crush on me, and he would often stand just outside my camper door and babble, muttering strings of words in an alien language that made absolutely no sense. Obviously, he suffered from mental problems like so many other homeless people.

Despite being a little frightened of New York's behavior, I treated him with respect and kindness, and only once did he ever truly scare me. While Sean was in bed one night and I was sitting nearby, playing my guitar, New York opened the door and stepped inside the camper. Knowing I had no way to maneuver around him and escape, I grew fearful for my safety. Luckily, Michael and Steve, sensing something was wrong, came by, saw New York in the doorway and hauled him away from my camper. I had to step outside and stop them from hurting him. They were both extremely protective of me and Seanie, but I didn't want anyone to suffer on my account.

New York disappeared soon after that episode, but I came to the conclusion that he had stopped by to tell me goodbye. His words hadn't made any sense at the time, but I believe that was what he was trying to say. Poor man. His illness seemed to always get the better of him.

In the early 1980s, it was clear that the number of people with mental disorders in the homeless community was growing. Ronald Reagan played a big part in this phenomenon. As governor of California in the 1960s and 70s, one of his goals was to open the doors of the state mental hospitals and release the patients back into their home cities and counties. His administration felt that it was unconstitutional for taxpayers to be forced to pay to maintain social programs for the mentally ill and the poor. He thought such programs were not worth the cost, time or effort.

In 1967, he got the state legislature to pass the Lanterman-Petris-Short Act, which abolished involuntary hospitalizations. In regards to mental health, it was one of the most short-sighted decisions in generations. Those who supported the Act argued that the state mental hospitals were in bad shape and were doing a poor job of treating the mentally ill. It would have been far more rational to have spent the money to improve the hospitals rather than let the mentally ill return to communities that were unprepared to handle their needs for accommodation and treatment. Funds to build housing for these people never materialized, so California suffered from an inevitable increase in homelessness along with a spike in violent crimes and incarcerations.

Reagan became president of the United States on January 20th, 1981, but one month earlier, Jimmy Carter signed the Mental Health Systems Act. It allocated money for the continuance of the federal community mental health centers program. The act included a provision creating federal grants for programs that promoted positive mental health. But when Reagan took office and Republicans took over the Senate, the Mental Health Systems Act was discarded and funds for mental health were block-granted to the individual states, who spent them as they desired, often unwisely.

Reagan never understood mental illness. He associated psychiatry and social welfare programs with communism. That prejudice carries on, in some circles, even to this day.

∾

DESPITE THE TENDENCY FOR HOMELESS PEOPLE TO LOOK OUT FOR each other, the streets of Santa Barbara were not always safe. There was a visitor to the Jungle lot who took advantage of the free coffee I would pass out on occasion. I only discovered afterward that he was pretending to be homeless in order to get close to his victims. He captured and attacked three women, including a mental patient who walked the streets, a schoolteacher at La Cumbre Junior High, and a young lady who was walking to her car after work. Only the third woman survived, though she'd been stabbed twenty-six times. Thankfully, she was able to identify her attacker, and another serial killer was taken off the streets.

I considered myself fairly lucky to have escaped the man's wrath, but then again, I never treated homeless men like predators and I never set myself up as a victim. Perhaps he determined that I wouldn't be easy prey. I made it a point in my daily life to treat everyone with respect, and by openly greeting strangers, I was able to assess each situation by the manner in which they responded. Since I delivered newspapers in the dead of night, I'd learned to be a quick judge of character out of necessity. Of course, my dog Schatzie gave me an extra layer of confidence. I knew she'd protect me with her life if need be.

One time I was servicing some racks in front of Sambo's on Cabrillo when I noticed a large woman pacing back and forth with her pants down around her ankles. I knew I should have refrained from engaging with her, but my sympathetic personality won out over my sense of caution. "Are you all right, my friend?" I asked. But the woman stared right past me as if I wasn't even there.

I turned aside to place my stack of newspapers in the rack, but I suddenly found myself shoved against the metal box. The woman leaned into me and hissed, "You are going to die before the sun rises."

The sun was just rising over the eastern horizon as she said this, and I knew I had to escape her clutches. I twisted my head around and growled, "Back off, bitch!" She let go and stepped away, whereupon I walked toward her with my forefinger pointed at her face like I was holding a weapon. Once she had retreated far enough, I called out to a few onlookers and asked if anyone had called the authorities to come help her. I needed to continue my rounds, so I didn't have time to wait for the issue to get fully resolved. Also, my back hurt from when I'd been shoved into the newsstand by the much bigger woman, so I decided to get into my truck and drive away. Hopefully, she got the help that she obviously needed.

Another morning, I was gathering up the unsold San Francisco Chronicles at the Greyhound bus station when a man with scraggly hair and a beard walked up to my truck and started throwing kernels of popcorn at my dogs. Schatzie and Tawny snarled and barked at him from the back of the pickup, obviously uninterested in what he had to offer. The man's face was all cut up and bleeding, so he appeared to have been on the losing end of some recent altercation. Nevertheless, I felt violated by his actions, and I asked him to stop it. I didn't want my dogs to retaliate and escalate the situation.

The lout leaned against my truck and told me to leave. I informed him that this was *my* vehicle and that *he* needed to be the one to leave. Without another word, he attacked. I found myself on the ground, and when he started to kick me, I rolled underneath the truck. His feet were unable to reach me there, but instead of staying where I was safe, my anger compelled me to crawl out the other side and confront him. I started hitting him as quickly as I could to keep him on the defensive. "Look what you did to me!" he yelled, pointing at the cuts on his face. I told him that someone else had given him those injuries, not me.

The man began walking away, and someone must have called the cops because a police car came around the corner and parked near us. I shouted out that the man had attacked me, and the police quickly seized him. As they were placing him in handcuffs, the man looked over at me and threatened, "I will get you when I get out."

For days afterward, I was too frightened to visit the bus station to pick up my papers. The man had to go to court, but his case was dismissed, so I knew that he was back out on the streets, lying in wait for me. I eventually resumed my full duties, returning warily to the Greyhound station, and when my attacker finally reappeared, a group of bystanders stepped forward and drove him off. Later, the police told me they'd seen the man stumbling up the center of the 101 freeway, and he disappeared from the city soon after that... just the latest mental patient to fall through the cracks of society.

~

ONE DAY I WAS CALLED INTO FRANKLIN ELEMENTARY FOR A meeting with Sean's teacher. Apparently, my son had been showing signs of Attention Deficit Disorder in the classroom. Not only was he disruptive and unable to focus on assignments or activities, Sean had also been reacting angrily when other students teased him about living in a camper. The teacher asked me if I would consider putting him on the drug Ritalin.

Naturally, I refused. I knew that many children were being pressured to take Ritalin to help teachers cope with classroom disruptions. I'd researched the drug and shuddered at the side effects, which included high blood pressure, rapid pulse rate, feelings of suspicion and paranoia, stunted growth and weight gain. Even depression was a possible symptom. The federal government classifies Ritalin as a Schedule II drug, like cocaine and methamphetamine, due to the high potential for addiction and abuse, so it is hardly surprising that we have a meth and opioid epidemic in our country. Because Ritalin is prescribed to so many boys and girls, parents falsely consider it to be safe and benign. Clever marketing and lobbying by pharmaceutical companies have made its use pervasive in our schools, impacting multiple generations of children, and seldom for the better.

Because I refused the teacher's recommendation, she determined that Sean was being neglected by his mother. The fact that we lived in a camper undoubtedly influenced her impressions. I was called back to the school for a second discussion on the subject, and when Sean and I arrived, I was shocked and angered to see that the teacher had brought a representative from Child Protective Services without telling me.

After introductions were made, I sat down nervously with Seanie on my lap. CPS, in my eyes, was the enemy. Many times, they'd taken children away from their mothers after suspecting they were homeless, even walking up to women who were in line to get free meals at the Salvation Army and seizing their offspring. My suspicions were confirmed when, before any other issues were discussed, the CPS employee questioned me about my drug use.

"What kind of drugs are you talking about?" I asked.

"Cocaine, for one. We need to talk about the fact that you are a cocaine dealer."

*What?* "If I was a cocaine dealer," I began, incredulously, "do you think that I'd be living in a camper, in poverty? I'd own a business downtown and would live in a house on the Riviera like everyone else in Santa Barbara who loves cocaine!"

This woman was an idiot. I wanted to argue further but decided it wasn't worth my time. I gave Sean's teacher a hard look, then stood up and took Sean by the hand. "I do not even take aspirin for a headache," I informed them. "We are out of here." I walked quickly to the door, fearful but determined. From that point, I resolved to get Seanie out of that school. His teacher had absolutely no idea what kind of life we lived. She just made the worst assumptions.

The next morning, I returned to the school, fully intending to withdraw Sean from the classroom and enroll him elsewhere. His teacher, however, walked up to me as soon as I arrived. She apologized profoundly for inviting the CPS representative to our supposedly private meeting. She hadn't expected the social worker to pounce on me with such force and incivility.

So I agreed to leave Seanie at Franklin. I asked the teacher if she'd like me to sit in the classroom while my son was there, but she told me that was unnecessary. After the incident with the CPS employee, however, I decided not to bring Sean to school in the camper anymore. People had too many misconceptions about parents with alternative living arrangements. Instead, I retrieved my motorcycle, which I had stashed at the newspaper warehouse, and I used the bike to transport Sean to school every day from that point onward.

~

ONE AFTERNOON, A SCREAM RANG OUT FROM THE JUNGLE THAT bordered the parking lot. Then came the words, "I do not want to die!" Michael sprinted across the railroad tracks in the direction of the woman's voice. I followed suit with Schatzie at my heels, and Roy left to call the police. As Michael and I approached the thick vegetation, a man dressed in black jumped out of the bushes with a broken bottle clutched in his fist. He waved it at us threateningly. Soon after, a woman with short blond hair ran out into the open. One hand clutched at her pants, which were down around her knees.

Michael came to a stop and grabbed my arm to pull me back. Together, we retreated to the parking lot. Schatzie, however, circled the man, barking and drawing closer to him until he lunged with the glass bottle. Thankfully, my dog dodged his attack, and the man slipped and fell right onto his ass. I then called out to Schatzie, and she returned to my side.

Soon, thanks to Roy, the place was crawling with the police. The perpetrator ran across Cabrillo Boulevard and disappeared. The cops didn't bother to pursue him or visit the camps in the Jungle to investigate the crime scene. They even told us they were familiar with the blond homeless woman and said that she *liked* to be raped. Before the officers left, however, we got the sense that they'd decided the Jungle and parking lot situation had escalated into a problem that the city needed to deal with, once and for all. Our days of being willfully ignored by the authorities were over. We were now in for the fight of our lives.

## ❧ 8 ❧

# A MEETING IN THE RAIN

Not long after the ruckus in the Jungle, the police showed up at 10 p.m., waking everyone up. I emerged from my camper, and the cops were taken aback when they saw me, for I was well-known around town as the Newspaper Lady. Nevertheless, they proceeded to inform us that, according to Municipal Code 15.16.080, camping was illegal in the City of Santa Barbara. Between 10 p.m. and 6 a.m., no one can sleep inside their vehicle within city limits. The law reads:

> *It is unlawful for any person to use any recreational vehicle for sleeping, human habitation or camping purposes in any of the following areas except as otherwise provided for:*
>
> *A. Any public park*
> *B. Any public street*
> *C. Any public parking lot or public area, improved or unimproved*
> *D. Any public beach*

I told the officers that we were not camping; the vehicles and campers were our primary residences... the only homes that we possessed. But my argument wasn't working on them. They told me to vacate the camper and go with my son to an all-night restaurant until it was time for me to go to work. My other option would be to go to jail, and if that happened, Sean would be taken away from me by Child Protective Services - a horror that no single parent should have to face.

I was shocked and angry at their brutal decrees. I had to wake my son from a sound sleep, put him in the work truck and drive him to Sambo's. I lay Sean down in one of the restaurant booths and covered him with a blanket. Then I ordered a coffee. I'd only managed to sleep for two hours before we'd been evicted. At least Sean was a heavy sleeper.

Michael and Steve soon joined me, and we passed the time until 2:30 a.m., when I had to go to work. Seanie rode around with me until school started. I gave him a bath in the warehouse sink, dropped him off at kindergarten and then tried to get some rest in the camper. My sleep was fitful and intermittent. Michael woke me after about two hours, and I used my motorcycle to pick up Sean from school.

Our small community held a conference that evening. Clu came by and we sat around trying to figure out what to do to resolve the situation peacefully. For the time being, we decided to stay in the parking lot. Every couple of nights, the cops would come around to wake us up and force us to leave our campers. Roy would throw open his door and scream at the top of his lungs, "Go ahead, you piggies! I'll pay the ticket with your tax dollars! I have a 'nut' check!" A diagnosis of mental illness meant that Roy was likely exempt from financial consequences. But the police were persistent. Being a single parent who had faced domestic abuse from Ross for years, I was furious that I now had to face abuse from the city and their men in blue - my supposed protectors. No end appeared to be in sight.

The harassment began to extend into my working hours. The police would drive past Mr. Monson's warehouse on Philinda Avenue and shine their headlights into the interior where my co-workers and I were stuffing advertising inserts into newspapers. It was their way of trying to break my will... to get me to move into proper housing or out of town. The rest of the staff started teasing me about my "criminal" reputation, which certainly didn't help my tired mind.

With how little sleep I was getting, I felt like I was holding on for dear life.

One morning while I was making my rounds delivering papers, I had to change a flat tire on my company vehicle. After resuming my route, I pulled into the 7-11 parking lot on the Mesa and hauled a couple bundles of the L.A. Times into the building. A trio of police officers looked up from their donuts and coffees as I entered.

"Aren't you getting tired yet, McCradie?" one of them taunted. His comrades joined in with the teasing.

"No!" I replied defiantly and looked them in the eyes. "If you were gentlemen," I continued, "you might offer to help me carry these papers. But since you are not, and considering how abusive you all are, I'm not expecting any help." I dropped off my load and exited the store with my head in the air and my middle fingers extended. I could hear them laughing as I got back in my truck and drove away.

After three weeks of these disruptions, I began to suffer physically and mentally from the lack of sleep, and Michael, Steve and Roy were looking even more ragged than usual. We knew we were parked on private property, out of sight and hearing from the rest of the city, and since it was not a public space, the police shouldn't have had the right to come into our area. Unfortunately, I felt too tired to put up an adequate defense against the authorities. I could barely see straight, let alone think straight.

When sleep is lacking, the brain and associated bodily systems stop functioning normally. One cannot concentrate or absorb new information. Nerve signals can also be delayed, decreasing one's coordination and increasing the risk of accidents. A person can become prone to mood swings, and if sleep deprivation continues long enough, one can start to experience hallucinations, seeing or hearing things that aren't there. It can even trigger manic behavior, mirroring the symptoms of bipolar disorder. I hadn't deteriorated that badly, but I knew I was beginning to fall apart. At least I knew I could count on my friends for support. We huddled together whenever we could and tried to help each other withstand the onslaught.

One morning, while it was still dark and I was feeling more tired than I had ever felt in my life, I was standing in the warehouse, assembling the day's newspapers when I couldn't take it anymore. I raised my face to the ceiling, shut my eyes and squeezed the tears out of them. Though the words were only in my head, I cried out to the heavens, "What am I going to do?"

Suddenly, the walls of the warehouse disappeared. I saw a bright light appear in the open sky, and from within that light came a booming voice that spoke, "I WANT YOU TO START A CHURCH!"

The sound echoed inside me as the warehouse reappeared. I looked down and my hands were still clutching sections of newspapers. To my right and left, my co-workers were still doing their jobs, tucking inserts into the L.A. Times. No one appeared to have seen me do anything strange. I stood there for a minute, stunned and a little freaked out. There were no drugs in my system, not even cannabis. Lack of sleep had to be the cause of the hallucination, but I felt there was more to it than that. I truly thought that God had spoken to me... and I needed to heed the message. This insight gave me a second wind, and with newfound energy infusing my body, I resolved to seek help for my friends... the people who lived on the streets. I would go to meetings around town and speak to the community about homelessness. That would be my church... my purpose in life... my calling.

However, after I completed the day's route and dropped Sean off at school, I immediately faced a huge complication. When I returned to the parking lot, Michael walked over and handed me an official-looking document. It was an eviction notice ordering to vacate the property. A police officer had presented Michael with it earlier that morning, and it was signed by the Amtrak train station management. *Amtrak?* We hadn't been exactly sure who owned the land, and now we had to simply hope the company could be reasoned with.

Clu and I decided to put on our best clothes and pay a visit to the train station. Both the manager and his assistant came over to listen to our pleas. I handed them the eviction notice, and while the manager perused it, I asked, "Who signed this document?" The assistant raised his hand. He told his boss that a couple of police officers had asked him to sign it, but he had no idea that he was unauthorized to do so.

The manager gave us back the eviction notice and informed us that the land we were using was not owned by the railway at all. It had been sold to Fess Parker and Bill Wright, who were collaborating with the city of Santa Barbara on plans to use the property for future development. Clu and I looked at each other and grinned. The police were not going to be able to enforce an invalid document.

We returned to Steve and Michael, shared the new information and then laughed until we had tears in our eyes. We could hardly wait for the police to come and try to wake us that night.

When they finally showed up, I shouted, "Out! Out!" at them. I told them their paperwork was no good, and they were forced to concede. We'd called them out on their ruse. As the cops drove away, Michael, Steve and I celebrated our victory. It felt tremendous; for the first time since the harassment by the police had started, we had won. I set my alarm for my normal 2:30 a.m. wakeup, and went to sleep a satisfied woman.

The next day, a police cruiser returned to the parking lot and out stepped one of my few friends who worked for the department. It seemed the police were looking to play nice this time. I couldn't fault their strategy, but I wasn't in much of a mood to be helpful.

My officer friend walked up to where I was sitting in the doorway of my camper and asked if I knew whose property we were squatting on. I let him know that we'd done our research, but we'd be fools to help the police learn the results of our investigation. They'd never shown any interest in helping us. In fact, the information was likely to be used against us.

The cruiser drove away, but I knew they wouldn't give up. Sooner or later, the police would learn that Bill and Fess were the true owners of the lot, and they'd ask the developers to evict us. We waited for the other shoe to drop, but when the cops showed up again, they had good news for us for once. The police had spoken to Bill and Fess, and the owners told them that we weren't bothering anyone. We were welcome to stay until they were ready to start building on the property.

~

WHILE DELIVERING PAPERS DURING THE HOURS OF DARKNESS, I encountered a different side of humanity. When people are sparse and not competing for space and attention, they tend to act differently. More laid back. This could even be said of the homeless individuals I encountered at night... those who hung out in all-night restaurants so they could beat the laws governing unconventional sleeping arrangements. I was always attracted to these weirdos, as they were to me. I'm not sure why. Perhaps because of my circumstances, I was hard-wired to treat them warmly and generously.

One such man was nicknamed "The Lone Ranger" since those words were stenciled on the doors of his blue pickup truck. In the back of his vehicle, he had mounted a large American flag, and every night he lived out his fantasy of being an undercover police officer, pursuing the drunk drivers that he spotted leaving the bars at closing time. He was also a dedicated L.A. Times reader and would snatch a copy as soon as it appeared in the racks each morning.

During my rounds one night, I decided to dip into the well-lit Sambo's restaurant for a cup of coffee. This time, I struck up a conversation with the Lone Ranger at the counter and listened to his stories. Before I continued my route, I fetched him a newspaper from my truck as a gesture of goodwill. From that point on, I made it a daily ritual to walk into Sambo's and drop off a paper for my favorite Santa Barbara vigilante before heading off down the road.

On one of these visits, I walked into the restaurant and saw a number of boatyard neighbors sipping their early morning coffees. The police must have conducted an overnight sweep of the camps in and around the Jungle, I presumed. It had been a few weeks since Fess Parker and Bill Wright had given us permission to stay on the property, but the police had apparently decided to enforce the municipal ordinance against sleeping in vehicles. In their minds, the law took precedence over any private arrangements we may have had.

Upon seeing me, the men leapt up from their seats and shouted that the cops were in the Jungle parking lot, trying to roust Michael and Steve from the premises. Even worse, the police had managed to get Sean out of my camper. I freaked. I ran out the door, jumped in my truck, made a sharp U-turn and sped down Cabrillo Boulevard in order to save my seven-year-old son. The Lone Ranger started up his own vehicle and roared down the boulevard right behind me, his flag flapping in the wind. We must have been a sight to behold.

Flying into the parking lot, there were no cops to be seen... or anyone else, for that matter. I feared the worst. Undoubtedly, Michael and Steve had been arrested and Sean had been delivered to Child Protective Services. But then the door to Michael's camper flew open and he and Steve stepped out. They had been successful at keeping Seanie from being carried off. In their version of events, the police had made Sean exit my camper, but my son always slept in the nude and couldn't find any clothes to put on. I had bundled all our dirty clothes together so I could do the laundry as soon as I got off work that morning. Steve had to grab his bathrobe and wrap it around Sean to keep him warm. When the cops announced that they were going to take the boy, Steve had thrust Sean behind him. He told the police that Sean was in his care while the kid's mother was working, and there was no way that he was going to give the boy up. Once they realized that Sean wasn't afraid of the two men, the officers got in their cars and left.

I turned to the Lone Ranger and thanked him profoundly for his loyalty. Then after checking in on Seanie and loading him and our laundry into my truck, I left to finish my newspaper route. I would have left my son at the boatyard, but I wanted to give Steve and Michael a chance to get some rest.

It was hard to focus on work in my agitated state, and as I approached State Street, I noticed a police cruiser driving up from the beach. Almost without thinking, I pulled over to the curb, jumped out of the truck and walked directly into the police car's path, screaming, "That's enough! Give me a ticket for sleeping in my camper! Do it!" I was furious. "I'll take you people to court for harassing us! Just give me a ticket or leave us alone!" I got down on my knees in front of the cruiser and would not let him pass. The cop had to back up his squad car and drive around me.

Afterward, I cursed myself for flipping out. I was just so angry and exhausted. I should have kept my cool, but when my child gets messed with, I become a tigress. Unfortunately, now those assholes knew that I was at my wit's end.

Seanie and I took care of the laundry before we rejoined Michael, Roy and Steve at the boatyard. Since it was a Saturday, I didn't have to take Sean to school. I was still tired, but Michael and Steve wanted to discuss a proposal. They'd found an ad in the paper for a corner property on Gray Avenue that some developers were renting out for just one hundred dollars a month. It would be a month-to-month agreement, and Mike and Steve thought the optics would look better if I was the one signing the contract.

I gave it some consideration. Our potential landlords, the Serena Company, had their offices in Carpinteria, so there was less of a chance that we'd be bothered if we parked our campers on the lot. The opportunity felt too good to pass up.

The developers asked for the first and last months' rent, which I was able to provide. When I went to sign the papers, I told them that I needed to park a small fleet of vehicles on the property for a short time. They didn't express any concerns, so Michael, Roy, Steve and I were able to move our campers onto the lot and finally get some peace. The police didn't bother us there... at least for a little while.

In the meantime, my boss was having a difficult time with thieves. Someone was breaking into the newspaper boxes and stealing all of his hard-earned quarters. No matter what preventative measures we took, we couldn't stop it from happening, and the police hadn't been any help so far. I eventually told Mr. Monson that if he gave me the night off, I'd patrol the racks and find the culprit. He agreed, even offering me a fifty-dollar bill if I were able to identify the thief.

I called up my friend Clu and asked if she'd like to take on this mission with me. Clu was completely game, so we dressed up in our leather biking outfits, took one of Mr. Monson's trucks from his fleet of delivery vehicles and parked ourselves in front of the Garvey Hotel on lower State Street. From there, we kept our eyes open for movement.

At 11 p.m., we saw him. Quickly, we ducked below the dashboard. Across the street was Mario - one of my former foster kids. He was pushing his bicycle up the sidewalk and giving suspicious looks over his shoulder before he stopped and used a crowbar to pry open the back of one of the boxes. His methods fit the profile of someone who knew the newspaper business. The kid knew what he was doing; after all, Ross and Phil had taught him everything he knew. Poor Mario. He was a bad seed. I'd been unable to work with him. Out of the six boys that I'd taken care of, Mario was the only one who could not keep it together. Clu and I gave each other a stoic look. It was time to go to the police and finger him as the perpetrator.

We drove to the station and asked to speak with the watch commander. After giving him the name of the thief and the address where Mario lived, the commander looked up from his paperwork and said offhandedly, "We noticed that you people have moved over to Gray Avenue." I looked at Clu, and she nodded, giving me permission to spill the beans about our month-to-month rental agreement with the Serena Company. The lease had been filled with lies, of course; the company had no idea we were sleeping in our vehicles. I didn't confess anything about our deception to the commander, but he was a smart man. He probably figured it out on his own. Perhaps our investigative work that evening had engendered some goodwill towards myself and my friends. I hoped the commander might look the other way regarding the Gray Avenue property, but I certainly wasn't counting on it.

We left the station feeling more disillusioned than inspired. Now we knew we were on the police's radar. How were we going to break the news to Michael and Steve?

The next evening, we were contacted by Sergeant Charlie Baker who announced that he had captured Mario in the act of using a crowbar to open up the lock on one of the newspaper boxes. Mr. Monson was terribly relieved. Clu and I were very proud of ourselves, and we took Steve and Michael out to Skandi's Restaurant to celebrate our victory. The establishment had a grand buffet of Swedish delicacies, and the meatballs were to die for. We stuffed ourselves for several hours, delighting in both the companionship and the food. All the while, however, Clu and I knew we had to update our friends on the Gray Avenue situation. We were not looking forward to it.

After the extended meal, we all piled into my Mazda station wagon - a vehicle I had recently purchased for seven hundred dollars - and on the drive back to the Funk Zone, I finally confessed that we were likely to have a visit from the police that night.

"Stop the car!" Michael screamed. I pulled the Mazda over and told him and Steve about our conversation with the watch commander the night before. After whining and cursing for several minutes, their brains settled and started to function rationally again. They told me to drive to Thrifty's - a drugstore downtown. The two men ran inside and came out with a load of "No Trespassing" signs and enough rope to encircle the lot we were leasing. Back on the property, they strung rope along the entire perimeter and hung signs every five feet so that no decent person could miss them. While that was happening, I went to my typewriter and typed up a letter to the city government. It stated that I had rented the property and hired Mike, Roy and Steve as security. I set the letter down next to my lease agreement, asked the guys to wake me up if the cops arrived, and then went to sleep.

Not long after, Steve knocked on the window of my camper to wake me up. Sure enough, there were five squad cars lined up along the front of the property with their red and blue lights flashing into the air. Steve and Michael approached the police, and when the cops tried ducking under the rope, my security team told them they didn't have permission to enter. They'd be trespassing.

The cops looked at each other, not knowing what to do. They walked around in circles for a while, then decided they needed to call their beat commander. The superior officer showed up next, got out of his car and surveyed the scene. My friends and I were standing in the yard. Along another edge of the perimeter, beneath a street lamp, the Lone Ranger had parked his truck in such a way that his American flag fluttered gracefully in the ocean breeze. It was a sight to behold.

Finally, the beat commander threw up his hands, and to our surprise, he shouted, "I love it! I love it! Nothing like this ever happens in Santa Barbara. It's usually about as boring as a tits on a witch's ass!" The man was laughing hysterically. The other officers thought he had lost it.

After this momentary lapse in decorum, the commander switched back to his normal, no-nonsense disposition. He asked us permission to step over the rope and come onto the property, and we granted it, though only to him. The commander took down our license plates and I gave him a copy of our rental agreement, plus the letter to the city I had typed up. Then he told the officers to clear out.

We had won that battle, but not the war. As expected, in a few days we received an eviction notice from the Serena Company saying that we had violated the terms of the lease agreement. Even if they didn't care whether we slept in our vehicles, they probably buckled under pressure from the police to kick us out. We had thirty days to vacate. Ah, well... at least those thirty days would be free of midnight raids and sleep deprivation. We would rest, and perhaps that would give us the strength to figure out what to do next.

~

ONCE THE THIRTY DAYS WERE OVER, WE FOUND OURSELVES BACK IN the boatyard. The community there hadn't grown any smaller in our absence. In fact, it seemed like there were more people living in cars in Santa Barbara every month.

One night, after having dinner at Carrows, we returned to the lot and I laid down Seanie for his nightly rest. Then I started making the rounds to check up on members of our close-knit family before I turned in for the night. In order to get seven hours of sleep, I had to be in bed by 6:30 p.m.

On my way back to my camper, one of the occupants of a white sedan walked up to me. I'd already made Jeff's acquaintance; Jeff was a poverty-stricken script writer who slept in his car with his girlfriend but was hoping to make a big splash in Hollywood someday. Tonight, however, Jeff handed me a flyer and asked if I would like to come to a meeting to discuss the laws regarding sleeping outdoors or inside one's vehicle within city limits. People were getting angry about receiving tickets and being thrown in jail for the simple act of sleeping outside. I was fairly interested, but I knew I'd already been identified by the police as an outlaw for living in my camper. I was afraid of getting involved in a civil fight, mostly because I knew they'd use my insubordination as an excuse to take Seanie away from me. Jeff's gathering would undoubtedly snowball into something much larger than a single meeting, I also knew, and I wanted to be left alone so I could lift my child and myself out of the poverty-stricken circumstances we'd found ourselves in.

I told Jeff that I was unable to attend. I was working three part-time jobs and felt exhausted most of the time. The meeting would also cut into my hours of sleep, which were precious enough to begin with. Jeff handed me a flyer for the meeting, in case I changed my mind.

A couple of nights later, I headed to Carrows for a cup of coffee to help me wake up before I started work at 2:30 a.m. I practically lived in that restaurant. She put me to sleep when the sun was setting and roused me in time for my early morning shift. This time, when I sat down in one of the booths, I pulled out a piece of paper and started jotting down notes while I sipped my coffee. I wanted to write a letter to the editor of the Santa Barbara News-Press... something about the problems that the city would be facing if more and more people were only able to find shelter in vehicles.

As I put down my thoughts, I paused to pull out Jeff's flyer. The front page read "Homeless People's Association" and "February 2nd, 1982, 6:00 p.m." *Association.* I toyed with that word. My extended family of Rubber Trampers was certainly an association of sorts. We'd made up unofficial rules to help us avoid tickets and arrest, like parking a good distance away from each other at night. Though we lived in our separate vehicles, we were not isolated. Most of us were equipped with CB radios so that if one of us were ever in trouble, we could call out on our special channel and get the help we needed.

The meeting was going to be held in the municipal parking lot on the other side of Santa Barbara Street from the Jungle. I became curious. Maybe I needed to do more than just write this letter. If I went to the meeting, I could read it aloud to the attendees and see if they had any feedback before I sent it to the News-Press. The event would cut into my sleep time, but I decided it was worth it. I was a rebel at heart, after all, and my community needed me.

On Tuesday, the day of the meeting, Sean and I sat in a warm and cozy booth at Carrow's and looked out the window. A rainstorm had swept into the city, and it looked like it would be sticking around for a while. It was absolutely pouring. I sipped my fifth cup of coffee for the day and wondered, *How could an outdoor meeting happen in the middle of this deluge?* I was skeptical, but the only way to find out was to drive to the municipal lot and see if anyone bothered to show up.

We ran to the truck and drove to the site. As we pulled up, I was astonished at what I saw through my wet windshield. At least twenty-five men huddled together, shivering and soaked to the bone, waiting for the meeting to start. This gathering really meant something to them, I soon learned. They were exhausted from years spent fearing that they'd be hauled off to jail every time they fell asleep. They wanted to organize. They wanted to fight back. Many of the men were Vietnam veterans who had lived out on the streets since they'd been released from the war. If these people were as serious as they seemed, then I believed they stood a chance of becoming a powerful movement. Besides, what else could they do besides prolong their brutal stalemate with the police department?

*Jeff Hess drawing of the first meeting of the Homeless People's Association*

I was immediately hooked. Ideas were thrown around at the meeting. Some were discarded, others were rousingly approved. I read my Santa Barbara News-Press letter to the assembly as quickly as I could, so as to not prolong the meeting. It was warmly applauded and approved for publication. Before dispersing, we set a date, time and an agenda for our second meeting. Officers had to be elected to oversee our new organization. When the meeting finally adjourned, Sean and I drove across the street and hustled into our camper to get ready for bed. Through the windows, we watched the other drenched attendees trudge to their respective tents and hooches in the Jungle where hopefully they could shed their wet clothes and stay dry for the rest of the night.

Jeff had done it. He and his girlfriend in the white sedan had given me a chance to make a difference. They'd connected me to a cause greater than myself, and little did I know, I would proceed to spend the next forty years of my life engaged in activism and advocacy for the homeless community.

~

THE NEXT WEEK, SEAN AND I PAID MY PARENTS A VISIT, AND MY mother smiled as she pulled out a copy of the Santa Barbara News-Press. There it was. My letter to the editor was the top story in the Voices section of the Sunday edition. It spoke of the growing number of people having to use motorhomes, campers, cars and pickups in order to shelter themselves because wages could not keep up with rising rent prices. It also warned the city government of the inevitable problems that would result if they chose to ignore the issue.

I was extremely proud. So were my parents, for that matter. My mother finally revealed that in her youth, she had also been an advocate for affordable housing, and she pulled out her own letter to the editor... one she had written for the same newspaper thirty-six years ago, in 1946, when the housing crisis was just as extreme and World War II veterans like my father were unable to find accommodations in Santa Barbara.

It stunned me. My life, in many ways, had been an echo of what my own parents had experienced. When I was just a six-month-old baby in their care, they were living out of a vehicle and struggling... not unlike my present-day situation, decades later. Perhaps I was destined to pick up the mantle of homeless advocacy and resume the fight for basic human rights in our city. It wouldn't be an easy burden. But seeing my mother's letter, so similar to my own, hardened my dedication to the cause.

Whether with a pen or a picket line, I knew I was going to keep fighting.

～

ON A BEAUTIFUL SUNNY DAY, THE HOMELESS PEOPLE'S ASSOCIATION met for the second time in the same parking lot on the corner of Cabrillo Boulevard and Santa Barbara Street. Our chief order of business was to elect officers. Edwin Kozdrey, Jr., who had once helped fix the lights on my pickup truck, was elected president. He was a nice young man who was solid in his belief that we needed to gather in strength to fight the tickets and harassment that we were constantly receiving from the police. His quiet determination and knowledge of legal matters would help solidify our group into a tight and efficient force.

We elected a vice president and a sergeant-at-arms, who doubled as security. Then they elected me to serve as both secretary and treasurer. Our newly-founded group was determined to take itself and our future seriously.

The sound of sirens suddenly disrupted our meeting, and we all turned to see a motorcyclist racing down Santa Barbara Street toward the Jungle. The biker revved his Ducati engine to taunt the two squad cars that were in pursuit, lights flashing. Quickly, we ran to the fence so we could catch the action. The cyclist took a sharp left turn onto the dilapidated Jungle road, which accessed the long row of trees and brush between Cabrillo Boulevard and the railroad tracks. It was badly rutted from years of government neglect and covered in debris, but the Ducati wove easily through the terrain. The cop cars attempted the same maneuver, but the first vehicle immediately struck a log, caught a bit of air and came crashing down, disabling his front end. The second cruiser slowed just in time before it became another casualty.

Having no love for the police, we all cheered to see the race come to a standstill. The biker flipped his Ducati around to face the officers.

Then he put his middle finger in the air and gunned it out of the Jungle, escaping back onto Santa Barbara Street and disappearing in the direction of the freeway. Needless to say, our meeting was adjourned for the day. We were ecstatic at the turn of events and unable to refocus on our agenda, but at least our laughter brought us closer together.

I learned that the mad biker had a habit of antagonizing the police. He would sidle up to a cop car, gun his engine and then take off down the road at top speed, practically begging the officers to chase him down. The cops would fall for it every time... or maybe they liked the thrill of the chase themselves. Eventually, the lawbreaker was brought down by the boys in blue, but not before giving us several stories to remember him by.

$$\sim$$

MEETINGS WITH THE HOMELESS PEOPLE'S ASSOCIATION WERE ongoing. We designed a logo and created a speakers bureau so that select members of the homeless community could educate students in public school classrooms or at local events. One morning at the boat-yard, Jeff came running up to me outside my camper. He wanted Clu and I to be part of a program produced by KEYT News that was tackling the subject of people who lived in their cars. Excited, we headed to the studio for our interviews. The show ended up being of great interest to the citizens of Santa Barbara, and the media began pulling us in on other occasions, calling us the "Car People".

Our president, who we affectionately named "Prez Ed", took a few men up to the courthouse to investigate the laws that governed our mobile lifestyle. They were able to capture many bureaucratic details, like how much money it cost taxpayers for the police to write us tickets and throw us in jail. The police told us they were aware of our movements, so it seemed like they were feeling threatened by our nascent attempts to organize.

*Prez Ed (photo by Bob Werling)*

Michael came up to me one day and told me he'd had all the activism he could stand for a while. The stress that the city was placing upon us had grown too heavy for him to handle, so he decided he was going to leave the Jungle community and take his camper to the Rincon Parkway. At the time, it was free for travelers to stay in their RVs there. Clu's boyfriend Steve decided to join him. Even Roy disappeared one day, and no one knew where he'd gone.

I didn't know what I was going to do without Michael and Steve. Besides being frequent babysitters for my son, they were like family. But the city had broken us apart. Clu was also devastated. She couldn't believe that Steve had chosen Michael's friendship over hers.

I no longer wanted to sleep in the boatyard parking lot by myself without the protection of Mike and Steve, so Clu and I cooked up a plan. She had moved from her little place on Santa Barbara Street into a small cottage on Carrillo along with her three Samoyeds. Across the street from her new place, I parked my camper and hung a sign in the window which said that if anyone had a problem with me parking there, they should go to Clu's front door and give it a knock. If Clu were home, she'd simply tell any concerned neighbors that Sean and I were sleeping inside the house. That wasn't true, of course, but it was a pretty good cover story.

At 2 a.m., I would drive my truck and camper to Carrow's for a cup of coffee, then head to Mr. Monson's warehouse. I'd have to transfer Sean to the back seat of my work truck while I made my rounds delivering newspapers, but he was such a hard sleeper that he'd immediately doze off again. After my shift was over, I'd wake up Sean, put him on my motorcycle, which I'd stashed at the warehouse, and drop him off at school. Then I'd swap my bike for the camper and head to the boatyard lot, where I'd put on a pot of coffee for me and my remaining friends. Sometimes I'd take a nap, play with Schatzie and Tawny, or just pull out my guitar and pluck away for a few hours.

When Sean was ready to be picked up, I'd drive the camper back to the warehouse, take my motorcycle to the school to retrieve my son and return to the warehouse to swap vehicles one last time. We'd spend the rest of the afternoon at the boatyard or at Carrows getting ourselves a meal, and then at 7 p.m., I'd park the camper across the street from Clu's cottage. This complicated routine proved to be the easiest way to dodge the police force and get a decent amount of undisturbed rest every night.

I missed Michael and Steve, but Clu and I drove down to the Rincon to pay them an occasional visit. Other times, we got on our CB radios and reached out from a distance. My handle was Royal Nibs - an alias I'd adapted from the pet name that my ex-husband Ross had sometimes called me: Nibs. I simply added "Royal" to it. Clu's handle was The Samoyed Lady, Michael's was Silver Bullet and Steve went by The Desert Ghost. When the two men moved from the Rincon to Point Mugu, further down the coast, we had to drive up to Shoreline Park in order for our radio signals to travel across the ocean and reach them. The separation of our family was regrettable, but the four of us had been connected far too long not to stay in touch.

*Michael Tice demonstrating his famous Tarzan yell at the Rincon*
*(photographer unknown)*

❧

A FEW GOOD THINGS CAME OUT OF OUR INITIAL OUTREACH EFFORTS. As I was bringing newspapers into a store on the Westside one morning, a man named Donald Olsen walked up to me and asked if I was Nancy McCradle. I nodded, and he explained that he worked as a department head in the city government. He'd seen our KEYT interview about the Car People and decided that he wanted to teach members of the HPA how we could work with the bureaucratic system to be more effective. That sounded perfect. The HPA wanted to spend less time fighting and protesting and more time engaged in community development.

Donald handed me his business card and told me to stop by his office at City Hall, which I did. He steered me toward a City and County Task Force that discussed local issues, such as the homeless, and the first time I went, they were kind enough to let me speak. I was new at this game and had a lot to learn, but I spoke about the necessity for shelter and the safety and health concerns of the homeless community. Then I went to the Moreton Bay Fig Tree Park on the corner of Chapala and Montecito Street to share the news. Members of our

Association had begun to hang out there underneath the overarching canopy and they were always eager to hear my perspective and glean any information coming out of City Hall. I never made a single move regarding homeless issues without getting a thumbs up from the HPA. It was the key to instilling a sense of self-empowerment in our members.

Soon afterward, I was contacted by a blue chip stockbroker who wanted to fund a fifty-bed shelter to help people living on the streets. Like Don, this businessman had also seen members of the HPA speakers bureau on television, and he asked me to set up a meeting between him and the city. It was an exciting development. I first brought the news over to the boys at the fig tree, and they were completely in favor of such a project. We sat in a circle while I tried to answer their questions, like what the term "blue chip" meant.

"Blue chips are commodities," I answered, "like gold, silver, wheat..."

"Sex," one person pontificated.

I looked around to find the joker, but he'd clamped his lips shut. That's what I got for being the sole woman working with a bunch of men, I supposed.

I worked to develop the shelter concept with my city contacts, but the project ended up competing with another idea proposed by the broker's girlfriend: a childcare center. Both projects had merit, but the child care center won out in the end, so we had to point our hopes in a different direction.

During the same week that I met Donald Olsen, another man approached me one afternoon at the Jungle lot when I was sitting by my camper. He reminded me of John Lennon, probably because of his aquiline nose and signature glasses. The young man introduced himself as Rob Rosenthal, a student in the UCSB Sociology Department who was working on his PhD. Rob wanted to interview me about the history of the Homeless People's Association, and he seemed like a nice person, so I invited him into the camper. I poured him a cup of coffee and he promptly produced a joint, so we immediately started off on the right foot. The two of us yakked for hours about the Ground Pounders and the Rubber Tramps... about my experiences living in my camper and the issues affecting the whole street community.

Rob became a real friend to the HPA over the next few months. I learned that an elderly philanthropist named Kit Tremaine had hired him to investigate some of the organizations that were helping different factions of the poor in Santa Barbara. While walking her dog every morning along Cabrillo Boulevard, Kit had started noticing all the people who emerged from the Jungle, and she became curious. She called up the University and eventually hired Rob to figure out what was going on.

Kit developed a keen interest in the Homeless Rights movement, and she had Rob arrange a meeting between the two of us. The philanthropist and I had lunch and discussed what it would take to get people off the streets. She was personally interested in me because we'd both had to deal with the effects of alcohol abuse by our husbands. Her husband died from his alcoholism, leaving her a significant stake in the Louisiana Oil Company. Besides being a writer with two books to her name, she was a prominent donor for many of the non-profit organizations in Santa Barbara.

Kit and I swiftly became fast friends and would go to lunch often. I thought she was a sweetheart, and I especially appreciated her friendship later in life, for one year after we met, my mother passed away after overdosing on estrogen and diet pills. In my mom's absence, Kit became the predominant maternal figure in my life, and I was so grateful for her presence.

~

As the Homeless People's Association became more prominent in local affairs, the media's interest intensified. The citizens of Santa Barbara appeared stunned that the homeless had enough grit and persistence to be able to organize. They firmly believed that the homeless were just a bunch of lazy addicts who were chemically disabled past the point of no return. Certainly, drugs were a factor in the community. Alcohol was the worst of their vices, but even the alcoholics had good ideas now and again, and if the drunkards could not implement those plans due to their handicaps, their healthier cohorts could do so. In my experience, I had never met a more creative, smart and resourceful group of people in my entire life. The men were mostly loving, eager to please and chivalrous, and I loved them dearly in return. They were the last to be considered when shelter opportunities arose, and that was how they wanted it. "Women and children first!" they would cry. That selflessness was why I was willing to advocate for them.

A journalist named Melinda Burns from the Santa Barbara News-Press contacted me and asked if she could do a story on the people who lived in the box cars at the Jungle. I asked her to hold off until I could secure permission from the residents. Surprisingly, they all agreed to be interviewed. I hadn't expected those reclusive souls to be media hounds.

Melinda's article turned out to be a well-crafted and insightful piece of writing. It was plastered across the front pages of the News-Press. The Associated Press also picked up her story and gave it national attention. The HPA was becoming a force that was recognized across the country as one of the most well-organized of its kind. Of course, the fact that President Ronald Reagan owned a ranch at the top of nearby Refugio Canyon helped to focus the media on Santa Barbara and its socio-political environment. We were well aware of the spotlight this gave us, and it stimulated the HPA to become even more outspoken in its public efforts.

More members of the housed community began to reach out to us and become part of the homeless rights movement, but we weren't embraced across the board. Outreach became of critical importance. Representatives from the HPA speakers bureau were called into the schools to speak about homelessness. The kids seemed to love hearing about the social upheaval that was occurring throughout the city. Other factions in the greater community preferred to ignore what was happening or were outright hostile to our presence. To them, the homeless were just ghastly to look upon. Hate mail was sent to the City Council by homeowners complaining about the deterioration of their scenic views. Emotions began to run hot in the city because we were not willing to hide anymore. We were making ourselves known, and in doing so, we ran the risk of generating hatred and fear in others. It's funny how some people react defensively when certain classes of people are trying to better themselves.

Most restrictions placed on the homeless served to make our lives tremendously difficult, but we weren't against every mandate. When the City of Santa Barbara passed a law making it illegal to drink in public - with the exception of permit holders, who put money into the city coffers in exchange for the privilege - the majority of us agreed with the initiative. It had been hard to walk anywhere in town without seeing displays of public intoxication.

One day, Rob Rosenthal came up to me in the boatyard and said that he'd finished his report on the homeless. It was time to do something with it, and he asked if I would accompany him to a city council meeting where we could meet our elected representatives. Susanne Riordan, who directed the Single Parent Alliance non-profit, would also be attending. I agreed to go, although honestly, I was scared to death. This would be my first encounter with the officials who I felt were responsible for countless attempts by the police to break my street family apart. I both hated and feared them. It was curious that I rarely received any tickets from city enforcers, unlike the rest of my community. When I drove my camper through town, sometimes the police would give me the peace sign as I passed. I'd respond by giving them the British gesture for "fuck you." Perhaps a similarly impassive attitude was what I needed to maintain if I was going to make it through this meeting without buckling under the pressure.

When the time came, I put on my best dress and heels and even curled my hair. Council meetings were held in the evening so that working-class people could attend and express their concerns about city policies. Sheila Lodge was the mayor and highest-ranking official present. Rob had put us on the agenda, and he introduced both Susanne and I. When it was my turn to speak, I walked to the podium and curtsied to the council. Then I spoke to them as if I were addressing my mother or father. The fear left me as I felt their honest interest in what I had to say. Many of them had seen a story on television about the origins of the HPA, and they were excited to finally meet one of its members. I think they were simply stunned that the homeless were able to get organized since they believed us to be just a bunch of bums and transients.

*Santa Barbara City Council (photo by Kevin McKiernan)*

Words spilled out of me. I spoke of my firm belief that criminalization was not the answer to solving the problem of homelessness. I explained how police harassment never actually resolved or changed anything except to make the lives of disadvantaged people miserable. When I finished, the questions flew. I did my best to answer them, then sat back down. No longer would I be afraid of these people. Maybe... just maybe... we could work together to make the streets of Santa Barbara a better place for its citizens, both the housed and the unhoused.

## 9

# PROTEST BOB

In 1983, a national conference on homelessness was held in Chicago. It brought together a diverse host of organizations that were working to address the issue. The philanthropist Kit Tremaine decided that Santa Barbara should be represented at the event, so she bought tickets for me, Rob Rosenthal and Susanne Riordan of the Single Parent Alliance and flew us out to Illinois for the weekend.

It was a lot to take in. Countless nonprofit organizations and government agencies had booths and tables spread out across the conference center. We spent three days attempting to make sense of it all, gathering contacts and attending workshops on housing issues, criminalization and nimbyism. It was reassuring that so many people were attempting to address the nationwide problem, and it felt cathartic to be able to commiserate with others about the roadblocks we faced in trying to get our solutions implemented. Too often, we advocates would be told, "Your proposal costs too much money," "We'll let the police handle it," "We'll write a new ordinance to curtail their behavior" or "We'll steer them towards other parts of the city so the tourists don't have to see *those people.*" We strategized how to circumvent these stubborn attitudes, sharing what worked in our communities and what didn't. Then at the end of the weekend, we consolidated the best ideas and gave them to the convention heads who would take our proposals to Washington, D.C. and an uncertain future.

In the wake of the Chicago convention, the nonprofit organizations in Santa Barbara began to coordinate a little more closely. An activist from the Latino-rights group called El Concillo reached out to the Homeless People's Association and asked for our help promoting some aspects of their agenda. We felt a little like political pawns sometimes, but the idea of multiplying our voting power was compelling. Kit and I went to several faith-based organizations to see if they were willing to help us with homelessness issues, and our efforts began to gain momentum from there. Representatives from these other groups began to show up at our meetings. The League of Women Voters became interested in our cause. The Grey Panthers - a group of activist senior citizens - came on board as well. Eventually, all these alliances resulted in the formation of a new nonprofit organization - the Homeless Coalition. They established an office at the bottom of Chapala Street next to the freeway and got to work.

I served as a representative of the Homeless People's Association to this new, larger entity, and once the Homeless Coalition moved into La Casa De La Raza on the Eastside, they hired me to be their office manager. The role required one to be in touch with the language of the streets, and I had all of the qualifications. For five days of the week, I was responsible for opening and closing the office, fundraising, answering phones and putting up with the homeless men who liked to hang out in the building and distract me. Mostly, the same guys showed up over and over again to use the phone or look for work, and at times I felt like I was running a daycare center. Still, they proved their worth on occasion by watching the desk whenever I had to slip out to run errands or pick Sean up from school.

I kept a log book that detailed which visitors came to the office and what the Homeless Coalition was able to do for them. One of my overarching responsibilities, however, was to be a public face and an over-the-phone voice for the organization, maintaining a cooperative tone with whichever government representative or coalition partner might walk through the door. Various facets of the city were fearful of our organization and the burgeoning homeless rights movement, so it paid to be as diplomatic as possible.

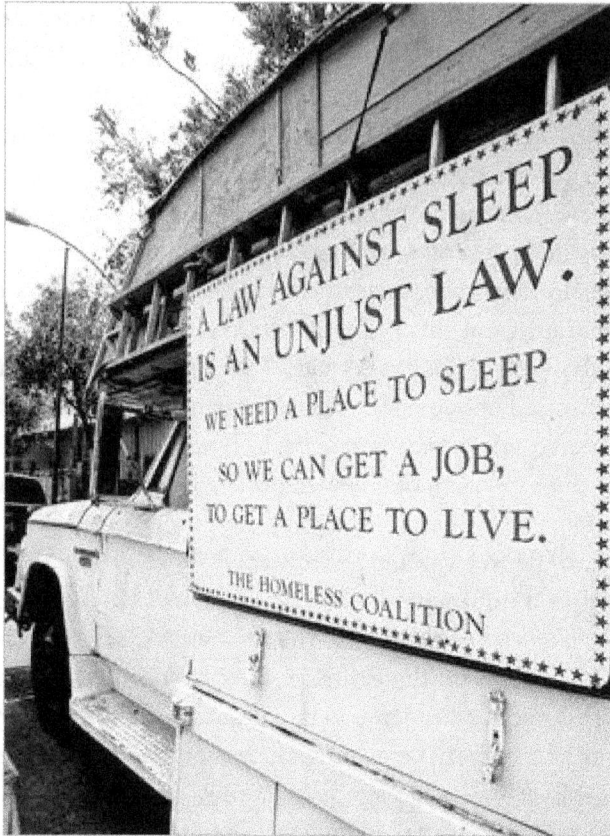

*Homeless Coalition sign on the side of Bob Hansen's truck (photo by Leslie Holtzman)*

My L.A. Times delivery job continued all the while. One day, my boss, Mr. Monson, called me into the office and asked if I'd like to start taking the newspaper returns over to the recycling center. His previous worker had quit on him, and a huge pile of old papers was stacking up in the corner of the warehouse. It would be bad to let them mold and fester. Mr. Monson would let me use one of the company trucks and I was welcome to keep the money. Despite already working two jobs, I agreed for the sake of padding out my paycheck.

The trucks were rated to carry a half-ton of weight, and I probably loaded them far beyond that. Some weeks it would take two or three trips to clear out the stack of papers, so I certainly got my fair share of exercise, and if I took care of it on Saturdays, seven-year-old Seanie would help out. I'd split the money with him so he could have an allowance. Some weeks the recycling center would pay $120 per ton of paper. Other times it was as low as $7, which wasn't worth the effort. Still, I continued these trips, knowing that the price would eventually go back up again.

One Friday, I dropped Sean off at school on my motorcycle and went to the warehouse to do a recycling run. The recycling center was located downtown on the site where the Summer Solstice Workshop currently operates. As I was emptying the truck, the manager walked up to me and handed me a piece of paper. On it was scribbled, "Robert Hansen" and a phone number. He explained that the number belonged to a man better known around the community as "Protest Bob" who wanted to join up with the Homeless People's Association and help out in some capacity.

Although I'd never met the man, I decided that Bob Hansen was no one I wanted to be in contact with. The HPA didn't need any protesters. I was protective of our budding organization, and we were working our way up through the administrative ranks of local government, trying to navigate within the system rather than outside it. Protesting was unnecessary and would be counterproductive to our current goals. I threw the number in the trash and promptly forgot about it. Perhaps I should have run the decision by the other members of the HPA, but that day I felt qualified to make a determination on my own.

A couple of weeks later, the same manager at the pay window of the recycling center asked me if I'd contacted his friend. I told him no and that I had no plans to do so. Protesters were a dime-a-dozen, and the Homeless People's Association was trying to work for civil rights in a more systematic fashion. He handed me Bob's number again, just in case, but again, I tossed it.

One early Sunday morning, I pulled up in my truck alongside the Santa Barbara Liquor store on State Street, and I wondered why a large group of homeless men were standing out in front of the place. It turned out they were waiting for me to arrive with my papers so they could talk to me. I got out of my vehicle, and while I was carrying a stack of L.A. Times to the front door, their designated speaker, a ginger-haired guy known as "Red Man", stepped forward and told me that I needed to meet Protest Bob.

I stared at the crowd, and they grinned disturbingly back. For some reason, I got angry. I threw up my arms and shouted, "I do not want to meet up with this asshole, okay? My word is final, so just leave me alone!" They laughed while I finished my work, got in my truck and drove off to the next delivery spot. *Jeez, Louise!* They just didn't get that a protester would ruin the relationships that the HPA had been forging with the city. *What a bunch of bull.*

A few weeks later, on another Sunday morning at 6 a.m., I pulled up to the same liquor store to make my deliveries. This time, the place was completely quiet. I slid the bundles of papers toward the back of the truck and grabbed the twine that was used to tie them together. Each paper at that time weighed four or five pounds due to all the inserts that were jammed in there. We'd worked for two days at the warehouse assembling them, and they were monsters. I was in terrific shape, muscular and without an ounce of fat on me because of all the lifting and throwing of these heavy bundles.

As I grabbed the slippery twine and maneuvered the stacks off the truck, I heard a long, drawn-out wolf whistle. Surprised, I dropped the papers and spun around. Across the street stood a tall man, about six feet in height with auburn hair and a beard, wearing Levi denim overalls like he had just walked off a Midwestern farm. Barefoot and scraggly, with dirt caked on his clothes and feet, he looked like he needed a bath more than anything. In his arms, he held a five-gallon bucket of ice cream that he must have scavenged from the dumpster near the Dreyers Ice Cream warehouse. For lack of a spoon, this lunatic was eating his dessert with a stalk of celery. Ice cream dripped down his face and the front of his overalls. I was nervous, knowing that the streets of Santa Barbara produce a lot of wingnuts, but I tended to my work so I could quickly get back in my truck and boogie out of there.

The man watched me for a while, then started to cross the street. *Gawd! Is he coming toward me?*

Schatzie stood guard in the bed of the pickup, hackles raised, and I knew I could count on her to defend me if the situation turned dangerous. I wished Tawny had been there as well, but my other dog had recently passed away from thyroid cancer. I kept the truck between myself and the interloper while I finished my tasks, and when I climbed into the driver's seat, he finally blurted out, "Do you want to get married?"

"God, no!" I replied. Schatzie leaned over me protectively, muscles tensed.

As I went to close the door, the man continued, obliviously, "Do you want to live together?" I couldn't believe this man was serious.

"I am just getting over a marriage," I told him, "So, *no.*" My rebound relationship with Duffy had also ended unsatisfactorily, so I wasn't interested in entertaining any romantic entanglements. I was happy living on my own with my son.

Undaunted, he asked, "Well, do you want to go out sometime?"

*Ugh.* "No!" The man just did not get it. I was trying to be as nice as I could, but all I could see was ice cream dripping down his beard and it was too much for me to handle. To put an end to the conversation, I told him, "If you run into me in a coffee shop and ask politely to sit down, I suppose it wouldn't be too dangerous for me to have a cup of coffee with you." I kept the possibility open because I was always interested in stories told by homeless men. Even if those tales were convoluted and contradictory, they were still educational.

With that, I closed the truck door and drove off to the Mini Mart, the next stop on my route. *Now, that was a strange encounter,* I thought. I'd met some strange characters on the street, but this guy was about the weirdest. Only after explaining this episode to some friends did I learn the truth: *that man was Protest Bob!*

~

ONE OF THE REGULARS AT VERA CRUZ PARK CAME UP TO ME ONE day and wanted to show me something. He and some friends had rented a shed from Tony's Body and Fender. With expressions of pride, they opened the shed and gestured to the mattresses they'd laid out on the floor. It was obviously illegal, but it would keep them safe from the elements for a time. I congratulated them on their ingenuity, but as I was studying their grinning faces, I noticed Protest Bob in their midst. *Was he part of this project, or did he just follow me to this little building?* I didn't ask. However, the man started to pop up wherever I went. I began to wonder if I'd picked up another stalker.

Bob Hansen integrated himself into the group of people who hung out at the Fig Tree. At least the man didn't directly come up and bug me again. Eventually, I got to feel as comfortable seeing him around as I did any of the others.

During this period of time, Lee and Sandi - the Native American couple who lived in their hootch in the Jungle encampment - came to me with a proposition. They wished to stay with me in the camper, and in exchange, they would babysit Sean while I was doing my newspaper route and while I slept. They'd even use my pickup to drop me off at work. Lee had become a trusted advisor for the HPA and his wife Sandi was a good friend, so seeing that I still wasn't getting enough hours of sleep with my current strategies, I agreed to their proposal.

It turned out to be an ideal arrangement. They loved to hang out at Sambo's restaurant drinking coffee until two in the morning while Sean and I slept in the camper outside. Then they'd drive me to work and hand me a coffee-to-go as I headed off to start my shift. They'd keep the camper stationed at the warehouse until I got off work. Then we'd head back to the Jungle parking lot and everyone would go about their business. Since there was room for four people to sleep inside the ten-and-a-half-foot space that I called my home, it worked out pretty well.

Lee was a survivalist and a veteran of the Vietnam War who professed to have served in the U.S. Special Forces. He said he was unable to claim his veterans' benefits because his paperwork was kept in secret files, and so far he'd been unable to obtain them. The stories he told about his tour of duty in the jungles of Vietnam were both outrageous and frightening. At one point, he said, he'd snuck off into the jungle and built himself a compound. The Viet Cong were afraid to approach his place, for he had placed severed animal heads on spikes along the perimeter. Lee had been honorably discharged from the service, but he suffered years of PTSD symptoms. Some nights, he walked the streets with his rifle after waking from nightmares about his time abroad. Lee was of mixed race, black and Apache - a combination which lent him a lot of shrewdness. His wife Sandi was of Arapaho ancestry, and the two of us women had a lot of fun together. I was glad to have their help raising Seanie, and they were fiercely protective of us both.

Sometimes we would park my camper beside the grassy area that held the Moreton Fig Tree. The place was often a hive of activity, and at some point, Ed and some of the other guys came up with the idea to get a city permit to put up an information table near the tree, on the corner of Chapala and Montecito Streets. At that time, permits were valid for use all twenty-four hours of the day. We put out written materials on homeless services to let people know the locations of bathhouses and lockers and where to apply for government programs that would provide financial assistance. Ed manned the space at night and kept an eye on any personal belongings that were stashed behind the table. The other homeless would take turns watching for police so that they could wake up their sleeping companions if the black-and-whites came around. That saved everyone from getting tickets.

Of course, Bob placed protest signs in the branches of the fig tree. The man seemed determined to draw as much attention to our corner of the city as possible, but there was nothing I could do if his antics were accepted by the rest of the homeless community.

Eventually, the police paid us a midnight visit. At least twenty police officers showed up to confront Edwin and order him to take down his table. Ed stood his ground. He pointed to his city permit, which was taped to the table, and informed them that they had two more weeks left of authorized usage. He dared the cops to take down the table themselves. Thankfully, the police declined to make that move, knowing that we had a legal right to maintain that space.

The next day, the city's attorney came by the fig tree to examine our permit. After determining that the table was legitimate, the government decided to just let the permit run out. Of course, before we could secure another one, they amended the permit rules so it could no longer be used around the clock like before. This was the game we played. Whenever we strove to become more visible, the city would work even harder to push us back into the shadows.

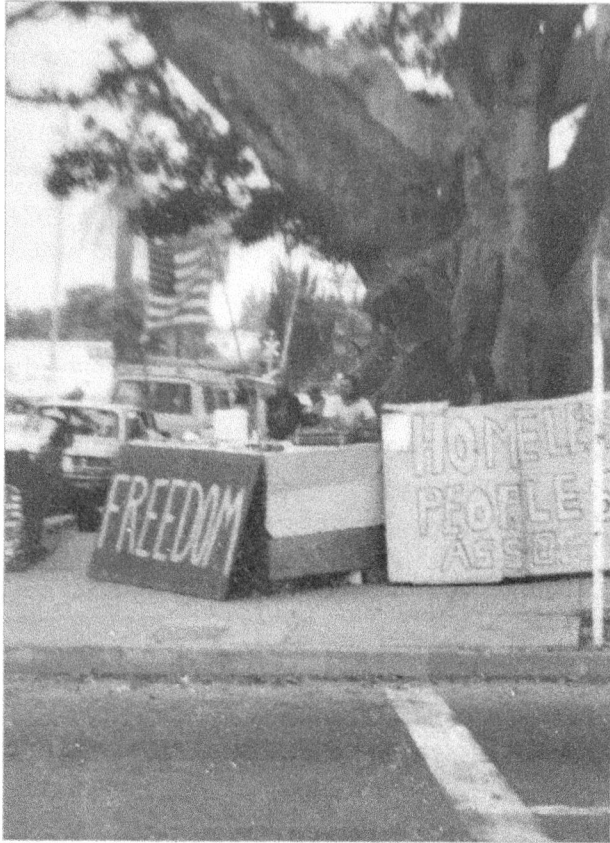

*The information table at Fig Tree Park circa 1983-84*

~

ONE EVENING, SEAN AND I WERE SITTING AT THE COUNTER IN Sambo's when the front door opened and the sound of bells caught my attention. In walked Protest Bob wearing a trench coat, yellow shorts and jingle bells on his shoes. He came over and asked if he could take a seat. That was fine with me. Despite his outrageous attire, Bob seemed to be on his best behavior, so I invited him to join us as we moved from the counter over to my favorite booth.

Sean was tired, so he put his head in my lap and dozed off, allowing Bob and I to get to know each other for the first time. Bob had just come back from Diablo Canyon where he and others had been protesting the nuclear power plant - the one that had been built on an active fault line. More specifically, he had just been released from jail after stepping over a barricade during the protest. So had several others. Apparently, it had been a grand old party.

That night, we talked about practically everything - religion, politics and of course, the homeless situation. It seemed that this weird man was more than just a protester. He was quite intelligent. He was born and raised in a comfortable, middle-class environment in Los Angeles and Torrance before coming to Santa Barbara in the 1970s. Like me, he was the black sheep and rebel of his family. I had yet to learn why he acted out so much and loved to stir up trouble, and I didn't know how he had come to live on the streets. Still, that night I realized how much I had in common with him, and we finally became friends. It was a very enjoyable evening, though at one point I looked at my watch and realized that I needed to get myself some sleep before work. I wished Bob a good night and took Sean to my camper so I could crash for a few hours.

My wake-up call came far too soon. I was rather groggy at work and didn't have Lee and Sandi to help out that day, so after taking Sean to school in the morning, I drove up to the Radio Square parking lot where I knew I wouldn't be bothered by friends or police. I gave the doggies some water and took a long, six-hour nap. Sean was now going to school for a full seven hours, so the extended break gave me a chance to get my strength back.

With Lee and Sandi frequently staying as guests, I rarely had the camper to myself in those days. Sometimes Lee's friend Billy would stay with us too and sleep in the front seat of the truck. That man was both delusional and scary. One night when we were parked by the Fig Tree, Billy and I were chatting in the front seats with Schatzie lying between us. The conversation took a dark turn, and suddenly a knife was in Billy's hands. He placed the blade against Schatzie's neck and told me that my dog was unhappy and wanted to go to heaven. I knew instinctively that if I freaked out, my dog would be killed. Somehow, I had to remain calm.

In the steadiest tone I could muster, I asked Billy what we could do to make Schatzie happy on earth again. He didn't think that was possible, but the delay allowed me to come up with an idea. I proposed that we play a game of poker, using a deck of cards I kept on the dashboard to determine Schatzie's fate. If I won, Schatzie would be allowed to remain on earth. *But if I lost...*

Billy was happy to engage in this gambit. I dealt the cards, and miraculously, I won! The crazy man put his knife away, and I never let Schatzie near him again.

Not long after this incident, Seanie and I were sleeping in the camper, which was parked next to the newspaper warehouse. Billy was staying with us again, and while we dozed, Lee sent his friend out to the dumpster behind McDonald's to see if he could scrounge up some hamburgers. Dumpster diving at that location was usually productive since the fast food chain always tossed their uneaten food at the end of the day. Thirty minutes later, I was woken by a knock on the camper door. Two policemen stood outside. They handed Lee a box full of McDonald's leftovers. "Here are the hamburgers you ordered," they said with a tinge of wickedness. "And by the way, we have Billy."

It turned out they had a warrant out for Billy's arrest. He'd accumulated too many tickets for sleeping outdoors, and now it was his time to spend a few nights in jail. Normally, I would have railed against the injustice, but this time, I was filled with a sense of relief. Something was quite wrong with the man, and I was afraid that worse things might occur in the future if he were allowed to stick around.

Protest Bob, on the other hand, became a closer friend as time went on. He began to hang out with us in the camper a lot. One time, Sandi and I were playing cards at the table while Bob was lying up in my bed, hanging out behind the privacy curtain. All of a sudden, the curtain flew open and out jumped Bob wearing my brassiere and a pair of women's undies. He did a hoochie-coochie dance in front of Sandi and me that had us in stitches. That was Bob for you.

Another time, the police came to the Fig Tree to harass the people manning our information table. Our permit for the table had not yet expired, but the officers wanted to know how many days were remaining. Bob strolled into the midst of this encounter with a dozen cigarettes in his mouth and two more sprouting from his ears. He didn't say anything; he just stood there, quietly trying to pull their concentration away from the table. The cops didn't bite. I think they realized that Bob craved their attention and they were reluctant to give him any. The man might have annoyed them enough, however, that they eventually gave up and left us alone.

Protest Bob had his positive moments. Unfortunately, at other times, he could be dreadful. One evening, I was quietly sitting in my booth at Sambo's when Bob and his friend Robbie Merritt walked in and sat down at my table. I wasn't in a mood for company, but they didn't take the hint. Instead, they launched into some textbook sexual harassment, trying to get a rise out of me. I kept my anger in check as long as I could, but once the subject of their conversation turned to blowjobs, I snapped. I seized two large glasses of ice water, stood up and poured the contents onto both their laps. I strode out of the restaurant with a big grin on my face as the men swore and made a commotion behind me. Ignoring them, I got into my pickup and drove my camper down the road. *Men!*

~

BARBECUE TIME AT LEDBETTER BEACH HAPPENED ON THE FIRST OF every month. That was when everyone received their disability and Social Security checks and could afford to buy food for the grill. The extended homeless community gathered there, and of course, I was invited to the festivities.

One of these afternoons, after soaking up my fair share of sunlight, I began to grow sleepy, so I headed up to my camper to take a nap. Sean was at school, so I wasn't likely to be disturbed. When I got there, however, I noticed that attached to my radio antenna was an American flag - nothing unusual, except that it was fluttering upside down. Normally, I would have interpreted that as a distress signal, but in this case, I knew it was Bob messing with me again. I took down the flag, turned it right-side up and attached it to the antenna on Bob's camper. *That guy...*

No longer tired, I walked back into the crowd, sat down and started chatting with my friends. I stared out into the ocean for a long time. Occasionally, Bob caught my eye and smiled. That was the day I let Bob follow me into my camper and we became physically intimate for the first time. I hadn't expected it to happen. I didn't think I wanted a relationship with anyone at the time. But through sheer persistence, Bob had managed to get under my skin. *So what happens now?* I wondered. All I could do was wait to see what would become of our unconventional dynamic.

~

OVER TIME, I LEARNED THE STORY OF HOW BOB HAD GONE FROM A middle-class existence to living on the streets of Santa Barbara. Robert Hansen was born in Los Angeles and raised in Torrance. He married his high school sweetheart Barbara and had a daughter, but his wife was unable to get him to settle down. Bob wasn't ready to buy a home together and help raise his child, and when nothing seemed to get him to change his lifestyle, his wife finally asked for a divorce.

Devastated, Bob retreated to Santa Barbara and lived in various apartments before switching to living out of one vehicle or another. He'd followed a pattern common with many men in which divorce and depression caused them to spiral into homelessness. When I met him, he seemed to have gained a degree of emotional stability, if not maturity. He was a genius in many ways, though dyslexic, and he suffered from obsessive-compulsive disorder. All the same, my boyfriend was a teddy bear of a man, and I came to love him thoroughly.

One day, Bob came up to me and asked if Sean and I would like to go with him to a family reunion picnic at a park in Torrance. Meeting his family felt like a scary prospect, but it felt like a really big deal to be invited. I had accrued two weeks of vacation from work and could use some of that time for a short road trip, so I agreed to go.

I had to tell Lee and Sandi that they needed to move out of the camper, even though they'd been helping me take care of Sean for a few months now. Our only other passenger on the journey south was Dego, a comedic homeless man who needed to catch a Greyhound bus from the Los Angeles bus station on Main Street in order to get back to Florida. Bob knew the city well, so he got behind the wheel of the pickup, allowing Sean and me to slumber in our own beds back in the camper.

I was roused from my sleep in the middle of the night when I heard the truck start up. Peering out the window, I saw that we were parked in front of the Greyhound station. But then I noticed that Bob was sleeping next to me. *Who, then, was driving the pickup?*

I leaned over the edge of the bed so I could peer through the camper's front window into the cab of the truck. Three unfamiliar guys were sitting in the front seat and had apparently managed to hot-wire the vehicle. Quickly, I shook Bob awake and told him that someone was attempting to steal the pickup. He immediately rolled out of bed, jumped out of the camper and ran up to the cab just as the thieves had started to turn the vehicle into the street.

By this point, I was standing in the center of my camper with my rifle pointed at the closed door, not knowing what to expect. It was only a pellet gun, but the robbers wouldn't know that. My hundred-and-twenty-pound German shepherd stood guard at my side. I'd been petrified when Bob left the camper, thinking the thieves would either shoot him dead or drive away and leave him in the dust. Either way, I'd be forced to defend myself.

Meanwhile, Bob banged on the glass of the cab window and told the men to get out of the truck. Shocked, since they were unaware that anyone was sleeping in the back, the thieves left without raising a fuss. I thought Bob had been tremendously lucky. He could have been shot or stabbed, and then who knows what would have happened to Seanie and me.

Further sleep was out of the question. The men had destroyed the pickup's ignition, but Bob figured out how to hot-wire the engine himself and get us going, so we headed off to Torrance and reached his parents' house a little earlier than we'd intended.

After my initial shyness, I hit it off with Bob's family. The picnic reunion in the park with Bob's many brothers and cousins was a fun affair. At one point, a soccer game was interrupted when the kids got the ball stuck in a tree. They tried shaking the tree and throwing objects after it, but they could not get it unstuck. Bob went over to try and get it free, but he was also unsuccessful. I finally got up from the grass where I was lying and ran over. I shimmied up the trunk, scooted along the branch that held the ball and shook it until it fell to the ground. Everyone stared at me as I climbed down, and I returned to my spot on the lawn with a big grin on my face. No one there knew how much of a tomboy I was, even Bob. I'd become a skilled tree-climber as a child since one of my favorite things to do at our house in Goleta was to climb the elm tree in the parkway, put my ear to the trunk and listen to its lifeblood flow beneath the bark.

The Great Soccer Ball Rescue became my claim to fame for the day. We returned to Santa Barbara in good spirits, and my relationship with Bob continued to deepen. He moved permanently into my camper and helped me to raise Sean. Reliability was not his strong suit, however. The man would disappear for days at a time, going out to drink with his friends on the street. He also took drugs whenever they were made available to him, and an entire book could be written on the difficulties he had coming back to himself after his psychedelic trips.

Whenever Bob vanished, I would be driving the streets of Santa Barbara a few days later and hear someone shouting my name. Looking into the rearview window, I'd see Bob chasing me down the road. His return appearances always left me emotionally confused, but I did my best to take the irregularities in stride. At least he wasn't cheating on me, as far as I knew. When thoughts of depression clouded his mind, Bob could lay down and not move for hours. I would coax him to join me for a bike ride, and that sometimes helped.

Our friends called us The Bob and Nancy Show. To the outside observer, our fights and intimate moments were tremendously amusing and overshadowed the lives around us. Even so, we were both loved. Our strengths and weaknesses provided enough drama to entertain the entire community.

From time to time, Bob would cook up large pots of stew to feed the homeless at Fig Tree Park. They dubbed him the "Mighty White

Hunter" of the dumpster dive set because he was one of the most resourceful men when it came to scavenging food that the city had discarded. Of course, during one of these meals, an illustrious member of our company named "Blind Burt" turned to the room and asked, "So who decided to put Alpo dog food in the stew?" Everyone instantly put down their bowls. They knew that a blind man had a much better sense of taste and smell than sighted individuals, so they looked toward Bob, who smiled sheepishly. Poor Bob. They tormented him about his culinary choices for months.

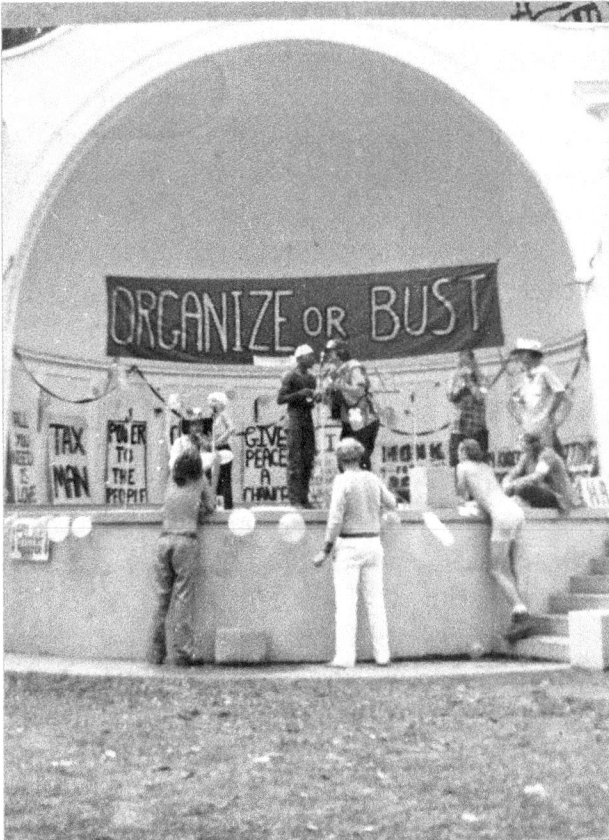

*Organize or Bust Rally at the bandstand in Pershing Park*

With the help of the Homeless People's Association, Bob once organized a protest party in Pershing Park. I negotiated a permit with the Parks and Recreation Department so we could use the bandshell, and we stretched a banner across the structure that read "Organize or Bust" in large letters. It was a raucous affair. We had a best-dressed contest, a worst-dressed contest, a joint-rolling contest, and signs that read, "Police Officers Register Here." The men got half-drunk and staged a three-legged race, and we laughed uproariously at their efforts. Street musicians took turns playing their guitars, and I sang some of the Beatles songs from my songbook.

Harry, a cross-eyed but inventive member of the community, was asked to join the worst-dressed contest, but he refused. He competed in the best-dressed contest instead and won, more because we thought he was a darling than because of anything spectacular that he wore that day. The award for the worst-dressed contestant went to a woman who got on stage, stripped off her clothes and danced around. We hustled her off the stage but granted her the first-place certificate that she so desired.

The whole event was wonderful. It brought forth more people who were interested in activism and joining the HPA. They saw how much fun our group was having and they respected the fact that the city had sanctioned the event by granting us a permit to host more than seventy-five people in Pershing Park. Volunteers helped clean up the park afterward so that we were able to get our deposit back.

The next time we gathered at the Pershing bandshell, I applied for another permit which came with an agreement from the Parks and Recreation Department to provide electricity for the event. This event was more music-focused. When we arrived and began setting up the speakers and soundboards, the Parks Department pulled up in a truck, walked over to a service panel, unlocked it and cut the power. When I tried to show them a copy of our permit that stated we had permission to use the outlets on the bandstand, they ran from me, hopped in their truck and drove off.

It was time to get creative. I told everyone that I would be back, and I went to Milpas Rental and rented a generator. *The hell with 'em.* We got to have our music and I promised myself that the city government would get a taste of our anger. People showed up that day who turned out to be professional musicians. They stood in solidarity with the movement for homeless rights, and our ingenuity in renting the generator impressed them, so they played an entire set for us.

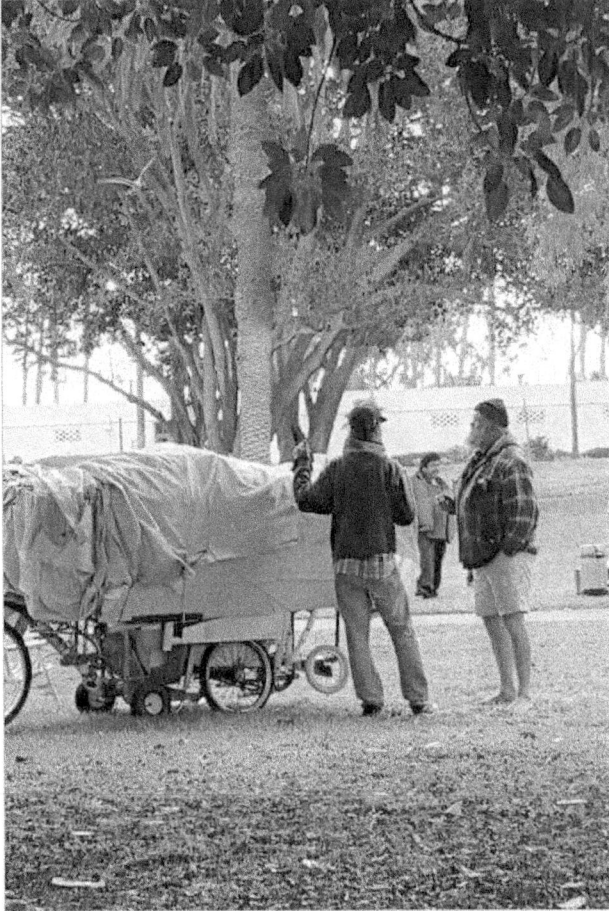

*Harry Davenport and his home on wheels with Bobby at Pershing Park*

My relationship with Bob continued to solidify. One night, he made an effort to impress me by taking me out to dinner at the Santa Barbara Inn. While we were eating, a young man sitting at another table appeared to recognize me. He got up, came over and introduced himself as the son of the manager of the Ladera apartment complex - the same kid who had stolen my boxes of belongings years earlier when

I was moving into Clu's apartment. I was a little taken aback, but he explained that he wanted to thank me for not reporting his crimes to his father. If I had done so, his dad would have beaten him within an inch of his life.

I stood up and gave him a hug, then told him I hoped that thievery was not in his future. He shook his head and shared that he had a wife and a child now. It appeared that he had set himself down a better path, and I hoped I had contributed in some small way to that change in direction.

*Nancy sitting on the lawn at City Hall (photo by Kevin McKiernan)*

~

SINCE BOB AND I WERE BOTH INTERESTED IN POLITICS, WE DECIDED to work on a friend's campaign for a seat on the City Council. Shelley Roulliard was a great lady, open-minded and caring, and we helped her by stuffing envelopes and making phone calls to potential voters. As we left her office one day, it occurred to us that we should re-register to vote ourselves, as our addresses had changed frequently over the years. The two of us walked into the county courthouse and filled out the registration forms. However, when we handed them to the clerk, she checked them over and said, "I'm sorry. We're not going to be able to process these. You need to have a physical address."

Because we lived in vehicles, we used a post office box to receive our mail. Apparently, that was not allowed if you wanted to register to vote. We tried to explain the obvious impossibility of having a physical mailing address in our situation, but the clerk would not budge on her interpretation of the law. Bob and I were shocked. The two of us were working on a political campaign, but we couldn't even vote for the lady! That meant none of our homeless friends could vote either.

Bob and I looked at each other. "It's time to get an attorney," I told him.

My boss Mr. Monson let me borrow his office, so I pulled out the telephone book and started making calls to law firms and non-profit organizations. No one seemed willing to represent two homeless people in a voting rights case. It took all afternoon before someone pointed me toward the Legal Defense Center. I rang them up and my call was answered by an attorney named Willard Hastings, Esq. At first, I spoke more broadly about the numerous city ordinances that curtailed things like sitting and sleeping - the basic human functions that homeless people needed to do in public. Mr. Hastings sounded uninterested. However, when I brought up the reality that the homeless were unable to vote in elections, the lawyer was hooked. He made an appointment for Bob and I to come to his office to discuss the issue further.

The offices for the Legal Defense Center were located in a former tea house on the corner of Garden and Canon Perdido. It was a quiet and beautiful property in the midst of bustling Santa Barbara - a perfect place for attorneys and clients to collaborate and work their magic to achieve justice. The organization was originally formed in 1970 to provide representation for students arrested in the aftermath of the anti-war Isla Vista Riots, and it played a prominent role in aiding garbage collection workers when they went on strike in the late 1970s and early 1980s. The LDC was supported financially by several philanthropists and by attorneys who volunteered their time to fight for the civil rights of those who could not afford lawyers.

Mr. Hastings welcomed us and sat us down in his office. The head attorney for the Legal Defense Center was a short, rotund man who we quickly found had a heart of gold as well as a wonderful sense of humor. Bob and I told him what happened when we went to register to vote. The man listened intently and appeared fascinated by the arguments I used to get my points across. At the end of the conversation, he was convinced to take our case.

The legal battle took only two weeks, but we won. Mr. Hastings managed to secure our right to vote based on a technicality - the fact that Bob and I had voted once before using a physical address in Santa Barbara. However, this victory did not take care of the Vietnam Vets who were unable to vote for their Commander-in-Chief, nor did it affect the rest of the homeless. We were still furious about their inability to go to the polls. A new case needed to be filed, but it was going to cost more money than the Legal Defense Center had available to devote to our cause.

Mr. Hastings arranged a meeting with interested parties to try and come up with enough funds to bring another suit to court. Generously, Kit Tremaine put up five thousand dollars to start the investigation. We selected four Vietnam veterans from among the members of the Homeless People's Association and filed a suit in their name. Willard warned us it would be a longer process this time. I didn't care how long it would take. Voting rights had become my passion, and I'd do whatever it took to win our case.

My job was to write letters and summon the media for interviews and coverage of our protests. Many other talented members of the Santa Barbara community came on board to help, among them the photojournalist Kevin McKiernan, Peter Marin - a writer from Harper's Magazine, and a trio of dedicated lawyers - Alison Adams, Dennis Flannigan and Glen Mowrer. Together, we plotted about how best to move our case forward in the courtroom as well as in the court of public opinion.

While the wheels of the justice system turned slowly, life moved quickly in other ways. I had managed to become pregnant in the midst of all this mayhem - a tough situation for any woman living on the streets. And Bob... Bob was my "teddy bear", but he didn't seem stable enough to convince me that he'd be a good father.

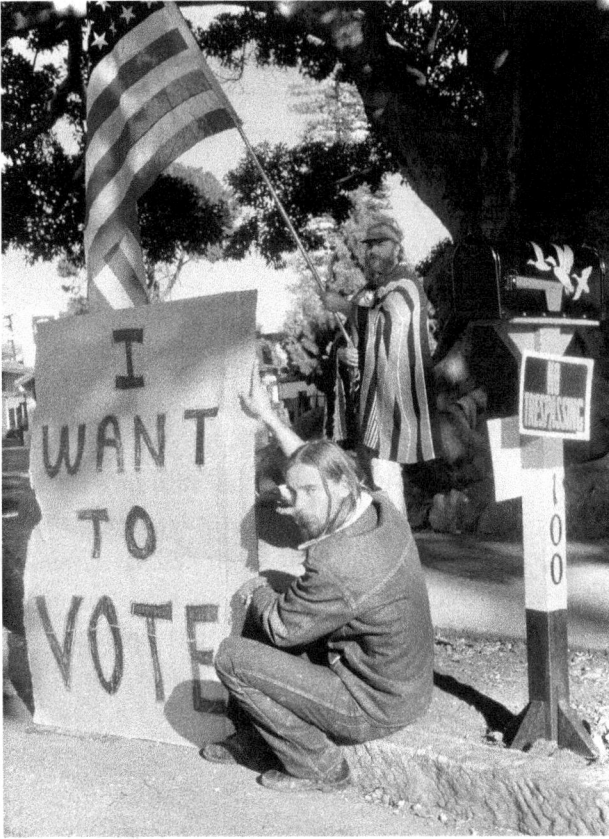

*President Ed and Bobby in 1984 (photo by Kevin McKiernan)*

Thankfully, I had Clu to support me through my pregnancy. My best friend had recently become homeless herself. Two men with brief-cases had knocked on her apartment door and handed her an eviction notice. The cottages on Carrillo Street were being demolished so developers could build office buildings. This was the latest trend in the Santa Barbara housing market because office space made investors more money than residential properties. Those who were evicted could apply for a government program that offered subsidized housing, but the waiting period was in the realm of six years... far too long to be of much benefit to people like Clu.

In addition, the "Standing Room Only" hotels in the city like the Garvey and the Victorian were being remodeled and upscaled to accommodate rich tourists. These budget hotels used to provide really cheap rooms, allowing homeless people a respite from the elements whenever they could scrape together enough money. Some of the working poor would stay there for weeks or months at a time. Now they too were disappearing. Affordable housing for low-income residents was being systematically dismantled, and the people thrown out were increasingly forced to live on the streets. *What were our representatives and planning commissions thinking?*

Clu had been given thirty days to leave her cottage. Her health was slightly impaired at this time because a chunk of the ceiling in the Sambo's restaurant had fallen on her head one night while she was drinking coffee and typing into her portable typewriter. The impact cracked a few vertebrae in her neck. After suffering for several days, Clu sued the restaurant chain and won a settlement that paid for her extensive medical bills. There wasn't a lot left over, and when Clu surveyed the current rental market, she knew the remainder would be eaten up in rent payments faster than she could replenish it. So instead of renting, Clu used her money to purchase a van that could be converted into a home for herself and her four Samoyeds. Those white, fluffy dogs were worth everything to her.

I wasn't happy that my friend had ended up on the streets like me, but I was grateful for the company during my pregnancy. She adapted quickly to her new situation and stuck by me the whole time. Women instinctively know how to do this whoever a member of their "family" is expecting, and I don't know how I could have done it without her.

*Clu and one of her Samoyeds in their van home (photo by Robert Bruce Duncan)*

❧

BOB'S BIRTHDAY FELL ON APRIL FOOL'S DAY, APTLY ENOUGH. TO celebrate it properly, the Latino rights group El Concilio de la Raza gave us a meeting space in the Westside Center so we could throw my favorite fool a party.

I had fallen in love with a song that could be sung as a round, and I had taught four men - Steve, Bob, James and President Ed - the words so they could sing it at the gathering. The practice sessions had gone well, and their voices blended beautifully. The song went, *"Love, love, love love. People we are made for love. Love each other as ourselves, for we are one."* I was so proud that I'd been able to tap into my musical upbringing in this way that I had tears in my eyes at the end of our last rehearsal.

However, when it came time to perform and the quartet huddled together on stage in the Westside Center, it was a train wreck. They'd forgotten how to sing the song as a round, but they plowed through the lyrics anyway, tripping over each other's cues the whole time. Unable to get them to stop and restart the song, I fell to the ground in embarrassment. The student Rob Rosenthal laughed and tried to comfort me, telling me how much he loved the performance. He was right. Regardless of my initial intention, it was still a crowd-pleaser. I gave up stressing about the debacle and joined in the merriment.

*Protest at City Hall with Don Hamilton and Bobby (in white cap) on left (photo by Kevin McKiernan)*

Next, James and two of his cronies ran up to center stage and started singing the Happy Birthday song to Bob. James had a big letter B painted on his backside. Ed had an O and Hopper had the other B. They sang, *"Happy birthday to Bob... Happy birthday to Bob..."* and every time they said the word "Bob", they spun around, pulled down their pants and mooned the audience while showing their letters. Our attorney Willard Hastings was there, howling uproariously. It was a good day, and a very fitting tribute to our irreverent friend, Protest Bob.

∽

1984 WAS AN ELECTION YEAR, AND AS THE SUMMER PROGRESSED, THE Homeless People's Association schemed about how our civil rights issues could be brought to the attention of the presidential candidates. We needed to be part of the national conversation.

My baby, however, was not going to wait for the next president to be chosen before she entered the world. By the time August rolled around, I knew her arrival was imminent. I was trying to save my energy for the ordeal that was to come, sleeping as much as I could. One evening, though, I stirred from my slumber, awakened by the sounds of giggling and raucous laughter. I rolled onto my side and saw that Bob had loaded up the interior of my camper with a bunch of Ground Pounders - namely, Cindy, Smitty and their associates. They looked like they were high on acid and ready to party. *Oh well,* I thought. *Might as well join in the festivities.*

I climbed down from my bed and took a seat next to Bob at the table. "Good morning, everyone," I said cheerfully. I reached for a lighter and my pack of cigarettes, noting that I had only one cigarette left. Lighting it, I sucked in my first hit of nicotine, only to have Bob angrily slap the cigarette from my mouth and onto the floor. It scared me so much that I jumped up and screamed. That made me fume. All these people were in my home, and I hadn't invited a single one of them. So I pushed open the door and jumped outside.

"Don't leave," Smitty pleaded. "You're about to have your baby!" I didn't care. I just wanted everyone out of my camper and back in their own camps. I started to walk down the sidewalk in the direction of the 7-11. My usual nighttime parking space was on the beachfront side of Cabrillo Boulevard, and the convenience store was only a few blocks away. There was money in my pocket... enough to buy a cup of coffee and a fresh pack of smokes.

I heard footsteps behind me and turned around. It wasn't Bob or another human... it was Boatyard Sam, a massive beast of a dog that was part Great Dane and part Black Lab. Usually, he stayed back at the boatyard and acted as a sort of security system. The monster trotted up to me and accepted a pat on the head. *Well, I guess I have an escort.*

Sam walked the rest of the way to the 7-11 with me. After purchasing coffee, cigarettes and a treat for my canine companion, we returned together to the truck and camper. I wondered what had caused that dog to appear at the moment in time when I needed him. Whatever the reason, I was grateful. I gave him his treat and headed inside.

Everyone, including Bob, seemed to have departed, except for Sean, who was lying in my bed. He slept so deeply that nothing ever woke him up until he was ready to start the day. *Why would Bob leave him alone in the camper?* I wondered. Regardless, I sighed with relief at the thought of getting some peace and quiet and decided to drive away before anyone returned.

I climbed into the driver's seat of the pickup next to Schatzie, started the engine and took my rig further down Cabrillo Boulevard to where Clu was sleeping in her van. Her preferred nighttime location was over by the beach volleyball courts. I parked behind her vehicle and climbed back into my bed to sleep until the sun came up.

When I awoke the next morning, Clu's van was gone. Clu knew that I could expect to find her in the boatyard parking lot by the Jungle, so I headed over there, parked my camper and joined the crowd of people she was hanging with. Like me, Clu also had a lot of friends on the streets of Santa Barbara.

I exchanged pleasantries with the group, but soon I grew restless and felt driven by an almost maniacal need to clean my camper. I told Clu that I'd be right back, and I drove out to the store to purchase some cleaning supplies. Harsh chemicals repelled me, so I bought Windex and vinegar. Green seedless grapes were ten cents a pound, and I purchased a big bunch of them to share with the folks back at the parking lot.

When I returned, I dropped the supplies off in my camper, then stepped out and asked the cluster of people around Clu's van if anyone wanted any grapes. As I walked toward them - *Bam!* My water broke.

Water gushed all over the broken asphalt of the boatyard. "Oh, no," was all I could say. Like a flock of frightened birds, homeless men scattered away from me, leaving only one man, Ed Mannon, who helped Clu fetch a towel. She wrapped it around me and placed me in her van. Then she got on her CB radio and asked if anyone with a landline could call the hospital and tell them she was bringing in a woman who was in hard labor.

I turned to Ed and asked him to find Bob. My partner needed to know his daughter was about to be born. Bob, I learned later, had climbed over the wall separating the Cabrillo sidewalk from the beach last night while I'd gone to the 7-11. He'd slept in the sand, intending to stay close to the camper and Seanie but perhaps conceding to my desire for some privacy.

Clu put Sean and Schatzie in her van, and then we drove to Cottage Hospital. My best friend was laughing at how the men had dashed out of the parking lot as soon as my water broke. It was indeed hilarious, but I was also sad that Bob might not be there to hold my hand while I gave birth to his daughter. Clu would have to be my breathing coach, and I was going to try and get permission for Sean to also be in the room with me.

As we pulled into the emergency room entrance, I saw they had a gurney waiting by the door. The attendants quickly clustered around me, and I had to wave them off, telling them I had a little time and could still walk. Apparently, the truck driver who'd heard Clu's call on the radio contacted the hospital and caused a bit of a panic, saying that my child could be born at any second.

I walked into the hospital, but my labor pains quickly intensified. The nurses wanted to put me in a bed and I told them that I needed to walk off the cramps. They weren't having it. Reluctantly, I laid myself down, and the nurses put a monitor on me. Clu sat in a chair and we explained to Sean about the pain his mommy was going through. When the doctor arrived, she checked in with Sean, who convinced her that he wanted to stay. Even though he was only nine years old, the doctor seemed to realize that he was mature enough to handle the experience. That made me very happy. My son was going to be able to watch his only sister being born.

As we were wheeled into the birthing room, Bob finally showed up. He was filthy and gripping a beer bottle with his grubby fingers. Who knows how or why he had managed to bring it into the hospital; I could only focus on the physical ordeal of labor.

Bob sat down next to me and held my hand. "It is time?" he asked. I nodded, and even though he was not in the best shape, I was glad he was there.

Clu told me she would leave and let this be a moment for my immediate family. I was so grateful to her for watching out for me, but a little disappointed that she wanted to depart. Sean was placed to one side of me, near my head. At one point, he asked the doctor to adjust the mirror so that he could see his baby sister come into the world.

The birthing was rough. My baby had a big head just like her father. She came out blue-skinned with the birth cord wrapped around her neck. The doctor quickly unwrapped her and called the nursery for help. By the time assistance came, the baby was pink again. She was going to be all right. A daughter, just as I'd known she would be. My life felt complete.

As the little one was getting cleaned up in the warming center, Sean asked me if he could name the baby *Krystal*. I looked over to Bob, who had wanted her to be called *Freedom*. "How about *Krystal Freedom?*" I asked the two men in my life. They nodded in response, so that was the name we put on her birth certificate.

After fussing over my child for an hour, I let the nurses take my little girl away so I could get some sleep. Later, once I'd recovered from my exhaustion, the hospital staff brought us to the cafeteria and fed us a steak dinner. If everything went well overnight, I expected that I would leave the hospital in the morning. Together, my family would return to my camper, and I would have Bob drive us to Fig Tree Park. My newborn daughter Krystal and I could rest and recover in the cool shade of that magnificent tree.

## ❧ 10 ❧

# THE FIG TREE MAILBOX

For most of the next three days, I lay in my bed in my camper beneath the shade of the fig tree. My body was exceedingly sore. Krystal's head had been quite large for such a little pipsqueak. Also, having a child at age thirty-nine was likely partially responsible for the slow recovery.

I had the door propped open so I could get cross-ventilation in the August heat, and that made it easy to hear another car drive up and park behind the camper. I peeked out the back window. *Oh, hell!* It was a squad car. *They'd better not be asking me to move or something stupid like that.*

I put up a barricade so that Krystal wouldn't roll out of bed and onto the floor, then went to the doorway. Outside stood Officer Kirby, one of the more friendly beat officers who patrolled the nearby beach and lower Santa Barbara. I asked him what he wanted. "I'd like to see Krystal Freedom," he said politely.

That gave me a smile. I told him to go into the park, and I'd bring the baby out to him. I wrapped Krystal up in a blanket, put a little stocking cap on her head and headed out the door. Walking over to Kirby, I told him to put his arms out. He did so, and I carefully placed

Krystal in his arms. He looked down at her. *Was that a tear I saw on Kirby's cheek?* Regardless, it was a beautiful moment.

It was also the last time we saw Officer Kirby in the Boulevard district. He put in for a transfer. Holding Krystal for just a few minutes convinced him to beg his superiors to take him off the beat where most of the homeless were. He'd had enough of trying to run the homeless community out of town, and the next thing I heard, Kirby was patrolling upper State Street instead.

One of our next visitors was Diane Erickson. She was a mental patient with bipolar disorder who was the only person to visit me during my hospital stay. Diane had a history with Bob Hansen. Supposedly, the two of them had a sexual encounter that produced a son. Bob refused to acknowledge the child, claiming that Diane also had sex with a second gentleman on the night in question. Thankfully, this all happened before Bob and I ever met. Her offspring was named John Jeffrey, and according to his mother, he was being raised by a prominent family not far from Santa Barbara.

Diane came to the door of the camper and asked if she could hold the baby. We all loved Diane, but she was prone to manic episodes and could act quite bizarre at times. Frequently, she went off her medication. This, I could tell from her demeanor, might be one of those times.

I invited her in, but I asked her to sit down and take ten deep breaths before I placed Krystal in her arms. Meanwhile, Bob was at the stove, cooking up a pot of soup for the men milling about under the fig tree. He was steadfastly ignoring Diane. It was amusing how uncomfortable Diane made him feel, especially when she danced about at parties, bragging that she'd had Bob's son.

Diane glanced at Krystal's head while she held her and noticed a triangular ridge that bordered the soft spot atop her head. Krystal had been born with it, but the peculiar feature freaked Diane out. She asked how Krystal had gotten it.

Bob stopped stirring the soup for a moment, then turned to Diane and said, "I beat her."

*Oh, Jesus.* Diane nearly threw Krystal at me, then rushed out the door, screaming in horror. I hoped that would have been the end of it.

After Bob fed the homeless outside, however, he picked up his daughter and was rocking her in his arms when the police arrived. Apparently, Diane had called 9-1-1, raving about a baby being beaten at Fig Tree Park. She tended to call emergency services a lot.

An officer walked up to Bob and watched him hold his baby for a bit. "Have you met my daughter?" Bob asked him. Someone explained that Bob had been tormenting Diane again, but no babies had been harmed in the process. The cop let Bob off with a gentle admonishment, and that was that.

≈

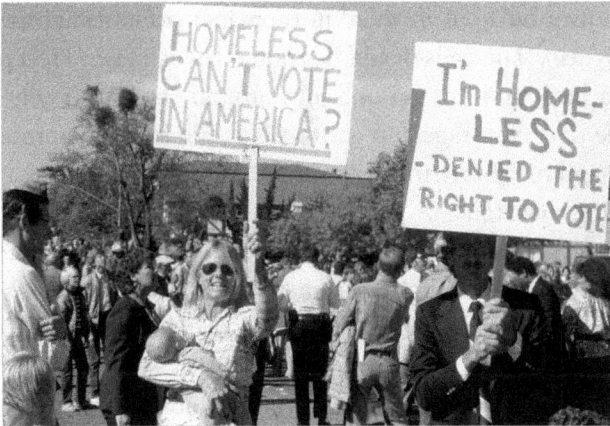

*Nancy and Krystal at six weeks old (photo by Kevin McKiernan)*

ELECTION DAY GREW CLOSER. ONE MORNING, ABOUT SIX WEEKS after Krystal was born, David Collier, Steve Austin and President Ed came up to my camper door while it was parked at the boatyard. I asked what the occasion was. The trio looked at me and said, "It's time to put up a mailbox at the fig tree."

What a great idea. It would be a remarkable act of protest and the perfect prop for a media event focused on the inability of the homeless to vote. Also, the post office had told them that if a mailbox was installed, they were obligated to deliver mail to it. I had to go to work, but I told them I'd let Bob know about their scheme.

Bob loved the plan. He had eighty dollars worth of credit at ACE

Hardware, and he let the guys use it to buy the supplies they needed: cement, four mailboxes, wood to make the posts, and screw bolts to hold the posts down to the cement foundations. Instinctively, we knew the city wouldn't approve of a mailbox being installed in their park, so we bought extra mailboxes in case one or two got hauled away by the Parks and Recreation Department.

Once the supplies were purchased, we reconvened at the boatyard and Bob got his handyman tools out of his old refrigerator truck. One section of the boatyard doubled as a storage spot for vehicles, and Bob had left his truck there while he was sharing the camper with me. It was uniquely modified; Bob had constructed a box on the rooftop with a trapdoor and ladder that led down into the vehicle. Whenever he needed money, he'd put in an ad in the paper promoting himself as an A-Z handyman. The calls would be routed to his pager. He'd phone his customers back and line up odd jobs around the city. Then he'd take his vehicle out of storage and get to work. He kept numerous tools in his truck, and his ability to repair doors, windows, roofs and appliances was amazing to watch.

Together, the group built a solid wooden stand and painted it red, white and blue. A beautiful black mailbox featuring an American Bald Eagle was mounted to it. President Ed decided that if anyone was going to get a ticket for staging this stunt, it should be him, so we proudly painted his name on top of the mailbox next to the eagle. No one would dare question our patriotism, at least. Before disbanding, we chose a date to install the mailbox on the corner of Montecito and Chapala right next to the fig tree.

The day before our protest event, I went into Mr. Monson's office and placed several phone calls to the media. I rang up radio stations as well as CNN, NBC and ABC News. They sounded in awe of our audacity, and I knew that they couldn't help but show up. Signs were quickly made promoting our plight and our cause. Voting was one of the most important freedoms in our country and barriers should not be placed preventing people from selecting their representatives, especially for something as ridiculous as using a P.O. Box for mail delivery rather than a physical address.

The next day, on October 18th, I helped greet the media as they arrived and moved them into position so that they could best capture the action. By the time the crews were finished getting ready, the park was filled with more cameras, tape recorders and microphones than I'd seen in my entire life. Any remaining open space in Fig Tree Park was taken up with news vans and satellite dishes. Some of the media had driven all the way out from Los Angeles. We'd done a stellar job at attracting attention, and now we were going to educate the world about the plight of the homeless.

While the cameras rolled, members of the HPA dug a hole, set the mailbox in place, mixed the concrete and poured it in. President Ed stood proudly next to the mailbox that bore his name, ready for questions. Whenever Ed was occupied, other Vietnam veterans were made available for interviews.

As the event wound down and just a scattering of media representatives were left, a conviction grew inside me that the City of Santa Barbara was going to tear down our mailbox as soon as possible. They were forever taking things from us. This would be no different.

I walked up to the KEYT News team and interrupted their packing to tell them the city was going to attempt to remove the mailbox that very night. We'd been protected by the presence of the media all day, but I knew within my heart that the city government was just waiting for the newscasters to go home and go to bed. The KEYT team mulled over the information I'd given them for a few minutes, and they liked the idea of catching the city in the act. Finally, they agreed to stay in the neighborhood. They told me they'd hang out at the 7-11 just around the corner for a few hours and wait for a call. Once they were alerted, they'd be back at the park and shooting footage within five minutes.

I thanked the news crew, then climbed into my camper. Bob told me he'd look after Sean so I could get some rest. The day had exhausted me. I snuggled up with Krystal in bed and quickly fell asleep.

Around 10 p.m., I awoke to shouts of, "Here they come!" I sprang from my bed, put up the barrier for the baby and jumped out of the camper. I searched for a dime in my pocket and felt my fingers close around one. *Good.* I was going to need it.

A police cruiser hurled down Chapala Street in our direction, sirens blazing and engines roaring. Others raced in from the Eastside, the Westside and the Beachside. You would have thought we were in the process of committing a felony. They stopped their cars by the fig tree, flanking the park on both sides of the corner. Bob quickly ran to the mailbox and clasped his arms around the wooden stand. At least ten cops got out of their vehicles, and as I watched, they pried Bob off the mailbox, put him in handcuffs and shoved him into a cop car.

I cleared my throat and in a loud voice, said, "Well, I guess it's time to call the media!"

Every police officer turned their head to look at me. They had not expected this. I walked confidently over to the payphone across the street and placed the call. No sooner had I returned to the park than the KEYT news van pulled up, cameras at the ready. I informed them that Bob had been arrested for hanging onto the mailbox, and I pointed to the squad car where Bob was being held. The reporters rushed over and started firing questions at the police.

The drama wasn't over. Soon, a worker from the Parks and Recreation Department walked up with a chainsaw. I stood with members of the Homeless People's Association among the roots of the fig tree looking on with alarm. *He was going to cut down our mailbox!*

I yelled out to the man, "Hey! You know that it's a federal offense to destroy a United States Post Office mailbox, right?" The worker stopped and looked at his chainsaw for a second. Ultimately, he realized I was right, and he shuffled back to his truck.

While we were wondering what kind of tricks the city government might try next, the cops decided to write Bob a ticket for failing to obey a police officer, then released him. We hoped that might be the end of it, but the city called Love's Towing. When the tow truck showed up, I tried to convince the operator of the unlawfulness of his actions. It didn't work this time. The truck driver prepared a chain in order to drag the mailbox out of the ground. That was hardly necessary; the cement wasn't even dry, and the Parks and Recreation worker could have probably pulled the post out by hand. It was all for show.

Angry, I decided we should put on a show as well. I grabbed the hand of one of the HPA members. He got the idea, and together we linked hands and made a circle around the root buttresses of the fig tree. As the metal chain was wrapped around the mailbox stand, I started to belt out "God Bless America". The others joined my voice in protest and the news cameras captured every moment. The operator got back in his tow truck, hit the gas, and we continued to sing as the mailbox flew out of the ground and was dragged down the street. It was quite a spectacle. The KEYT news team was grateful that they had stuck around, and they thanked me for getting them that story.

*Nancy, Sean and Krystal in front of the El Dorado camper*

The next morning, we installed the second mailbox from our backup supply. Unfortunately, that same afternoon, an irate citizen in a brown pickup truck jumped the curb, drove across the sidewalk and plowed down the mailbox. It was a hit-and-run. We were upset, but we knew we had done our job to educate the public. We decided to let the mailbox idea go. It was time to come up with a new scheme... some new type of street theater that could rally other people to our cause.

~

ON THE EVE OF THE 1984 ELECTION, A FEW OTHER MEMBERS OF THE HPA and I attended a meeting at the Legal Defense Center with a host of sympathetic attorneys. We knew Ronald Reagan would be visiting Santa Ynez to cast his ballot, and for that reason, we were encouraged to drive there to raise some signs and make some noise. Cameras would be everywhere, and it was a valuable chance to educate the public about how the homeless were barred from voting.

My friends and I knew how to put a plan into action fast. We headed to Fig Tree Park and started making signs and selecting the ten people who would fit in the back of my camper. Some of us felt apprehensive about going into north Santa Barbara County, knowing how conservative the populace was there compared to the city of Santa Barbara itself. The crowds surrounding Reagan wouldn't be too friendly to our cause, we believed. Nevertheless, we prepared to leave the next morning after I finished my rounds delivering the L.A. Times. I laid down that evening with the intention of getting a good night's sleep. Voting Day was likely to test everyone's endurance, and I needed to be ready for whatever came our way.

Trouble came a lot sooner than I expected. I awoke to a commotion outside of my camper, and I wrapped up baby Krystal and stepped out to see what was happening. Horns were blaring at the intersection where Chapala Street hit Highway 101, and I realized, *Oh, no. Those idiots have gone and shut down the highway. During rush hour, no less.*

Back then, traffic on the 101 was forced to stop at four traffic lights as it passed through Santa Barbara. For decades, the lights had been the last impediments standing between motorists and four hundred and thirty-five miles of uninterrupted highway. Knowing this, a squad of homeless men had waited on Chapala Street for the signal to turn red. Then Bob, Scotty, President Ed and other members of the HPA moved into the crosswalk with their newly-made signs and blocked the northbound lanes of the 101. Rush hour traffic came to a standstill.

By the time I arrived on the scene, tempers were flaring. People leaned on their horns and swore at the homeless activists. Deva, a Native American songwriter, stood in the highway median and vigorously waved an American flag. I watched as a woman stepped out of a Volkswagen Bug with a beer in her hand, cursing up a storm. What a show. I was dismayed, for I knew that soon we'd be losing the bodies that were supposed to be holding up signs in Santa Ynez the next morning, but I also understood my friends' need to act. The highway shutdown showed how desperate and angry we had become in the struggle to attain our voting rights.

By the time the police arrived, traffic had backed up all the way to Ventura. The cops stood on the edge of the freeway and tried to assess the situation. Meanwhile, the driver of a semi-truck lost his patience and maneuvered around the first row of cars in the northbound lanes. He inched his way up to Scotty, the mastermind behind this spontaneous act of protest, but Scotty put his chest up against the grille of the semi and defiantly pushed back. The man was stockier than most and not afraid to do what it took to help his friends on the streets, but needless to say, he was unsuccessful in his attempt to stop the vehicle. His shoes slid across the pavement as the truck inexorably pushed him forward. In an act of bravery or sheer lunacy, Scotty decided to try a different tactic. He dropped to the ground and lay down in front of the semi, daring the driver to run him over.

Instantly, the cops ran and scooped Scotty off the asphalt. No one was going to die on their watch if they could help it. Scotty stiffened his body to make it harder for the cops to carry him, but they still managed to drag him and the other members of the HPA off the highway. Deva was scared of the police and ran off with the American flag. The other protesters were placed under arrest and loaded into the squad cars. With Bob, they didn't have to work very hard because they knew he wanted to be arrested.

Soon, half of our Santa Ynez team were on their way to jail. It would be up to me, I knew, to recruit more bodies and make sure that the Voting Day protest still took place.

~

AFTER MY NEWSPAPER ROUTE THE NEXT MORNING, I RETURNED TO Fig Tree Park to rally the remaining troops. Seven people climbed into the camper and I drove up and over San Marcos Pass into the Santa Ynez Valley. I parked as close to the polling station in Santa Ynez as the Secret Service would allow. As I feared, the residents glowered at us and our protest signs, but we held them up high and attempted to engage the crowd in dialogue.

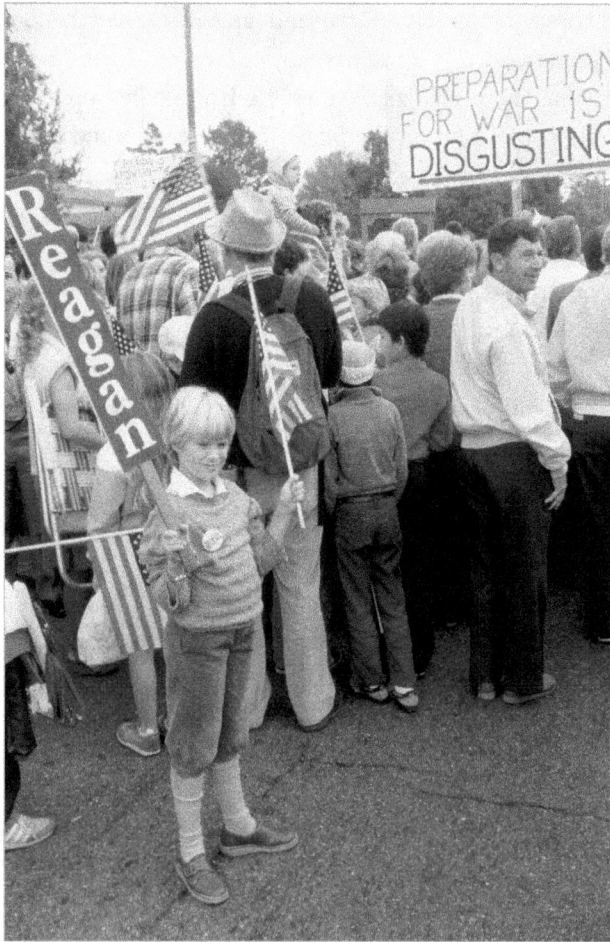

*Protest and patriotism in Santa Ynez (photo by Kevin McKiernan)*

In the middle of all this, my son Sean approached me and said that one of our HPA members, James Magruder, wanted to talk. I found the blond, athletic young man nearby. He looked at me and simply pointed upward. I followed James' eyes and saw a metal streetlamp - one that was about twenty feet high.

"I want to put my sign up at the top of the pole," he stated.

"How are you going to do that?" I asked.

"I'm gonna shimmy to the top and stick it up there," he responded stoically.

I was skeptical, but I told him he'd better wait until President Reagan got in his car and the motorcade of black vans started to move out of the neighborhood. I didn't want him to be shot and killed by the Secret Service.

James took my advice, and the moment the President climbed into his car, James stuck the stick-end of the cardboard sign down the back of his jeans, shimmied up the pole and attached the sign to the horizontal beam. It read, "HOMELESS CAN'T VOTE IN U.S.A.!"

He was surrounded by a cadre of sheriff deputies within seconds. Kevin McKiernan, our photojournalist friend, took his picture up there. James began to climb down but stopped midway as he suddenly realized how much trouble he was in. I felt terrible for the young man, who seemed torn with indecision. Eventually, his arms gave out and he could not hang on anymore. He slid the rest of the way, and when he touched down, the men in their tan outfits grabbed him and pulled him away from the crowd.

Sean started to cry, for he loved James dearly. "They are going to hurt him, mom," he wailed.

"No, baby," I reassured him, "they will not. We'll get the attorneys to have him released tomorrow."

James was the hero of the day, and Kevin's photograph made it into Time Magazine. There was little more we could do after that. Our team piled into the camper and headed for home.

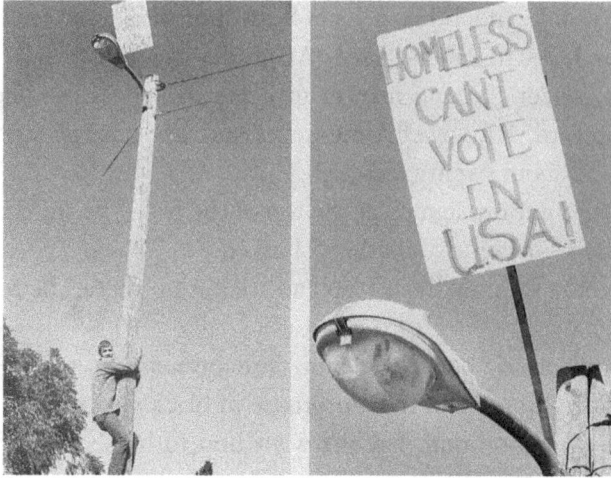

*James Magruder, about to be arrested in front of Reagan's polling place on November 6th, 1984 (photo by Kevin McKiernan)*

The following day, James walked into our circle at Fig Tree Park, beaming. We all cheered for him and patted him on the back. It was a nice moment in our ongoing battle for voting rights. The bailing out of the highway blockers from jail took longer, but Kit Tremaine and his fellow lawyers got it done. At the next city council meeting, the homeless lawbreakers sat proudly in the front row. We'd become media darlings, and the camera shutters clicked whenever we stood up to speak. The news channels were hungry for more episodes of civil disobedience, and the fame our protests brought inspired the HPA to use guerrilla theater tactics more and more often as the fight for justice continued.

∾

DESPITE OUR ADVOCACY AND OUR HOPES AND DREAMS, RONALD Reagan won re-election in 1984. Nevertheless, we continued to fight for homeless rights through direct actions, like marching to the gates of Reagan's ranch on Refugio Road to protest city ordinances, as well as through the courtroom. Thanks to the tireless efforts of the Legal Defense Center and our media campaign, we won our lawsuit, *Collier versus Menzall,* in the appellate court in December of 1985. Homeless people were finally guaranteed the right to vote in California, though the rights of people nationwide were not yet secure. The voter registration application in our state was changed so that people had more freedom as to what they would write down as their home address. From that point on, Bob wrote, "Moreton Bay Fig Tree" as his voting address, and I used the boat storage yard for mine.

*The march to Reagan's Ranch (photo by Kevin McKiernan)*

Our victory was invigorating, but I suffered some personal setbacks and tragedies around the same time. My mother passed away when Krystal was just a year old. She'd been taking diet medication to lose weight and estrogen supplements in an attempt to stay young. Her doctor was a real pill-pusher, and six years earlier, those medications had given rise to dozens of blood clots that found their way into her lungs. My mother survived that ordeal and was prescribed blood thinners, but in August of 1985, her heart rate shot up to 247 beats per minute. My father rushed her to the hospital, but it was too late. She was gone.

Then toward the end of the year, my newspaper job disappeared. My boss, Mr. Monson, lost his contract with the L.A. Times, throwing seven people at the warehouse, drivers included, out of work. My position at the Homeless Coalition only earned me four hundred dollars a month, so what little savings I had evaporated within weeks. I was sitting in Carrows one morning, not knowing what to do, when the waitress said I had a phone call. I picked up the phone, and it was Kit Tremaine. She'd heard about my employment issues and asked me to meet her for lunch somewhere. That was sweet of her. Kit was becoming something of a surrogate mother in my mom's absence, and I suppose she saw me as a sort of surrogate daughter, too.

We met at the I-Hop downtown. During our meal, Kit revealed that she wanted to give me a gift of five thousand dollars. It was not to be shared, just used to benefit myself and my children. I was taken aback. Reluctantly, I told her I was unable to accept it. I told her that she already took care of the homeless community by donating to the Legal Defense Center, and I didn't feel worthy to receive anything more for myself. In truth, I prided myself on my financial independence a little too much to take her gift. The idea of accepting someone's charity felt almost unbearable.

Kit became upset at my refusal. She said that I'd come to my senses and accept a gift eventually, if not for myself, then for my offspring.

Soon after, I got a call from my father with good news. I'd applied for a job with the package-delivery company Purolator Courier six months ago, and they finally wanted me to come in for an interview. The meeting went well, and I was able to start work right away. I knew it would be a wonderful job because I loved to drive and make deliveries. I was also well aware that I would not get paid for at least two weeks. This was not a mom-and-pop operation that could advance me the money from my future paycheck like Mr. Monson would have. So how was I going to be able to feed Sean during this period? I had no idea.

On the morning of January 28th, 1986, I was too poor to even afford a cup of coffee, let alone breakfast, so I borrowed some change from a homeless panhandler and sat in a booth at Carrows, sipping my drink slowly and wondering if I should swallow my pride and take Kit up on her generous offer. A police officer sat at the counter, taking a break from his patrol, and I decided to walk up to him and ask, "If someone offered you five thousand dollars as a gift, would you take it?"

The cop looked at me strangely and answered, "You bet! I'd be in Mexico tomorrow!"

With that, I rang up Kit and said, "I'll accept your gift. I really do need it. I'm completely broke."

She invited me to come to her house immediately to view the take-off of the Space Shuttle Challenger on her television. I left Krystal with Bob and drove up to Kit's adobe dwelling on Coyote Road. The two of us relaxed on her couch and watched the shuttle prepare for liftoff. Then we also watched as it blew up in midair, killing all of the astronauts on board.

We sat there, stunned, in shock and grief for several minutes. There was nothing either of us could say. But eventually, I had to excuse myself so I could pick up Sean from school. Kit handed me the check and asked if it would be enough to get me into proper housing. I told her that even with my new job, I wouldn't be able to afford rent in Santa Barbara, so I was going to use the money to survive until I received my first paycheck with Purolator. Then I'd use the rest to buy a motorhome; *that* felt like a more secure future for myself and my children. Kit was slightly disappointed, but she accepted my decision along with my sincere thanks.

Her gift came none too soon, for the timing chain on my truck was wearing out and the camper was getting rather crowded with Bob and I, plus my two growing children. My father loaned me four thousand dollars to supplement Kit's donation, and with that money, I was able to find the recreational vehicle I was looking for: a twenty-seven-foot, 1979 Pace Arrow. Ed Mannon wanted my pickup and camper, so I sold them to him for five hundred dollars. Now I had a solid roof over my head... one that would last me and my offspring for several years and not be subject to the dictates of any landlords.

Little did I know that this vehicle would propel me toward the biggest adventure of my entire life.

## ✣ I I ✣

# A WALK ACROSS AMERICA

I n the summer of 1960, my parents purchased a twenty-three-
window Volkswagen van so we could take a cross-country road
trip to visit my grandmother and our various uncles, aunts and
cousins in Bristol, Connecticut. I was fifteen years old at the time. My
four siblings and I had to squeeze into the back seat like sardines,
while my baby brother Jimmy was consigned to a cardboard box on the
floor between my mother and father.

The journey seemed endless, especially on the way back to the west
coast. To avoid having to face the chaos that my younger siblings
fomented in those close quarters, I stared through the window into the
countryside and tried to tune out the rest of my family. One afternoon,
my eyes were trained on the shoulder of the road. Patches of gravel
and mown weeds whipped through my vision and I fell into a sort of
hypnotic trance. Suddenly, a set of ghostly footprints began to appear
along the ground. One print after another, though I couldn't tell if they
were truly set into the earth or floating above it somehow. *Where did
they come from?*

I knew I shouldn't be seeing this sort of otherworldly
phenomenon, so I shook my head to clear the vision. My brain must
have been playing tricks on me. Even so, a clear idea had risen to the

surface of my thoughts, and it remained there after the apparition outside the window had faded.

I turned to my mother. "Mom! Guess what?"

"What, dear?" she replied.

"I am going to find a man someday who will walk across the country with me."

My mom looked at me patiently. "That's nice, dear."

Dad, who had an adventurous nature, was much more excited about the idea. "That could be very educational. You might have a lot of fun doing that."

The moment stuck with me for decades, though I never came close to being able to explain how it happened.

~

IN THE LEADUP TO THE ELECTION YEAR OF 1988, THIS MEMORY FROM nearly thirty years earlier rose to the surface. It happened while Bob and I lay in bed in the RV after tucking our children in for the night. This was usually our time to make plans for the next day, when there was space for our thoughts to settle. In this case, however, the plan was bigger than anything else we'd ever conceived or considered. I turned to Bob and shared my memory, then proposed that we actually make it happen - a great walk across the United States. We would take a support vehicle with us so that our kids and animals would be safe and protected.

To my delight, Bob immediately became excited at the prospect. However, he wanted to steer it toward political purposes. It would be "The Santa Barbara Homeless and Poor People's Peace Walk" - a way to create media exposure and fight for greater homeless rights in an election year. We would try to make it to Washington, D.C. in time for the "Housing Now" rally that organizer Mitch Snyder was holding in November. I was a little disappointed that the Walk wouldn't be a private adventure, but with Bob's passion buoying our efforts, at least I knew it stood a much greater chance of happening.

I let Bob run with the idea, and he immediately started organizing meetings to bring some key players on board. Fundraisers needed to be scheduled, flyers had to be made and a support vehicle had to be purchased. A Native American man named Robert Duncan - who we dubbed "Indian Bob" to avoid confusion with my partner - was recruited because of his experience completing similar walks across the country. Two other homeless people - a couple in their early thirties named Chuck and Katrina - latched onto the idea of the Walk. Chuck, a blond, athletic man, wore camouflage clothes all the time and pretended he had been in the service. I found him a little frightening, while Katrina was a thin, unhealthy-looking woman with mousy hair who acted completely subservient to Chuck. Something was off about the two of them, and they clung tightly to Bob right from the beginning, which caused me some concern.

The fundraising initiative started to take off. Bob and Indian Bob set up a table on State Street so they could pass out the flyers I'd made and ask for donations. An out-of-service school bus was bought with the funds, driven to the boatyard and outfitted with shelves and a six-burner propane stove so it could serve as a support vehicle. Everything seemed to be going well until Bob made a huge mistake. He gave Chuck and Katrina responsibility for looking after the cash box. Donations would thereafter flow through them and each week they were supposed to report the tally.

During the meetings that followed, I began to grow suspicious. The reports from our treasurers were incomplete and they squirmed a little whenever I tried to pin them down on details. Something wasn't right. I went to Bob and told him Chuck and Katrina were skimming off the donations, but he refused to believe me. I couldn't understand the hold they had on him, but perhaps Bob was afraid of losing them since no one else had committed to undertaking the cross-country journey with us.

Chuck and Katrina soon realized that I was a danger to their scams, and they needed to get rid of me. First, they convinced Bob that they needed to borrow the typewriter I'd used to write letters in support of our project. Then the precious stones and trinkets that I'd collected for my daughter started to disappear from the RV. I'd been saving an assortment of rings, bracelets and necklaces for a time when Krystal was older and could take care of them. Jewelry was wasted on me because I was too active; necklaces were constantly breaking and bracelets slipped off my wrists when I wasn't looking. But I liked the thought of my daughter wearing them someday. Now they were going missing from the drawers and cabinets, and Katrina was my chief suspect.

The fundraising had been effective and we should have had nearly seven hundred dollars in the kitty, but the treasurer reports didn't reflect that. I finally put my foot down. I told Bob that as long as Chuck and Katrina were involved, I was done with this project. I needed to protect myself and the kids, so I drove away from the boat-yard in my RV and left him to deal with those two. I was sure their hold over Bob would strengthen, but my partner wouldn't take my objections seriously, so what could I do? A bad outcome was inevitable.

I didn't stop all communication with Bob in the weeks that followed, but he refused to open his eyes to what was happening. Chuck had convinced him that I was jealous of Katrina. That wasn't the case at all - I was just angry that I'd been unable to protect Bob from their schemes.

The Walk was scheduled to begin on Martin Luther King's birth-day, January 15$^{th}$. The bus was fully outfitted and they'd raised close to a thousand dollars to help pay for food, gas and supplies. The two Bobs were itching to leave and the rest of the crew were excited to send them forth from Santa Barbara. By now, I'd committed to letting the Walk go on without me. I was worried about losing my job, for one thing. Purolator Courier had long since gone out of business due to competition from FedEx, but I'd resumed working for Mr. Monson after he signed contracts to deliver the USA Today and The New York Times. I didn't want to jeopardize that income, and I also needed to watch over my son, who had developed a defensive streak and was starting to get into fights at school. If I was going to lose Bob over my decision to stay, so be it. He'd already stopped talking to me because he knew how much I hated Chuck and Katrina. I missed Bob and I missed our friendship, but I also felt grief that my dream of walking across America had been effectively stolen from me by him and his homeless cronies. The loss of everything broke my heart.

One evening close to the departure date, I drove down to Fig Tree

Park to check in with friends. One of the guys informed me that Katrina had told Bob I was screwing all the men here just to get back at him. That did it. I was overcome with a desire to grab Katrina by the neck and beat the crap out of her. She had taken everything from me... my boyfriend, my desire to help plan the Walk and my daughter's jewelry. All the hate came bubbling to the surface. I announced I was going to the boatyard to take care of that woman, but as I stormed off, Ed Mannon grappled with me and threw me to the ground. He tried to get me to come to my senses, saying it would be far better to wait for Katrina to come to the fig tree and into *my* territory. He reiterated that there were only two weeks left before the Walk was due to happen and that I should calm down. He was right, so calm down I did.

A week later, Chuck and Katrina disappeared from Santa Barbara with the cash box. My prediction had come true, as I knew it would. Both Bob and Indian Bob were mortified. Postponing the trip would be a disaster because we'd already arranged a goodbye rally at De La Guerra Plaza with the city, and all the media were scheduled to attend. Now our funding had vanished. The Walkers wouldn't be able to make it as far as the Arizona border, let alone Washington, D.C.

Bob was furious, but mostly at himself because he had put so much faith in those two traitors. He came to me full of remorse at having let them take over his life, explaining that he'd been afraid of having to do the Walk on his own. Those fears had come to pass regardless. I took pity on him and told him I would play my guitar and sing at the rally if that would help. The famous local musicians Tom Ball and Kenny Sultan were also scheduled to play, so I felt jazzed to be part of the lineup.

To his credit, Bob decided not to give up on their mission. He and Indian Bob set up another table on State Street and determinedly set about raising more funds for food and gas, ultimately coming up with one hundred and fifty dollars in time for the downtown rally.

The event at De La Guerra Plaza was a rousing sendoff. The media turned out as promised and the musicians kept the atmosphere jubilant. While I was playing "Scarlet Ribbons" on my guitar, Krystal climbed up onto the stage and sat at my feet - the perfect prop to enhance the emotions that the song brought forth. The girl was a natural performer who'd obviously inherited those genes from my side of the family. She loved singing and dancing, whether a crowd was there to watch or not.

*Bob "Protest" Hansen the day before the Walk (photo by Kevin McKiernan)*

That night, with Bob once again lying by my side in the RV, I felt sadness wash over me. My decision to remain behind in Santa Barbara had not changed. I was grateful that we'd patched up our relationship, but when Bob departed on his trek the next day, I was going to miss him with every fiber of my being.

~

ON THE MORNING OF MARTIN LUTHER KING'S BIRTHDAY, WE gathered at the fig tree and formed a prayer circle. Twenty people, including Sean, Krystal and myself, were going to take part in the first leg of the journey to Carpinteria. The men had built an imitation of a covered wagon out of two bicycles, using bent PVC pipe to replicate the arched roof. It was designed to be pulled, rather than ridden during the Walk, but when we set off from Santa Barbara, Krystal was able to perch atop the front seat and wave to passing cars as they cheered us on. Bob followed behind in the support bus.

Together, we trekked through Montecito and Summerland, holding protest signs and soliciting donations from sympathetic citizens. By the time we reached a campground in Carpinteria, a miraculous thing had happened - the kitty had grown to four hundred and fifty dollars. The chances of Bob reaching the East Coast had grown significantly.

That evening, I went with Krystal and Sean to a bus stop and took public transportation back to Santa Barbara. Unfortunately, I was so emotionally overwrought that when I got on the bus, I left a backpack containing my camera on a bench in Carpinteria, and I never saw it again.

Meanwhile, back at the Carpinteria campground, a rainstorm struck in the middle of the night. People had been dozing in their sleeping bags outdoors when the deluge hit. Some relocated underneath trees for shelter. Bob fled to the school bus. Needless to say, the next morning had to be spent at the laundromat drying out their clothes and bedding before they could continue.

The Walkers reached Rincon Beach on the second day and Oxnard on the third, where employees and clients of the local women's shelter accompanied them to the outskirts of town. On the fourth day, they camped across the street from Pepperdine University in Malibu. Students were generous with their donations and some of the Walkers were invited to speak at a University social science class. Eventually, the police informed them that they'd overstayed their welcome, so they moved onward toward Venice Beach.

Over the next few weeks, I distracted myself with work and childcare, but I couldn't shake the feeling that I might have made a mistake by not going on the Walk. As a child, I'd convinced myself I was meant to trek across the United States with a man, and Bob was the only person I'd ever met who could pull it off. Besides all that, I missed him, and I drove down the 101 several times to check on my partner and his companions before they progressed too far east.

My twelve-year-old son Sean helped keep me focused on the present, but not for the best of reasons. A friend of his had been bringing marijuana to school, and after classes were let out, the two of them would head to the edge of school property to smoke a joint. Sean wanted to return the favor, so he got ahold of some LSD during a gathering at Pershing Park and shared it with his friend. Afterward, the other boy's parents grew concerned at their son's strange behavior, so they took him to a doctor and did some blood tests. Traces of LSD were found in the boy's system, and he was forced to point the finger at Sean, not mentioning that he'd been providing Sean with marijuana all this time.

Sean was charged with supplying LSD to another child. This was bad. Sean had been shuffled around from school to school by the district administration several times over the years whenever troubles arose, and I didn't know what the consequences would be this time. He seemed unable to think about the results of his actions, and I had a feeling it would only grow worse from there.

The next day, I picked up a copy of the Santa Barbara News-Press and sat down in Carrows to read the headline: "Walk Slows to a Crawl". When I saw that, I knew that I had to stop being afraid of the Walk. I needed to be there, both for my own sake and to make sure it was ultimately successful. I drove down the Pacific Coast Highway and found the caravan members at Leo Carrillo Campground. Over three weeks they had only progressed as far as Venice Beach because the bus transmission had taken a dive. They had to use most of their funds to put in a new clutch plate and throwout bearing, after which they decided to return to Malibu to rest up for the next leg of the journey.

I noticed that several citizens of Venice Beach had joined up with the group and were planning to accompany them across greater Los Angeles. Most of the Walkers appeared to be on LSD and were as high as a kite. That convinced me that rules would have to be made to corral these new personalities and make sure they all made it to the other side of the continent alive. I would make their safety my responsibility.

I showed the newspaper headline to the Walkers, and that sobered them up a little, giving them the motivation they needed to put an end to their Malibu beach vacation. I told Bob I was going to head back to Santa Barbara to make preparations for myself and the kids. Like it or not, my motorhome was going to have to come on the trek, and it needed new tires.

I went to Mr. Monson, who understood my need to take a leave of absence without my having to say anything. He told me to go, and sensing my anxiety, he reassured me that my job would be waiting for me when I returned. I thanked him profusely and asked him for six more weeks of work, which he granted. He was a great man who knew how to take care of the employees who were loyal to him.

Over the next month, I had fresh tires installed and I outfitted the RV with the supplies I'd need to host Bob, Sean and three-and-a-half-year-old Krystal while on the road. I'd asked Bob to keep me updated as to his location, and I received a letter saying he would wait for me on a road outside Palm Springs. It was time for my children to join the Walk.

I drove out there, knowing that I'd have to return to Santa Barbara myself to earn some additional money and train someone to do my newspaper route in my absence. Getting Sean out of the school system for a while also seemed like the right thing to do. He needed to be in a new environment for his own sake as well as his teachers'. I left my kids with Bob and made sure to instruct him not to have anyone cut Krystal's hair. It was a beautiful blond color and I wanted her to be able to grow it out. He promised.

It was hard to leave my children behind, and Sean was a little frightened to be separated from me. He chased me down the road when I drove away, and I had to pull over and reassure him that I'd see him soon. In four weeks, we were planning to meet in Show Low, Arizona on Easter Sunday - Sean's favorite holiday. Sean's grandmother Jane lived there, and we'd be able to visit her before moving on.

Back in Santa Barbara, I checked my mail and found a letter from the District Attorney's office. It specified that Sean and I needed to attend an arraignment hearing arranged by the D.A. to discuss the drug-furnishing complaint. My stomach dropped. Sean was hundreds of miles away and I had no ability to retrieve him by the date listed on the letter. How was I going to get out of this mess?

I brought the directive to my attorney at the Legal Defense Center, Willard Hastings, who had a mischievous twinkle in his eye after he read it. "That's easy, Nancy," he attempted to reassure me. "You haven't seen this letter. You have to go on the Walk. In fact, you've already left, haven't you?"

I was not entirely comforted. I still had four weeks left of work before I could leave town and I was scared that would give plenty of time for the police to come after me once I failed to show up at the arraignment hearing. The days passed slowly as a result. One afternoon, I received an envelope in the mail containing a bunch of blond hair along with an apologetic letter from Bob. He said that a woman on the Walk had been unable to keep Krystal's hair from tangling, so she cut it. I was upset, but I knew it would grow back again.

My departure date would be two days before Easter Sunday, I determined. In the meantime, I worked, hid from the authorities and slept. My final paycheck brought my savings up to six hundred dollars, which I hoped would be enough. I closed out my account at the bank and received a stack of twenty-dollar bills. Now I needed to stash it carefully. I'd be traveling with people who might be untrustworthy, and I couldn't afford to make the same mistake Bob had made with Chuck and Katrina. This money wasn't for the rest of the Walkers; it was for myself and my kids.

I came up with a plan. In the bookcase of the RV was a photograph album. I pulled it out and methodically slipped a twenty-dollar bill in between each pair of back-to-back photos. *Not bad, huh?* I told myself. No one would be able to figure out why I was able to buy fancy tailor-made cigarettes or purchase treats for my children whenever we rode into a community.

When my departure date finally arrived, I was greatly relieved. I woke up at 2:30 a.m., and instead of going to work, I walked into Carrows to supply my body with the caffeine it needed to make it all the way to Show Low. Then at 4 a.m., I escaped town under the cover of darkness and set off to find my family.

~

BY THE TIME I REACHED VICTORVILLE, THE RV WAS NEARLY OUT OF gas, so I exited the highway in search of a station. I passed two hitch-hikers with backpacks by the side of the road, and that gave me an idea. If those men were still looking for a ride after I filled up the motorhome tank, we might be able to take shifts behind the wheel and

I could get to my destination sooner. Provided they knew how to drive a motorhome, anyway.

After gassing up, I found the hitchhikers sitting in the same spot. I pulled up next to them, threw the RV into park, opened the door and leaned my head out. "Is either one of you capable of driving this rig?" I asked. Smiles appeared on their faces and they nodded eagerly. "Come on board, then," I said and waved them inside.

I soon learned that Jay and his partner Steve had just been discharged from the Marines and were trying to get to New Jersey. Knowing that, I told them what I was looking for. I needed to get to Show Low by Easter Sunday and I couldn't pay them, but I could cook them meals while they drove. They could head off on their own once we reached my destination.

The political concept underlying the Walk intrigued and excited them, so I was convinced they'd be safe companions. They were extremely grateful, for they'd been waiting for a ride out of Victorville for the last four days. I asked them to drive me to the Arizona border. Then we'd rest for the night and travel the remaining distance the following day. Jay took the wheel and I went to curl up with my German shepherd Schatzie to take a nap. *Life is marvelous,* I felt. I was where I was meant to be.

After a few hours, the voices of Jay and Steve drifted into my dreams. "Nancy, we're approaching the Arizona border. Should we stop?"

"Of course," I answered groggily. "Let's have some dinner, and then you guys can get some shut-eye."

Jay flipped on the turn signal, headed down the next exit and found a place to park. I shook off my weariness and started making us a meal. After supper, the two men passed out, and I returned to bed to get a bit more sleep.

Before my guests arose the next morning, I woke up and got behind the wheel. Following the map, I took us into northwestern Arizona and drove as far as I could. Jay switched stations with me as we approached the White Mountains and the town of Show Low, but unfortunately, we traveled all the way through the small city and out the other side without seeing any signs of a dilapidated-looking bus with a bunch of crap hanging all over it.

I felt both disappointed and extremely anxious. *How could we have missed them?* By now, night had fallen and I wasn't sure what to do. The lights of a semi-truck flickered in the distance along the highway, coming closer. Quickly, I grabbed the CB radio and hit the speaker button. "Hey, Big Guy!" I spoke into the microphone. "Have you seen an ugly old school bus parked along the road anywhere near here?"

The driver's ears happened to be on and he responded, saying he'd seen one about seven miles ago. They must have been approaching Show Low from a different direction. I was ecstatic. My kids had been without their mother for nearly a month.

We found the bus at a turnout, and no sooner had I pulled up alongside than Bob came walking out with Krystal in his arms. My baby grasped ahold of me and gazed up with her beautiful eyes. Sean was already sleeping, and I knew better than to try and wake him up. Our reunion could wait until morning.

I introduced my two hitchhikers, and they were invited to roll out their sleeping bags along the ground next to the other Walkers. Then Bob, Krystal and I climbed into my motorhome and held each other closely until sunrise.

The next day, Sean emerged from the support bus and gave me a big hug. I handed him and Krystal a pair of Easter baskets that I'd purchased in Santa Barbara, both filled with goodies and toys. The smiles on their faces were the best thank-you presents I could have received.

One of the guys made a pot of cowboy coffee, and I sipped a small cup of the stuff while assessing the state of the homeless crew. My biggest question was: *Where had all the Walkers gone?* There had been twice as many when I'd seen the group outside of Palm Springs. Now only seven remained.

Over breakfast, Bob and the others explained that one week earlier, they'd held a meeting at a place called Devil's Canyon. By that point in the journey, many of the Walkers had grown angry. Back in Palm Springs, the kitty had become flush with donations, thanks to the local advocates. But the purse strings had been held tightly, and several of the trekkers felt it was only fair that the money be divvied up among them. Half argued that this would be disastrous for the Walk; the support system would disappear if people were spending the donations on themselves. But the others felt that the seven hundred dollars raised in Palm Springs was being unfairly withheld from them. They couldn't see how they still benefited from the abundance of food and tobacco. Even the group's resident cartoonist, Jeff Hess, was being supplied with pens so he could illustrate their adventures in his many art books.

The meeting resulted in a split decision. As a compromise, they agreed to split the money in half. Those who wished to support themselves individually decided to leave the group and undertake a Walk of their own along a different route. They left, using a shopping cart to carry their belongings and leaving the other seven to venture on to Show Low without them. The kitty was lighter now, but still intact.

Of course, the rebellious splinter group never made it to the East Coast. The last we heard, a photographer reported seeing them trudging back to Los Angeles, broke, with nothing but a liter of alcohol and a carton of eggs between them.

At the end of breakfast, the two Marines asked if they could travel with us for a time, and we agreed. That brought our total up to ten people. Together, we walked the seven remaining miles to the outskirts of Show Low. I carried the American flag proudly, but toward the end, I felt a sharp pain along my vertebrae. My efforts had resulted in a pinched nerve, leaving me in agony for a few minutes. I surrendered the flag to another Walker, knowing my flag-bearing days were over, at least for this trip.

We left the support vehicles outside the city limits and entered the town, seeking Sean's grandmother's house. It was the first time Sean had seen his relative in a long while. Sadly, it would also be the last time because Jane was suffering from the onset of Alzheimer's Disease. The woman could barely recognize us, which made our reunion bittersweet.

~

THE NEXT DAY, WE CARRIED ON TOWARD THE NEW MEXICO BORDER. I quickly learned the patterns of movement that the Walkers had settled into. The support vehicles would head two miles down the road. Then the drivers would get out, lock the doors and walk back to the others, meeting them halfway. That gave everyone a chance to set their feet on the ground and walk the same distance, even if they were moving backward at times. Once we reached the bus and the motorhome, we'd make sure we all drank some water or juice to hydrate ourselves.

Meetings were held to discuss the day's activities, clear the air of any grievances and go over any budget issues. To support the mission, the Walkers collected any aluminum cans they found along the highway, then cashed them in to collect the deposit money when we passed through major cities. The guys would also donate blood plasma for cash, which they'd spend on alcohol more often than not. We used the bus as our kitchen and for food storage while my motorhome carried everyone's personal belongings and provided shelter for my children. It was insane how many locals came to talk to us. The majority of them also contributed funds and gifted us with food and clothing. There were so many offerings that we found ourselves having to donate most of them to social service agencies in the smaller towns we passed through.

Everyone had a job to do. I interviewed the Walkers, collected handwritten submissions and worked on a newsletter using the old typewriter that we'd managed to retrieve from Chuck and Katrina before they abandoned us. I also made sure the group was fed, gave out bandages for blisters and looked after people's hydration and health. These responsibilities gave me an excuse to not have to attend the daily meetings, even though they were a priority for Bob. Meetings were important, but they were a "free for all" affair with arguments breaking out every few minutes. Most of the friction had to do with the aluminum cans we were picking up. Some people felt they were collecting far more than others, and so they thought they deserved more money in their pockets. They were oblivious of how monies were carefully spent for the common good. Others wanted a reward system for simply donating their time to the Walk. The arguments grew intense, and it was obvious that something had to change, but no one was able to come up with a satisfactory compromise. So the yelling and screaming continued.

The next big city along our path was Gallup, New Mexico. To get there, we had to trudge through the snow and cold across Native American reservations where the residents felt no qualms about chucking aluminum cans out of their windows as they drove by. We couldn't walk five feet without picking one up and adding it to our stores. Some of the cars pulled over and offered us rides, for the drivers assumed that no one would go walking outside in winter temperatures if they didn't have to. Naturally, we had to turn them down.

Our route ran parallel to Interstate 40, though we had to walk along the shoulder of the highway when side roads weren't available. I'm sure we were a scary-looking bunch of people to most observers, but many locals would find themselves overwhelmed with curiosity and come up to chat with us despite their initial misgivings. As the only woman in the group, I was asked to do advance work for the Walkers. Before the group reached the next community, I would recruit a partner and drive ahead into town. We would find a coffee house, borrow their phone directory and call up social service agencies, the police department and the media. It was important to make sure we weren't surprising the local sheriffs because they could have made our lives very difficult.

The media could come out to meet us when we entered the town, and all that exposure helped to bring in donations of food and money, replenishing the kitty. Sometimes, people would cook meals, then invite us to sit down in a community park and break bread with us. My assumption that the citizens of the United States were cruel and indifferent to the plight of the homeless was fast diminishing. In fact, people seemed angry that so many were forced to live on the streets.

We kept in touch with KEYT back in Santa Barbara, as we were still media darlings and could count on sympathetic coverage. CNN News reported on our progress as well. Homeless people marching for the homeless - it was a story that sparked the imagination and would hopefully result in real national change.

We also retained support from key players in our hometown: Kit

Tremaine, Peter Marin of Harper's Magazine, Chuck Blitz and, of course, the Homeless Coalition. Peter had contacts with New Mexico State University in Las Cruces, and he made arrangements so that we could stay on the university extension campus in Grants and recuperate for a few days. He also decided to take a train and come see us in Gallup. Being a writer, the story of our walk across America was right up his alley.

We made it to Gallup just in time for his arrival, and Peter walked with us sixty miles to the city of Grants. I was truly happy to see a familiar face from back home. Homesickness had begun to affect my spirits, but I knew that every step of the Walk was one step closer to returning home.

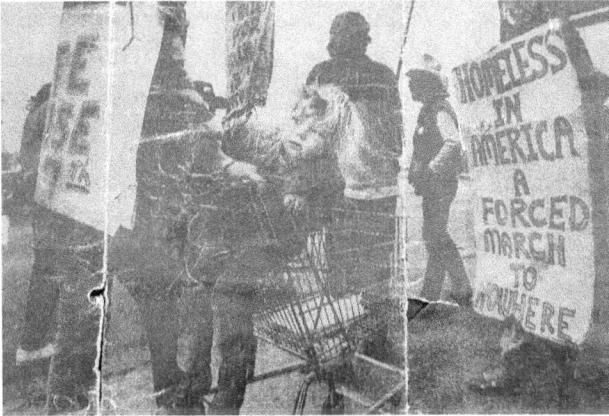

*Krystal Freedom, en route to the University of New Mexico campus in Grants (photo by Mark Holm of The Journal)*

When we reached the university campus, I was more than ready to rest. My back was still in excruciating pain from the pinched nerve I suffered in Show Low. Peter helped find us vagabonds a place to set up camp, and the crew settled down to nap or cook up some food. Soon, I was approached by a reporter for the Campus News. She asked to pull me aside for an interview - a common occurrence, as I was the only woman in the group. We sat down a ways off from the others, and it was such a relief to talk to someone of my own gender. I'd been among men since leaving Santa Barbara, and all too often they ganged up and tormented me. Bob usually instigated it... reacting out of jealousy, perhaps, because I was receiving so much attention from the others. I had to fight back with regularity, and the stress was enormous at times. So talking one-on-one with another woman was such a pleasure.

Women can become close and empathetic very quickly. During the course of the interview, my new friend noticed that I was experiencing some extreme pain. She asked me what the matter was and I explained what happened on my first day of walking when I tried carrying a heavy American flag. Ever since then, I felt sharp pains whenever I moved my body in certain ways. It became almost impossible to breathe.

The reporter looked hard at me and said, "I'm a chiropractor by trade. If you'll allow me to give you a treatment, I'll come back after I write up our interview. We'll see if we can't get you some relief.

*Where do these miracles come from?* I thought. The treatment was a success and I felt leagues better than before. She'd given me my old self back.

After a few days, when it was time to leave Grants, the campus gave us a send-off celebration and accompanied our group to the edge of town. Peter needed to get back to Santa Barbara, so he said farewell and wished us the best. The rest of us hit the road and got back to work.

Along the way to Albuquerque, we stopped at a highway rest area and Sean wandered off to explore the terrain. He came back with a red-headed and bearded homeless man that he'd met previously on the streets of Santa Barbara who was currently hitching rides to another part of the country. The drifter was interested in joining the group, so we nicknamed him "Irish" and welcomed him aboard.

During our long trek across the country, we noticed that a surprising number of people were traveling back and forth between the East and West Coasts looking for new lives. Some had lost their jobs in their hometowns so they were headed to the western states where there were plenty of opportunities. In 1988, the minimum wage in California was five dollars an hour, which seemed like a lot to most people. However, that amount couldn't cover the cost of rising rent prices. The immigrants couldn't afford housing, so many people we encountered were hitchhiking back east, disillusioned by the cost-of-living and hoping for more sustainable opportunities. Their plight was eye-opening to us. We'd make meals for these people, give them whatever we could afford and listen to their tales of how society was mistreating the common American worker. There was plenty of sorrow to go around.

We made it to the west side of Albuquerque in the late evening. The drivers found a mesa where they could park that looked out over the city. One of my fondest memories of that time was when we stood at that vista and I felt a small tug on my arm. I glanced down to where my daughter was excitedly pointing to the shining spectacle of the city landscape, lit up by thousands upon thousands of streetlights and signs.

"Look, mommie! The stars are on the ground."

Krystal was unrelentingly cute. I had to chuckle.

The next morning, I drove into the city to do some advance work, checking into a coffee shop and jotting down all the phone numbers I needed to call. The remainder of our group stayed back on the mesa and rested. My recruitment efforts were successful, and when we awoke the next day, not long after sunrise, we were greeted by a large group of people, including activists and local media, who wanted to walk with us through the city. It was a grand procession. That afternoon, we were able to take care of our errands efficiently, cashing in our aluminum cans, and the guys donated more blood in exchange for twenty dollars apiece. We camped on the east side of Albuquerque and continued onward the following morning.

Interstate 40 had never been ideal for us to walk along, since doing so was technically illegal. However, it was the best way for us to gain public attention and solicit donations. Sometimes the state troopers would drive alongside us, flashing their lights protectively in dangerous areas with low visibility. But for some reason, whether it was due to politics or policy, they never made direct contact with our group. They just wanted to keep us safe.

The Texas border grew near. Tucumcari was the last remaining town in New Mexico of any significance, and as we approached, we reflected on our days pushing through the pelting snow and talked about the struggling workers we'd met along the way. Outside of the small city, we found a place to camp atop another small, flat mesa that held an abandoned, rusted-out gas station. No sooner had we gotten settled, however, than we were paid a visit by an entourage of state troopers. I could already sense that these men had a completely different attitude than the others who had escorted us along our journey, and when a tall, rigid man got out of the lead car, I walked up to him to try and defuse the situation before any of the more short-tempered Walkers got involved.

Officer Harold Bittinger was a real screamer, yelling at me that we'd be arrested if we tried walking down the interstate into his community; we needed to drive the final distance. He was one of those people who felt he had to be pushy and combative to get his point across. I tried to explain to him that we were on a national walk and had to progress on foot every step of the way. There were no other routes into Tucumcari for travelers coming from the west, so it wasn't as if we could choose a side road to walk on. None of my arguments made any headway with the state trooper. He called us a bunch of stubborn mules and repeated that we would be arrested if we went ahead with our plans. Then he got back in his vehicle and drove off. *Okay, then.* None of us thought that the Walk was going to be free of arrests or police confrontations, so we didn't feel all that threatened by the trooper's edict.

The next morning, over cups of cowboy coffee, we strategized how we were going to deal with Mr. Bittinger. We decided it would be best to split into two groups. One would walk along the westbound side of the highway and another would take the eastbound. We'd also stagger each person twenty yards apart from each other so we could plausibly deny that we were coordinating our efforts. I would drive my RV in front of the group so that if most of them were arrested, my children and I would stand the greatest chance of staying safe.

We set out, fully intending to make it into the Texas Panhandle by the end of the day. But as soon as I pulled up in front of the Walk and parked alongside the highway, a squad car approached. It was Mr. Bittinger. *Oh, hell.* It was up to me to deal with him.

I got out of the RV to greet him as patiently as I could, but he immediately started raging. "I thought I told you people to not walk along the freeway!" he blustered. "I said I would have to arrest you!"

"But *I'm* not walking," I responded coyly. "I'm not disobeying any of your orders. My children and I are simply driving into town, as you said."

Mr. Bittinger then ordered me to tell the other Walkers to get into my motorhome and drive into town, but I informed him that I had no authority to do so. Each individual here would be making their own choice whether to walk or not, and there was nothing I could do about it. Jeff the cartoonist came up to support my arguments and to show the trooper his book of drawings, as if the documentation of our journey might sway or calm the man. Mr. Bittinger didn't want anything to do with him.

"You are not to walk another step toward Tucumcari," he told the artist.

Just then, Indian Bob approached, pushing a shopping cart with a banner that read "Homeless and Poor People's Walk to the White House". He didn't pay much attention to Mr. Bittinger; he just looked at us, shook his head and pressed on.

The trooper noticed the Walkers on the other side of the freeway and started to understand our strategy. Since he was just one man, there was only so much he could do. His face got red as if he were about to have a stroke, but then he refocused his attention on Indian Bob. He had his target.

Mr. Bittinger ran up to Indian Bob, grabbed his shopping cart and threw it into the ditch, banner and all. His face twisted in rage, the trooper put Bob in handcuffs and declared that he was under arrest.

"That's not the way a police officer should be acting," Jeff called out, but his words only made Mr. Bittinger angrier. He marched Indian Bob into the back seat of his squad car, then got in the front so he could call dispatch and report to his superiors.

Colin - one of the main Walk organizers - arrived and told me to get my camera. I dashed inside the RV, grabbed it for him, and my friend started taking pictures. All of a sudden, Mr. Bittinger jumped out of his vehicle and screamed, "You took my picture!" Colin insisted that he hadn't, but the trooper seized my camera and tried to yank out the film, but in his rage, he was unable to figure out how to do so. In frustration, he threw the camera to the ground as hard as he could.

That kindled my anger as well. It was an expensive new camera, and he had no right to break it. I told Mr. Bittinger that if it was broken, he would have to buy me a replacement. The trooper didn't answer. He simply staggered back to his car and drove away with Indian Bob looking anxiously at us through the back window.

It looked like our plans for the day had changed. Now instead of simply walking through the city, we needed to walk to the county seat and try to free Indian Bob.

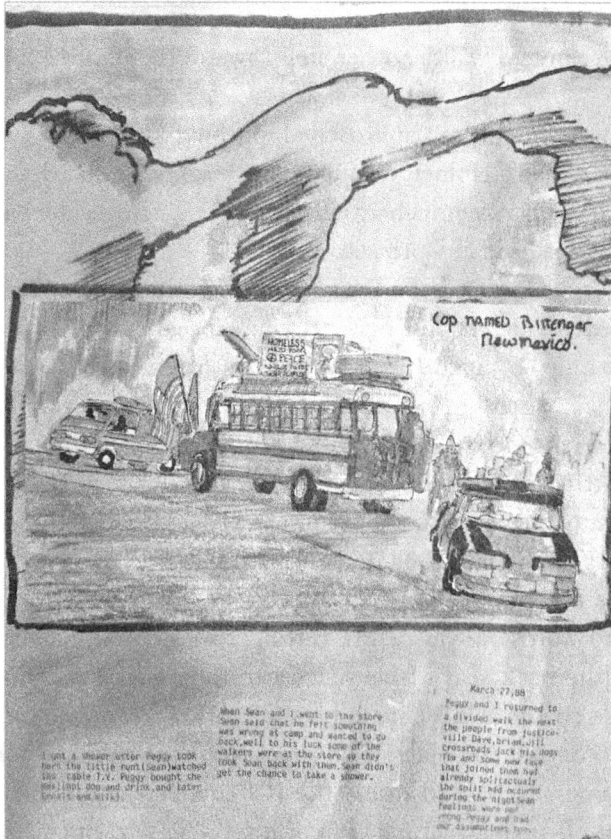

*Jeff Hess' illustration of the Mr. Bittinger encounter*

~

TUCUMCARI IS THE SEAT OF QUAY COUNTY WITH A POPULATION OF around six thousand people. It sits beneath Tucumcari Mountain and was built in 1901 on the site of a Native American legend.

The story revolves around an Apache chief, Wautonomah, who was nearing the end of his life. He picked the two fiercest braves and ordered them to fight to see which one would succeed him. Tonopah and Tocom were sworn enemies who were both vying for the hand of the chief's daughter, Kari. In the course of their combat, Tocom was mortally wounded. Kari was in love with Tocom, and she flew out of the bushes where she had been hiding. She grabbed Tocom's knife, then killed Tonopah and, out of grief, took her own life. Wautonomah looked sadly down upon the result of his ill-fated decisions. He took the same bloody knife and stabbed himself in his heart, crying, "Tocom! Kari!" as he did so. His dying words were merged into "Tucumcari" - the name held by the town and the neighboring mountain today.

Back along the highway, our group gathered around the support vehicles and determined that we needed to head to the City Plaza and fight for the release of our brother, Indian Bob. We walked proudly up to City Hall, then set up a soup kitchen out front with tables, bowls and utensils to share with the community. Our homemade tomato soup was a big hit. Colin went inside the building, called up the CNN newsroom and spoke loudly into the receiver so that any government bystanders could hear what he was reporting. My partner Bob marched back and forth in front of the doors, chanting, "Release our brother!" over and over again. Jeff ran around passing out flyers and showing off his cartoons to anyone who gave any interest.

The citizens of Tucumcari gathered in droves, hungry for drama. Even the local reporters were fascinated; nothing like this had ever happened in their boring town in living memory, and they eagerly scribbled down the details. They interviewed me for the town newspaper, of course, and one of the reporters let slip that they were fairly pleased by what was happening. They all hated Mr. Bittinger. The man was trying to run for public office and his efforts at gaining publicity were causing him to act like an asshole toward everyone in the community. Any embarrassment that the state trooper suffered today would be well-deserved.

The authorities in town must have been disturbed and annoyed by our presence, for they stuck Indian Bob in front of a judge only two hours after we arrived. They interviewed him in court and decided he was harmless. More importantly, I think they recognized how much national media support we had, for they released him as fast as possible. They even gave us a map showing us the fastest way out of town.

Reunited with our brother, our group packed up the soup kitchen, held a quick meeting and then departed the City Hall grounds with the citizens of Tucumcari cheering us on. We crossed the state line in triumph and entered the Panhandle of Texas. New adventures awaited us, but I knew our encounter with Harold Bittinger would be one of my fondest memories. He may have been an asshole, but he was truly dedicated to his job, and the successful outcome of our encounter was worth all the hassle that he caused. If the details of our journey ever became fuzzy in future years, I had one piece of physical evidence to remember Mr. Bittinger by: his image, preserved on film in my still-functioning camera. Colin hadn't been entirely truthful with the officer that morning, and I certainly hadn't been inclined to admit anything to the contrary.

## 12

# THE TREAD WEARS THIN

The walk through Texas was psychologically hard on us, as we looked a lot more like hippies than cowboys. The natives seemed either frightened or repulsed by our group, so we had to work particularly hard to make a good impression and educate the communities we marched through. At one of our first camps, however, a young woman pulled up in a red pickup truck. When I went to greet her and introduce myself, she asked if we smoked pot. I said yes, and she gleefully pulled a joint out of her pocket to share with us. She told me she would have gotten in big trouble if her father knew she was here, but to show a measure of solidarity with our cause, she was willing to take the risk.

Another day, we were walking along the interstate when a Volkswagen bus approached us. It was filled with an assortment of beatnik figures and they invited us to come to their "Peace Farm". We consented to their offer and soon found ourselves in a truly peaceful setting. It lived up to its name, as it also had a farmhouse, a barn and a silo like any other Texas farm. They invited us to relax and spend the night. All might have been well, but Bob convened one of his infamous meetings. I refused to attend, shutting myself inside the motorhome with Sean and Krystal while the same old arguments erupted outside over the collection of aluminum cans. It was crazy. The debate over the distribution of can money threatened to tear the group apart, but we couldn't afford to stop collecting. It was how we paid for gas for the support vehicles as well as fresh vegetables in order to keep the Walkers healthy. I couldn't contribute funds to feed everyone because my personal stash of six hundred dollars was diminishing rapidly. So the fighting was destined to continue.

We left the hippie commune the following morning, and I'm sure they never forgot us. We had brought war to their "Peace Farm".

As a tribute to these struggles, one of the Walkers built a statue of an aluminum god using an upside-down coffee pot for a face, an aluminum torso and aluminum cans for its arms and legs. The legend was that somewhere down the road, this idol was destined to produce a miracle that would save the Walk and put an end to our conflict over the collection of cans. Then everyone would be happy at last. In the meantime, we continued our scavenging. Bags of cans dangled off the roof of the bus, and we would earn three to four hundred dollars every time we cashed them in at a recycling center. It was hard work, but undeniably profitable.

A friend of ours, Eve Fowler, contacted the group and requested to join us to take pictures. She was a photography student and an acquaintance of Peter Marin who was studying photojournalism. We waited for her at one of the mile markers along the highway, and as soon as she stepped off the Greyhound, I knew it would be a joy to have her company, as I was tired of being the only woman among the Walkers. She gave an update on the splinter group that had mutinied at Devil's Canyon in Arizona, reporting that she'd come across them slinking back to Santa Barbara, and she commended us on our endurance and resilience.

The journey was tough on Eve at times because the illustrator Jeff developed a crush on her. She handled his attentions stoically, however, with an air of professionalism. Better still, she walked alongside us and took notes and countless photos.

In the Texas Panhandle, we learned what walking in the noonday heat was like for the first time. When we'd traveled through the high-elevation terrain of New Mexico, we'd had to deal with snow and severe cold. Here, we were forced to contend with temperatures of 105 degrees at midday, which compelled us to find shade and take breaks from noon to 4 p.m. every afternoon.

Creeks and rivers were few and far between. Instead, we passed lots of pastures that were ruled over by herds of cattle or sheep. One day, Jeff ran up to us after doing some reconnaissance on a nearby property. "Want to cool off in a Texas hot tub?" he asked.

We changed into bathing suits and Jeff led us up and over some barbed wire to a pair of cattle troughs. It wasn't as appealing as Jeff led us to believe. Looking into the water, we saw a lot of cow slobber and other debris. "Just push the slobber away," Jeff told us, "and hop in!" He was originally a farm boy from Iowa, so his standards were slightly different from those of your typical Santa Barbara resident.

We were so hot at that point that we put our reservations aside and made the plunge. It certainly served to bring our body temperatures down... enough that we were able to climb back over the fence afterward and resume our pilgrimage.

Word reached us that reporters from the KEYT radio station in Santa Barbara were going to meet us at the capitol building in Oklahoma City. I was excited, for I missed home very badly and it was comforting to hear that there was enough demand for updates about our adventure that the station was sending a crew out to interview us. Oklahoma City would be the halfway point between Santa Barbara and Washington, D.C., and we calculated that we should be able to reach the city by Memorial Day weekend. After learning this news, the crossing of the Panhandle seemed to take forever. I couldn't wait to be back in my hometown, but I accepted that every step I took eastward down the highway was another step closer to Santa Barbara... chronologically speaking, if not geographically.

During one of my phone calls with KEYT, after I had updated them on our progress, they informed me that two Santa Barbara women, Peggy and Diane, wished to catch up with us and join the Walk. I was eager to have these ladies enlist since Eve couldn't travel with us for the full distance, so we arranged to have their Greyhound bus drop them off at a specific mile marker along the I-40. It was great to have additional female companionship... at first. But soon,

Peggy and Diane would cause more problems within our group than ever.

I continued to isolate myself in the motorhome, working on the newsletter during Bob's daily meetings, for it was difficult to have to listen to arguments constantly erupt about the aluminum cans. Now, however, a new point of friction was arising. Peggy and Diane started to train their focus on the group's alcohol consumption, which became an issue whenever we passed through a city and the men converted their blood plasma donation money into booze. For the next few days following these transactions, the guys would wreak havoc with their raucous behavior, but they thought they had every right to do so since it was their private earnings. The new female recruits tried to place controls over their drinking, but it didn't go over very well. The men pushed back, believing that the only way to relax after a grueling day pounding the pavement was through a bottle of booze. I eventually learned that the women were part of a national group of sexual abuse survivors, and alcohol was the bane of their existence. This was understandable, but trying to force the guys not to drink during rest breaks was a losing proposition. It became just one more thing to fight over during meetings.

One day, I was trying to get some work done on the newsletter in the RV when the screamfest outside reached a fevered pitch. Despite the racket, a slight noise *inside* the motorhome caught my attention. I turned from my typewriter and saw the aluminum god figurine sitting on my couch. One arm had been positioned casually, resting along the back of the couch, and one of the figure's legs was crossed over the other. I had no idea how he'd gotten there. Still, I was seized by the need to put him to good use.

I grabbed the sculpture by the neck, walked to the door and threw it open. Then I pitched the aluminum god into the air and thundered, "Thou shalt have no other gods before me!" The figurine struck the ground with a loud clatter and everyone at the meeting fell silent.

As people's shock subsided, a realization spread over everyone that the aluminum can issue had become a fiasco. It had taken over the Walk's focus and eclipsed what the event was supposed to stand for. So they finally came to a compromise: from now on, the kitty would be kept at a maximum of four hundred dollars. If the cashing in of cans brought the total above that amount, the excess would be distributed among the Walkers. Not only did this arrangement stop the infighting, it gave the men an even greater incentive to pick up cans along the way. Now all we had to do was make Peggy and Diane a little less afraid of the alcohol consumption. Their concerns had cast a cloud of nervous energy over the group, but because they both had suffered some horrific childhood experiences, they did not seem likely to drop the issue.

At one of the "stab labs" in Texas, I was finally tempted to donate some blood myself, for I'd finally run out of savings and could no longer buy any treats for myself or the kids. The other guys tormented me in the lead-up to the procedure, exaggerating how big the needles were and how much it would hurt. By the time it was my turn, I was truly scared and stressed out, but I needed the twenty dollars. To my relief, however, the process was smooth and reassuring. The doctors gave us a physical to make sure we were good candidates for donating. Thanks to all the walking we'd been doing over the last few months, we were in wonderful shape. Everyone's blood pressure was low. Mine was 102 over 68, with a pulse rate of 58 beats per minute. I was still very thin, without an ounce of fat on my body. All the walking had been good for me as well. As a child, I'd learned the Native American technique of walking slightly pigeon-toed. That kept my shoes from wearing out as fast as the others', and I never had to deal with blisters. Of course, when I tried teaching this skill to the men, they refused to listen to a woman's advice.

After our physicals, we laid out on the warm beds and held out our arms. The blood was extracted and then spun in a machine so they could separate out the plasma. The remainder was put back in our veins. After I was bandaged up, I was told I could go down the hallway to the food area, where I'd be given orange juice and a hot dog. I slid off the bed and started in that direction, but my knees immediately gave out from underneath me. The next thing I knew, I was lying sprawled on the floor, having fallen flat on my face. I must have blacked out from all the stress of going through the donation process for the first time.

The nurses picked me up off the carpet, put me in a chair and brought over some food. I wasn't too badly bruised, and I recovered quickly. It was worth it. With twenty dollars in my pocket, I was able to purchase some treats for Sean and Krystal as well as a carton of tailor-made cigarettes for my efforts.

*"The Imagine" (photographer unknown)*

We made steady progress through the Texas Panhandle. In another town, I handed a flyer to a desk clerk at the police station as part of my advance work, informing him that our group would enter his community in two days. I reassured him that we had no intention to pillage the townsfolk or cause trouble, and he promised me that he'd pass the message along to the chief. After that, I checked in with local media and asked the city government if any of their social service divisions could help us with donations.

Two days later, just before we reached the town, the skies grew dark and we thought it would be more prudent to set up camp for the night instead of continuing into the city. Rain seemed likely. As we were pulling sleeping bags out of the support bus, our group was suddenly surrounded by police cars. The chief wanted to know our business, and after the purpose of the Walk was explained to him, he turned to me and asked why we hadn't informed the town that we were coming. I assured him that we definitely *did* tell the station we were approaching. Thankfully, one of the police officers stepped forward and confirmed my story, and the chief apologized. He also told us that this was no safe place to camp. A massive thunderstorm was on its way, with lightning and even the possibility of tornadoes. He urged us to follow him into town to a community park that had a huge open-air shelter. If we slept in the middle of the shelter, he thought we would be fine.

Quickly, we packed up the sleeping bags and headed for the park. And thank goodness we did, for the heavens opened up that night. It was hard to sleep with lightning bolts striking the ground right outside the shelter. The thunder was deafening... as loud as I've ever heard in my life. But we survived to walk another day.

The final city on our route through the Texas Panhandle was called Shamrock, named after the clover species that possessed luck-granting properties in Irish tradition. I handled the advance work as usual, and we were invited to camp for the night on the front lawn of a church. It was a nice evening, so Bob and I decided to sleep outdoors with our sleeping bags. Krystal laid down contentedly between us.

Later that night, we were woken up by the clinking of glass and several shouts from our campmates. Someone was throwing beer bottles at us! Jeff jumped up first and yelled fiercely at the ruffians, "There's a baby sleeping with us! Do you want to hit her?"

Our attackers turned out to be military officers who had strayed off base and were looking for entertainment at our expense. After drunkenly voicing some choice words about hippies and the homeless, the situation settled down and the soldiers wandered off. Needless to say, it was hard to sleep for the rest of the night. Some of our crew took shifts playing security in case our assailants returned. The rest of us slept fitfully. On the morrow, we would cross into Oklahoma where we hoped we'd receive a warmer and more hospitable welcome.

~

WHILE DOING ADVANCE WORK IN ELK CITY, OKLAHOMA, I MET UP with a compassionate woman from their social services department and conveyed a request from the Walkers. The guys were looking for fresh veggies and meat, having long grown tired of the cans of tuna that were a staple of our meals on the road. They hoped the city could provide some vouchers for food, and thankfully, the city employee came through. The proviso was that she needed to accompany the shoppers to make sure that the one-hundred-fifty-dollar voucher would be spent appropriately.

I invited the woman back to our camp and asked our group for some volunteers to go on a grocery run. Colin and Indian Bob raised their hands, so they left and came back a few hours later with an outrageous assortment of items. Some were essentials, thankfully, but they also brought back a five-pound bag of sugar and a ton of raisins. Since the social worker would have stopped them from buying alcohol with the voucher, they'd come up with a sneaky workaround. By letting the sugar and raisins ferment in a five-gallon bucket with some yeast, in ten days they would have a potent batch of "raisin jack" - a type of booze they'd learned to make from their comrades in jail. I was quite upset, as I had done all this advance work only to have my efforts hijacked and directed toward getting the men drunk again. But I decided not to say anything. I'd just have to be watchful so that it never happened again.

The guys ended up being too impatient to wait ten days for full fermentation, and they drank the concoction after only three. What a waste. If they'd made it properly, it could have been a good brew. Regardless, I refused to taste the stuff.

The group progressed into Elk City and headed for the address of a homeless shelter that the police had given us. We picked up a few more Walkers there, including another Native American man. It was normal for people to come and go over the course of weeks and months on the road. Some well-intentioned Walkers couldn't handle the community rules or the consistent task of walking twenty miles each day. Peggy and Diane dropped away, taking a Greyhound bus from Elk City back to wherever they came from. They'd decided the Walk was not for them because they couldn't control how much alcohol consumption was going on, and honestly, it was a relief when they departed. We did better without the constant drama.

After we left Elk City and continued down the highway, we came to a park where the guys decided we should spend the night. A sign prominently warned us that there was no overnight camping allowed, but most of the Walkers didn't care. They laid their sleeping bags out across the tops of the picnic tables and prepared to get some shuteye. I didn't want to be in violation of any county ordinances, so I took my children and parked a half-mile up the road where I thought we'd be much less likely to be disturbed.

Around midnight, I was woken by the sound of insistent knocking. I dragged myself out of bed and opened the RV door. There stood a middle-aged, bespectacled woman from Child Protective Services flanked by two two police officers. I asked what I could do for them, and the woman informed me that they had a report that my boyfriend and I had been sexually abusing my children. *What????*

Immediately, I knew where that accusation had come from. It had to be those two bitter women, Peggy and Diane, who were mad and angry that they couldn't fulfill their dream of walking with us to Washington, D.C. To lash out, they were attempting to have my children taken from me. Even from a distance, they'd found a way to cause mischief.

First, the social worker wanted me to wake the kids so that they could be interviewed. I tried to rouse Krystal, but she was out cold and could not be wakened. After several attempts, I went back to the woman and explained that I couldn't do it without being violent with my baby. "Who is being abusive now?" I taunted.

The woman gave up on Krystal but asked to talk with Sean alone. I agreed and exited the motorhome. Sometime later, the social worker emerged and told me how charming my little boy was. Sean had explained the Walk to her and had affirmed that he would never let anything abusive happen to himself or to his little sister. He was just the witness I needed to convince the woman that I wasn't a child molester.

Still, the police wanted to have words with Krystal's father. I explained that Bob was a half-mile away at the picnic grounds, and I had them follow me in the RV back to the encampment. I shook Bob awake and explained to the confused man what was going on. He took a few minutes to settle into the interrogation process and form coherent answers to their questions, but ultimately, Bob was able to convey that Peggy and Diana were suffering from childhood trauma and wanted to get back at us because they had to abandon the Walk. I asked the woman what proof they had that we were child abusers, and she explained that the report stated that Krystal kissed her parents on the cheek with her tongue out. *Unbelievable.*

The CPS worker, realizing her case against us was substantially weak, did not force the police officers to seize our children. However, she did ask me to come back to her office in Elk City the next day so that we could continue our conversation. We made an appointment, but after she left, I laid in bed, sleepless for several hours. I wanted to strangle Peggy and Diane. With luck, I'd never see them again in this lifetime. More seriously, I fretted over the consequences of not showing up for that appointment. We had to get to Oklahoma City by Memorial Day Weekend because Paul Vercammon and the KEYT news team from Santa Barbara were scheduled to meet us there. The idea of disobeying the authorities was frightening, especially since my children were involved, but soon we would be out of their jurisdiction. Continuing down Interstate 40 felt worth the risk.

A few days later, we came to a bridge over a gully, and on the railing sat a very large, very dejected-looking young man with blond, curly hair. He must have weighed four hundred pounds, but his head was lowered as if the weight of the world rested on his shoulders as well. He wouldn't say where he'd come from or where he was going, but after speaking with him for a few minutes, we asked the young man, William, if he would like to join our company. A smile of gratitude beamed across his face, and he wholeheartedly embraced his new family.

William was told that he would have to walk, just the same as the rest of us, but we'd start him off slow and increase his mileage gradually until he was able to do the full twenty miles a day. He tried hard, but the blisters on his feet didn't make it easy. A lot of the time, we let William drive our advance vehicle - the RV of mine that Jeff, an avid Star Trek fan, had dubbed "The Enterprise."

William's weight proved a hindrance to his walking ability, and we had to give him a lot of encouragement to keep going throughout the day. When his birthday approached, I told him I would bake him a cake if he was able to walk twenty miles in one day. To our delight, he finally did it. It was a vindicating moment for him, not to mention a morale booster for our entire team.

*The Walk (photo by Newsday)*

THE POLITICAL SITUATION IN OKLAHOMA WAS BOTH FASCINATING and disturbing, particularly in regard to the rights of Native American populations. One day, in a small town outside of Oklahoma City, an

Arapaho woman sat down and introduced herself to me. I was shocked to hear how the indigenous population was treated. If a Native American chose to seek employment and live outside of the reservation, they would lose all their federal welfare benefits. That made it very difficult for them to get ahead in greater American society.

Also, in the 1980s, whenever they left the reservation, they were under curfew. Police officers would receive a twenty-dollar bonus in their paychecks for every Native American caught outside after 10 p.m. One night, two members of our Walker group, including one indigenous gentleman, were discovered after curfew and came running toward our encampment with the local police hot on their trail. We quickly stashed them inside the Enterprise where they couldn't be touched, and the disappointed officers had to retreat back to town, thwarted from collecting their bounties.

Meanwhile, the newsletter was finally nearing its completion. I pestered the Walkers until they each gave me a short biography, then finalized the layout and typed out each section on my old portable typewriter. Oklahoma City represented the halfway point of our journey to Washington, D.C., and I desperately wanted the newsletter to be printed out by then.

When it came time to do the advance work in Oklahoma's capital, Bob asked if he could assist me for a change. I suspected he was jealous of Colin Atherton, but I didn't mind; I was happy to show him my strategies for getting the most out of our sojourns in civilization. We drove to the capitol square and found a squadron of bikers chatting with each other. Bob and I started passing out flyers that explained the goals of our Homeless and Poor People's Peace Walk. I was eager to get the media involved, but all Bob wanted to do was visit Salvation Armies and rescue missions in order to solicit free goods for the Walkers. None of those organizations were interested in helping us, however. I quickly grew frustrated at my inability to stop and make phone calls to TV stations and newspapers as I was used to. Bob's sense of priorities was keeping me from doing my job.

Some of the people gathered on the capitol grounds were members of a caravan that sought food and clothing donations they could bring to victims of civil wars in Central America. I told them that we had a surplus of canned and dry goods in our bus kitchen, and we worked out a deal where they'd take the excess off our hands tomorrow in exchange for fifty dollars. It was a good deal all around.

Before leaving the capitol square, I received information about a Jesus House in town that might be able to donate some additional items to our cause. The day was growing late, and I was still annoyed that we'd failed to connect with media and government services. I didn't want to return to the Walkers empty-handed, so I told Bob we had to at least pay the Jesus House a visit.

We followed the directions we'd been given and pulled the RV into the parking lot of a large school that had been converted into a drop-in center and shelter. Two women met us at the door. They accepted our flyers and listened to our situation for a few minutes, then ushered us inside and brought us to a bustling office. Somehow, we had stumbled upon the statewide Homeless Coalition of Oklahoma. They immediately put their resources to work. Their media manager was assigned to convince the local outlets to attend our press conference tomorrow, and community members were contacted so that they could walk into town with us in solidarity. In the space of just a few hours, we had our itinerary all planned out. They even took our newsletter and printed copies for us. *Amazing.*

Bob and I needed to return to the Walkers, but before we left, the Jesus House representative invited our group to stay in their shelter for the duration of our stay in Oklahoma City. It was more wonderful news on top of all their generosity.

The next morning, members of the Homeless Coalition met us on the west side of Oklahoma City and walked with us toward the capitol grounds. We passed by the KEYT news team and I called out to their News Director, Paul Vercammon. He made a *shush* gesture because we were currently being taped, so I averted my eyes and kept walking. It was just exciting to see familiar faces from Santa Barbara again.

The streets in front of the capitol building were filled with throngs of people for Memorial Day Weekend. There happened to be a biker rally happening as well, and before our press conference, I spent time walking among the motorbikes, admiring the various Harleys, Hondas, Triumphs and Yamahas. Thanks to all the visitors, as well as the citizens of Oklahoma City, our press conference was well-attended. All the Walkers spoke, including Sean and Krystal. Soon after the event, however, the winds picked up and the clouds started to turn black. Paul Vercammon mentioned that a storm was coming through, and he hoped it would not be accompanied by tornadoes. Thankfully, the worst-case forecast failed to materialize. While the KEYT news team packed up their gear, we made the food exchange with the Central American Contra supporters and received fifty dollars to add to our coffers, as promised. Then before any rain could spoil our spirits, we headed for Jesus House to rest up for the second half of our cross-country journey.

Ruth Wynne and Betty Adams walked out of the old school building to greet us. Although they were not technically Catholic nuns, they were affectionately referred to as Sister Ruth and Sister Betty by the employees and residents. The two friends had first opened the Jesus House in 1973, using a storefront building at Reno and Walker Avenues and feeding the homeless using whatever resources they could glean from food banks and dumpsters. When the two-story abandoned school was donated to the organization, things really got cranking. Women and children slept on the top floor, while men took the bottom. Residents of the shelter were given jobs to do, and rather than being paid in cash, and volunteers received cigarettes or vouchers for clothes. Some people prepared donated food in the fabulous cafeteria-style kitchen, serving three meals a day with roast beef, potatoes and veggies. Desserts abounded for those with a sweet tooth, and if the Walkers didn't have an important job to do, we could have stayed at the Jesus House forever. Other residents worked in janitorial services, sorted clothes at the donation center or ran the registers at the community thrift store. The Oklahoma City police department kept a small office in the Jesus House, and the presence of a local officer helped instill a sense of order and civility on the premises. I thought that was a magnificent idea, and I didn't detect any inkling of trouble while we were there.

One night during our stay, I lost track of little Krystal. We searched everywhere for her. Finally, I opened the door of one of the porta-potties that had been placed on-site to reduce pressure on the building's plumbing, and there she was, holding a squirming little boy in a bear hug while trying to give him a big, juicy kiss. That was my three-year-old.

In gratitude for everything Sister Ruth and Sister Betty had done for us, we asked them what we could do to repay them. They told us that one of the biggest issues impacting the homeless in Oklahoma was a ruling that said they were not allowed to collect food stamps. The Jesus House had been trying for months to find a workaround, but the way the law had been interpreted, citizens of Oklahoma needed to have a physical address. Thankfully, our group included several well-educated activists, and we told the two women that we would get to work on this sad state of affairs. Food stamps were a federal program and were meant to go out to all native-born and naturalized citizens of the United States if they were below a certain income level. Having a physical address was irrelevant.

The Santa Barbara Walkers were well-versed in street theater, and Colin, Indian Bob and Protest Bob were chosen to lead the charge. The next morning, we drove to the federal building - the same one that would be blown up by domestic terrorist Timothy McVeigh in 1995. I slipped inside to monitor the situation, and our trio of troublemakers began their protest, raising signs and screaming for attention. In short order, they got it. Guards surrounded and questioned them, and after an hour, a government employee came outside to investigate further. The three of them were escorted up to the social services department, and after a short conference, a book of federal guidelines was hauled out and the State of Oklahoma was shown the error of their ways. They agreed that their interpretation of federal laws was wrong and that even people without a physical address should be able to receive food stamps. Our group of misfits had won.

They released us, and we were able to drive back to Jesus House and proudly announce to Ruth and Betty that their residents could start applying for the food stamp program. The Homeless Coalition of Oklahoma was astonished that three people could rewrite state policy in a day. They saw us as heroes. But we simply knew an important truth: sometimes you have to embarrass your leaders in order to effect change in your community.

~

WHEN IT CAME TIME TO FINALLY LEAVE OKLAHOMA CITY, SISTERS Ruth and Betty presented us with two large bags of dog food, plus cartons of cigarettes and other essentials they thought we would need on our trek. We loaded up the support vehicles, and right when we were about to crank up the engines, I saw something that made my heart sink a little. Shuffling toward us, suitcase in hand, was one of the most miserable specimens of the human species that I'd ever seen. He was tall and lanky with a giant nose that gave the impression that he was a product of inbreeding or an actor from the movie "Deliverance". I hoped he wasn't planning on coming with us, but unfortunately, that was his desire, and we had a policy that we'd take on anyone who wanted to join our cross-country adventure. I knew he would cause some trouble on the Walk, and unfortunately, I was right. Noel was not that bright, and he sashayed as he walked, which elicited jeers from the rest of the gang, including my son Sean. But that day, we threw Noel's suitcase into the RV and welcomed him aboard.

It was hard to say goodbye to the capital, but we headed onward to Tulsa, the second biggest city in Oklahoma. The Walkers set up their usual appointment with the stab labs so they could exchange their plasma for alcohol. It was a disruptive cycle, but it did force everyone to get a physical on a regular basis, and keeping track of our members' health was a real benefit. Most of the men would drink themselves silly in the cities, leaving me and the few remaining sober individuals to handle interviews with reporters. I'd use the money to buy a carton of tailor-made cigarettes and something nice for Sean and Krystal.

I wished the men would use their money on footwear because the condition of their shoes was deplorable. At this point, most of them were walking on stubs. Thankfully, Tulsa had a shoe factory that donated two pairs of tennis shoes to each Walker. Tulsa's generosity had come in the nick of time. Newly outfitted, we marched onward to Missouri.

*"The Imagine" in Miami, Oklahoma (photo by Miami News-Record)*

~

AS WE NEARED THE MISSOURI BORDER, WE DISCOVERED THAT THE I-44 was about to become a toll road for a stretch, and pedestrian traffic was not permitted on that section. To avoid the tollbooth and police interference, we detoured onto side roads through the southeast corner of Kansas for a brief distance. It took about twenty minutes for us to pass between the "Welcome to Kansas" and "You Are Now Leaving Kansas" signs, which we all found extremely amusing.

Soon after we entered the state of Missouri, however, Bob left the Walk.

He and another Walker wanted to check out the "Russian and American Peace Walk" - another grandiose outreach effort that was taking place concurrently with our own cross-country journey. The purpose of their walk was to foster a climate of trust between the citizens of both nations. They also wanted to educate people about how many billions of American dollars and Soviet rubles were being spent on mutual annihilation rather than for the betterment of our societies. This second group of walkers was not following our same route, so Bob and his friend loaded some supplies into the school bus support vehicle that we called "The Imagine" and set off on their own adventure to try and find them.

Ultimately, the Peace Walk did lead to a number of positive steps that made it easier to limit stockpiles of war weaponry. But the immediate result when Bob left was that I felt abandoned. And then everything seemed to go wrong.

First, we stopped at a park for lunch and accidentally left Minnie - our tiny mascot Chihuahua - behind when we departed. Further down the road, we made camp, then noticed that the Enterprise had a flat tire. Eve and I decided to hitchhike back to town to see if we could find someone to fix it for us. Being women, we figured we were the most likely people in our group to get a ride.

We were picked up almost immediately. Unfortunately, after getting in touch with a number of tire shops, no one wanted to come help us. It was a split rim job, and those can be dangerous to the mechanic if heavy precautions aren't taken. No one wanted to do it without a cage to protect themselves. Eve and I finally shrugged and decided to walk back to camp. First, however, I wanted to return to the park where we'd had lunch to see if we could find Minnie.

When we arrived, I headed toward a family at a picnic table and asked if they'd seen a little black dog running around. They replied in the affirmative, saying the little creature was last sighted in the direction from which we'd entered the park. Eve and I went running back to the park's edge, calling for Minnie. The weeds were tall along the boundary, and we soon witnessed a tiny, black object jumping through the grass, bounding toward our position. Minnie threw herself into my arms and began licking my face with joy. I was so happy to find her. Eve had tears streaming down her own face and sobbed, "It's just like watching a Disney movie." With the Chihuahua safely in my arms, we continued down the road to our campsite.

Soon after I placed the little dog in Krystal's arms, our camp was visited by an irate gentleman who said we had no business parking on his property. We tried to explain that we'd been told that camping there was acceptable, but he wasn't inclined to be charitable. He called the police.

When an officer arrived on the scene, we showed him our flat tire and said we couldn't leave until it was fixed. At first, the cop told us we'd be arrested if we didn't depart immediately. I walked up to him and argued that it would take forever to incarcerate us. He'd have to get CPS involved because of the children and Animal Control involved because of our pets. "Besides," I reasoned, "I thought police officers were supposed to help people in trouble, not threaten them."

He looked at me warily and asked, "Do you have any money to get this tire fixed?" I assured him that we certainly did. So he went back to his vehicle and radioed headquarters. They made a phone call and dispatched a mechanic who was able to fix the tire without a cage for just forty dollars. The officer then escorted us to a campsite where we would be safe from harassment. I was relieved, but the feeling of missing Bob weighed heavily upon me.

Since we now had a viable place to camp, our group made the decision to pause for a few days and rest up. After learning from locals about the many caves in the area, we decided to find a company that would give us a tour of the underground terrain. We were reasonably close to the Meramec Cave System outside of Stanton, so we withdrew some money from the kitty and headed there. It was the largest tourist attraction in the State of Missouri. Once used as a hideout for Jesse James, the large cavern was also appropriated as background scenery for the Batman television show. The tour was fascinating, and when our guide turned off the artificial lights, we truly understood the concept of darkness. It was one of the highlights of our walk across the U.S.A.

After four days, we finally packed up our camp and returned to the I-44. Bob had not yet returned, and it would be easiest for him to look for us along the Interstate. That night, we were just settling into a new location when a white Cadillac pulled up to our campsite. A man got out and told us that the media in Jefferson City, Missouri wanted to arrange an interview. They'd been following us on CNN - a news outlet that I called periodically so that they could keep track of our progress. The stranger wanted to drive a representative of our group to a local watering hole so they could talk with the Jefferson City media over the phone. I volunteered to go with the man.

After making sure my kids were looked after, I got in the Cadillac, and soon we were racing down back roads through the dark forests of the Ozark Plateau. After a time, I grew slightly nervous, not having been told that the phone would be located twelve miles away in the middle of nowhere. So to keep tensions low, I chatted with this Southern gentleman about the Walk and answered all his questions.

Thankfully, the ride was legitimate. We pulled up to a bar, and the man ran inside and told the owner to call up the Jefferson City news team. I got on the phone and gave the interviewer an audio version of our usual press release. When he asked why we weren't walking through Missouri's capital, I apologized and explained that we had to stay on a route that had been mapped out for us. We had adjusted our route so we could travel northeast to New York City where the National Coalition for the Homeless was waiting for us. Also, Bob was planning to catch up with us somewhere along Interstate 44. To satisfy their desire for video footage, I invited the Jefferson City newscasters to meet us on the I-44 the next day.

The following morning, I awoke to find we had a slow leak in another tire. Plus it was raining. At least the rain was warm, so we decided to start the day's route a little early. The Enterprise would drive ahead into the next town and find a gas station that could plug the tire while the rest of the group proceeded on foot.

Little did we know that the light rain would become a downpour. We had no jackets or raincoats to protect us from the deluge, so when the Jefferson City media found us along the highway, we were soaked and shivering. They turned on their cameras and interviewed us anyway. I sensed that we impressed them with our stamina, which had remained strong despite everything that nature was throwing at us. We could have loaded everyone up in the support vehicle, had it been available, but we were obligated to walk every step of the cross-country journey. No cheating.

When we arrived at a highway rest area, Eve and I staggered into the women's restroom and shook ourselves dry. It was a good thing that we'd done so much walking over the last few months because less healthy people might have succumbed to hypothermia. The rest area janitorial employees kindly gave us a box of plastic garbage bags, which we fashioned into raincoats. They weren't perfect, but at least they helped us retain more of our body heat.

Our next stop was the city of Rolla. Once the Enterprise returned with its freshly-patched tire, I climbed aboard with my children and headed into town. The Walkers would arrive at the edge of the city in less than forty-five minutes, so I didn't have much time to get the advance work done. First, I drove up to the police station with a flyer in hand and gave my spiel. The cops went to work immediately on our behalf. They set us up with a dorm at Columbia University so that we'd have beds, showers and access to a cafeteria for food. Krystal and Sean's eyes bulged when they saw the buffet line. The rest of us were simply floored by the generosity of the community. We were interviewed by the local media and felt incredibly well-rested by the time we returned to the interstate.

*Indian Bob (Robert Duncan), dumpster diving for McDonald's hamburgers in Rollo, Missouri (photo by Newsday)*

Bobby finally came back. He had missed our grand reception in Rolla, but at least he was able to witness the grand sight of the Gateway Arch in the city of St. Louis. The six-hundred-and-thirty-foot arch was built in 1960 to honor the exploits of the explorers Lewis and Clark, and it remains both the world's tallest arch and the tallest human-made monument in the Western Hemisphere.

The city gave us permission to station our vehicles and sleep in the park directly below the arch. Some of the more creative Walkers scavenged cardboard boxes from the local dumpsters. They cut them into squares two feet across, drew letters on them and set them on the lawn facing the monument. When their task was finished, I took my kids on a ride to the top of the arch. We walked to the window of the observation room, and when I looked down, I squealed with joy. Excitedly, I called for everyone else in the room to look down. There, spelled out on the lawn far below us was our rallying cry, "HOUSE THE HOMELESS!"

Not a bad way to commemorate our travels through the Western States before we crossed the Mississippi and officially entered the East.

## 13

## IN THE BIG CITY

Beyond the Illinois border, we started to learn about the plight of the farmers. Due to the severe drought in 1988, wheat and corn crops were failing across the state. Farmers were unable to provide for themselves, but their vulnerability gave them a degree of empathy for our situation and what we were fighting for. We sat down with several of them and shared our experiences. Many farmers lamented the end of their way of life, and the fragility of the American Dream mythos gave us common ground. We had our housing issues, and they had their drought issues, but they both touched upon one thing - the vulnerability of the human experience in the face of the seeming ambivalence of the United States government.

One day, as we were walking past a farm, a woman ran up to our entourage, breathless and frantic. She quickly explained that her son and husband had climbed inside a tank to clean it out, but they both succumbed to the methane fumes that remained inside the vessel. Bob and Jeff rushed over to her property and were led to an eight-foot-high metal tank with an opening on top like a manhole cover. Apparently, it was meant to hold the hydrogen chloride that would be mixed with water to enrich the soil periodically. A ladder bolted to the side of the tank led from the opening down into the dark interior. I don't know what had possessed the farmers to climb down there without breathing protection, but for whatever reason, they were now in a heap of trouble.

Jeff tied a rope around his middle for safety and wrapped a scarf around his nose and mouth. Then he descended the ladder into the tank. Both the farmer and his son lay comatose on the floor, so he untied his rope and secured the father with it. Bob hauled on the rope, and with Jeff's help, they managed to extricate the man from the metal chamber. The rope was lowered a second time, and the sixteen-year-old boy was pulled up next.

After Jeff climbed back up the ladder, he and Bob noticed the victims beginning to stir. They survived, but if the wife had waited for the fire department to arrive, she very likely would have lost her family.

By the time the fire trucks got there, Bob and Jeff had already said their goodbyes and were working to catch up to the rest of the Walkers. The pair of them hadn't waited around to receive any more praise. The fact that they'd managed to save two lives that day was reward enough.

Our journey through Illinois wasn't punctuated with too many positive moments like that one. For the most part, the miles felt endless and the novelty of walking alongside a highway had long since worn off. Still, we kept a consistent pace of around twenty miles a day, although in one instance, we walked a full thirty-two miles to reach a particular campsite. I wished I had an oil can to lubricate my joints after that endeavor.

In one small city, an incident came up that smacked of veiled racism. A group of cops suddenly appeared as we were walking, rushed up to Alfred Lee, an African-American gentleman, handcuffed him and threw him in a vehicle. We had no idea why this was happening. Alfred was a sweetheart. As the cop car drove off, one of the officers explained that earlier that day, a woman was approached by a black man selling a boxed and sealed DVD player. The box looked intact, so she paid for it and took it home, only to find it had a brick inside. She called the police, who went searching for suspects. Poor Alfred, because of his dark pigmentation, was an easy mark.

We went down to the police station to vouch for our fellow Walker because he had been with us the entire day. Thankfully, the cops released him to us. It was a sad incident, but at least the consequences were not more severe than that.

When we reached Springfield, Bob and I paid a trip to a farm that his former wife Barbara had inherited. During the time they'd been married, the two of them had raised rabbits on the property and had even owned a Shetland pony. After three years of working the one-acre farm, however, they moved back to the West Coast to take care of Barbara's mother, and the land was finally sold. The visit brought forth heavy feelings in my partner, and he seemed relieved when we finally left and rejoined our companions.

Along our route through Illinois, we kept our eyes open for creeks and rivers where we could hydrate, clean our bodies and, because it was midsummer, indulge in a refreshing swim. One morning, after walking ten miles, we pulled over along the side of the highway where it crossed a stream. I took a quick dip in the water, then returned to the vehicles to watch over Krystal, who was now almost four years old and napping in the back of The Imagine.

I was preparing some food for the other swimmers when I heard a knock on the door of the schoolbus. A well-dressed gentleman stood outside, and I greeted him cordially before asking his business. It turned out he had seen the carts and vehicles and was curious about our efforts. I handed him an informational flyer and answered his questions, and the more I explained, the more excited the man grew about our Homeless and Poor People's Peace Walk. He was a minister at a church in Indianapolis and said it would be wonderful if we could speak to his congregation. He would even run a fundraising campaign in exchange for our stories. I thought that was marvelous. We'd give him a call once we reached the Indiana border and found a payphone.

After the minister left, I continued making lunch, finishing just as the ravenous Walkers were returning from the waters below the bridge. They gobbled down everything I could give them, and then we hit the road once more.

~

AFTER CROSSING INTO THE STATE OF INDIANA, OUR FIRST LARGE CITY was Terre Haute. I preferred the smaller towns where it was easy to do the advance work. Government agencies and charity organizations were easier to find when there wasn't a maze of streets to negotiate. First, I would head straight to the police station and let them know we weren't there to cause disruptions to their community or any sort of trouble. I'd notify the media in case they could be persuaded to cover our story. More often than not, they showed interest in our cause and would even help encourage the townsfolk to visit us wherever we stopped or made camp.

My attitude toward the people of this country changed a lot over the course of a few thousand miles. I had started out on the Walk thinking that everyone hated the homeless. But so far on our journey, I'd found that the majority of the population were kind, generous and similarly worried about homelessness and the lack of affordable housing. Of course, there were usually a few brats in every community who would call us names and shout, "Get a job!" That was a joke. Not a single one of those people could have done what we were doing, walking all the way across the United States to bring the homeless issue into focus during an election year. We *had* a job... a really good one.

A couple days from Terre Haute, we awoke to a terrible realization. Colin Atherton had stolen the kitty and disappeared. Three hundred and fifty dollars was gone. Indian Bob, who was in charge of the kitty, had tucked the remaining fifty dollars into his wallet, so at least we had enough gas money to make it to Terre Haute. After we arrived in the city, however, we didn't know what we would do.

We were devastated. Colin had been one of the main organizers of the Walk, and we didn't know what could have possessed him to sneak into the Imagine bus and steal from his fellow Walkers. He hadn't been feuding with anyone. Perhaps it had happened because we were conveniently close to Florida, where Colin had some roots, and he'd seized the opportunity to pursue some personal objective down in the Sunshine State. Regardless, we still missed the guy, and not simply because he always made a pot of cowboy coffee for the group first thing in the morning. He'd put coffee grounds straight into a pot of water and boil it for a bit. The grounds would remain on top, but by adding a bit of cold water, they'd sink to the bottom and then you could ladle yourself a mug of bitter coffee without any trouble. It helped all the Walkers get going in the morning. I would motivate them further by driving two miles up the road with the bus and setting up a table with water, juices, sliced oranges and more coffee. That had been our daily routine, *but now*...

A little heartbroken, we shouldered on and limped into Terre Haute. I knew we would have to stay at the local homeless shelter to try and recoup our losses. After getting the group settled, I called the media, and they came to do a story on us. One fortunate result is that a woman came to visit our group at the shelter and presented me with a check for fifty dollars. She said that God had told her to give it to us. Many miracles occurred on our walk across the country similar to that one. I could only deduce that we were meant to make it to our destination.

During our stay at the shelter, the guys learned that the facility needed a ditch dug so that they could replace their sewer lines. Immediately, they grabbed a bunch of shovels and excavated a ditch for our new friends. It was fun to help people like that and it gave the Walk a secondary reason for being.

I called up the minister in Indianapolis and told him we'd made it to Terre Haute. He admonished me at first, saying that I hadn't given him much time to put together a proper fundraiser, but after I explained that the stealing of our kitty had pushed us into survival mode, he understood and said that he'd see what he could do.

Before leaving the shelter, our group also took care of some painting and plumbing. Protest Bob's experience as a handyman came to good use, and the shelter employees were extremely grateful that we stayed for as long as we did. The media continued their coverage of our efforts, and all that positive exposure paid dividends down the line. On the way to Indianapolis, people would pull over in their vehicles and press five or twenty dollars into our hands. I had to believe it was a result of local news organizations being sympathetic to our cause.

We kept up the aluminum can collecting regardless of how big our kitty grew. It provided us with gas and food money, which supplemented what we received in food stamps. Whenever we crossed a state line, we'd apply for food stamps again and replenish our supplies. I would receive about two hundred and thirty dollars because of my two children, and I would always take them into grocery stores so that they could pick out something that they desired for themselves. I didn't want them to think that stealing was an option. Colin had set a bad example, and we didn't need anyone following in his footsteps.

We arrived in Indianapolis and found our way to our friend's church parking lot. To our amazement, the minister had organized a potluck dinner for us with the help of his congregation. They seemed to enjoy breaking bread with us, and afterward, we sat down and told them stories of our adventures. We answered dozens of questions and emphasized how important our mission was.

The message was well-received. By the time our audience dispersed, we had seven hundred dollars in the tip jar. *Ha!* Too bad Colin hadn't waited to steal the cash box until after we'd finished hobnobbing with the church folk in Indianapolis.

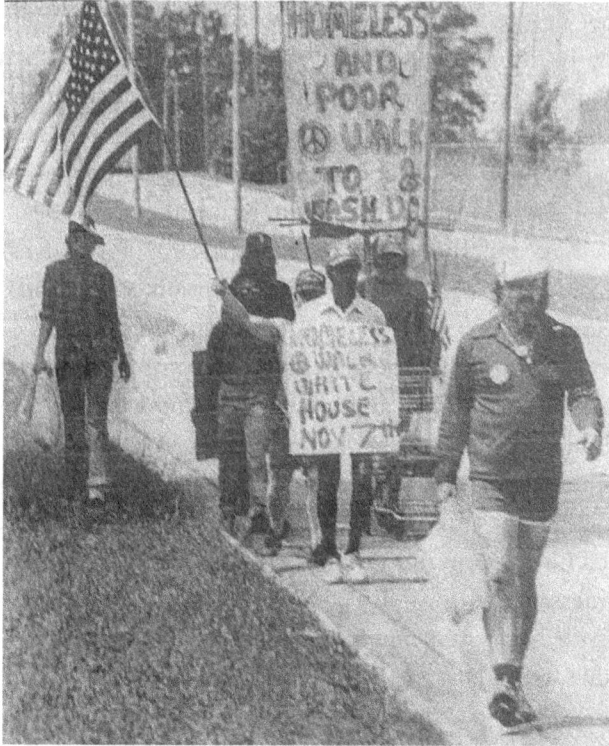

*Bob Hansen in Richmond, Indiana (photo by Jeff Bond of the Palladium-Item)*

∼

NOT LONG AFTER PASSING THE BORDER BETWEEN INDIANA AND Ohio, we glimpsed a rest stop up the road and decided to use the facilities for an extended break. We parked, and I lowered the kitchen table connected to the side of the bus so I could begin preparing dinner: meatloaf with mashed potatoes and veggies. It was my birthday, and I wanted a better meal than our usual. Tonight, the Walkers would feast.

As I peeled potatoes, the guys went rummaging through the trash, looking for aluminum cans. Everything was going smoothly until, all of a sudden, our vehicles were surrounded by deputies from the local sheriff's office. They were bullish and rude, demanding that we pack up and leave at once. Maybe they simply didn't like our looks, but it made me angry. That was no way to communicate with people.

I walked up to one of the deputies, gave him a flyer and explained our mission.

He wasn't impressed. "We want you off this property now!" he bellowed.

I struggled to keep my temper as I turned to Jeff. "Call CNN News," I told him. Then I informed the cops that we were supported by national media, who would be here shortly to document their harassment.

As we waited for Jeff to return, more arguments came into my mind. These cops were out of their jurisdiction. The rest area was a state facility, and they worked for the county. So I let them know that in order to move us, they'd have to call the state troopers. They argued vehemently with me, saying that they were perfectly capable of patrolling this facility, but we held our ground, knowing we were in the right.

Meanwhile, Dan Rather's office was getting an earful from Jeff about our predicament. We knew we had the power of the media behind us, and we weren't afraid to use it when necessary.

The standoff lasted until state troopers finally arrived. They weren't mean to us like the sheriff's deputies. Instead, they politely asked us to go, explaining that the workers who ran the rest area were upset because we'd scavenged the aluminum cans that they normally claimed for themselves. It appeared we had disrupted the natural order of things around here.

So, we packed up and restarted the support vehicles. My birthday dinner was ruined, but I didn't much care. I hoisted the American flag as I prepared to walk, and I taunted the cops, saying, "What do you expect from people who gunned down their own children?" - a reference to the Ohio National Guard who participated in the Kent State Massacre in 1970. I couldn't help myself. We strode out of there singing, *"And crown thy good with brotherhood from sea to shining sea."*

~

THE WALKERS MARCHED ON FOR SEVERAL MORE WEEKS ACROSS THE length of Ohio, past fields of corn wilted by the ongoing drought.

When we took breaks at the highway rest areas, we refrained from raiding the trash bins for aluminum cans so the deputies wouldn't give us any more trouble. One day, a distinctive individual approached us while we were hydrating in the shade. He was tall and lanky with alligator boots and a broad stetson hat, and despite his tough demeanor, the man still had a good air about him. Deciding we were interesting enough to have a conversation with, he sat down and asked us a number of questions about our backgrounds and our mission. Then he proceeded to tell us about himself.

Our visitor alleged that was a retired CIA agent for the United States government. After he'd given up his badge, he'd purchased a seven-acre farm with the intention of settling down and taking care of a few animals. "You want to know who killed John Fitzgerald Kennedy?" he asked. Of course, we did, and the man revealed that it was President Johnson who issued the orders. Something to do with a Texas oil deal. I supposed it could have happened that way, but one never knows who to believe with these conspiracy theories.

The guy must have been eager for human companionship, for he invited us up to his ranch. We were open to hanging out with a cowboy for a spell, so we followed him back to his property and were quickly introduced to his small menagerie. He showed us his six-month-old bull calf and bragged about how dangerous the creature could be if anyone set foot in the field he was grazing in. I made sure to keep an eye on Krystal in case she tried to make a new friend.

The self-described former agent also owned a blue-and-gold-feathered macaw named Alex who had a vocabulary of around two hundred and fifty words. The bird would carry on a conversation with any of us who paid him the slightest bit of attention. In another pen was a herd of pigs, while several sheep had free rein over the rest of the farm. For a retired government employee, this piece of land probably felt like heaven on earth, if a bit lonely at times.

On the third day of our visit, the cowboy decided that Bob needed to lose the hippy look. With Bob's permission, he cut the protester's long hair and shaved off his beard. The next time Bob tried to pick up Krystal, the little girl screamed. She didn't recognize her father after such a drastic makeover.

The rest of the Walkers complained about the conservative attitudes of our host, so we finally decided it was best to get back on the
road. We thanked our benefactor and continued east toward the city of
Columbus. The local police still harassed us occasionally, but Jeff the
cartoonist had become our secret weapon. He'd drawn pictures of
everything we experienced along our journey, so when the cops started
poking their noses into our business, Jeff would pull out his book of
cartoons and entertain them with anecdotes from our adventures. By
the time the cops looked up from the pages, the rest of the Walkers
would be down the road and out of sight. "I think we've been had," one
of them might remark. But Jeff always managed to catch up to the
Walk without too much trouble.

In the capital city of Columbus, we parked our vehicles in the
parking of the homeless shelter, and the men slept inside. Women and
children were not allowed, but I didn't mind. I liked sleeping in the RV
with my children, especially when the men weren't around to create a
ruckus.

To our good fortune, the city was putting on a free laser light show
in a downtown park that evening, so some of the guys made plans to
see it. Sean wanted to go, and the men promised me that they'd take
good care of him. I wish that had been the case. Unfortunately, the
Walkers purchased alcohol and gave some of it to the thirteen-year-old
boy, who stumbled and fell down the bleachers during the show. They
retreated to an alleyway after the show to continue their drinking, and
that was where the police found them. After some interrogation, the
cops learned the men were part of the Walk for homeless rights. They
put Sean in their car and brought him back to me at the shelter, where
I tucked him into bed so he could sleep off his condition. I was so
angry at the rest of the Walkers that it was hard to fall back asleep
myself.

The next morning, while we were preparing to depart the shelter, I
discovered that Sean had broken his elbow when he fell down the
bleachers. I told the rest of the Walkers to go ahead while I drove my
son to the children's hospital. The nurses treated Sean's elbow and put
it in a cast. Since I didn't have insurance or any money on hand, I tried
to explain my situation with a flyer, and the hospital employee told me

they'd mail a bill to my post office box. For some reason, it never arrived.

We drove back to rejoin the group, and Sean showed off his cast. He was required to keep it on for six weeks. Everyone wrote their names on it with special messages, some of which were compassionate and others too crude to mention.

The incident served to remind me of our fragility - a condition that extended to our pets as well. My dog Schatzie was getting on in years, and she was diagnosed with stomach cancer just before the Walk began. I didn't expect her to live through the journey from coast to coast, but somehow, she kept going.

One time we accidentally left Schatzie behind during a lunch break, just like we had left Minnie. Once we realized what had happened, Bob told me to get into the support vehicle and we raced back to our lunch spot. Unfortunately, Schatzie was nowhere to be found. Bob recognized how upset I was and refused to give up. We drove back and forth along that stretch of highway until we finally spotted her. The dog had been following the Walkers' footsteps, trying to reunite with her family.

Bob pulled up alongside my canine companion and we lifted her onto the bus. Schatzie climbed into my lap and let out a long sigh, while I cried tears of relief. It must have been bewildering for the animal to have been left behind. She was my protector and my rock, and the Walk would not have been the same without her.

～

THROUGH THE ROLLING HILLS OF WESTERN PENNSYLVANIA, WE marched onward. Most afternoons, I would park the bus a couple of miles ahead of the Walkers so I could start dinner and have it ready by the time the group arrived. One time, a carload of young men stopped to chat. I asked if they were "hillbillies".

"Yep!" they said, laughing.

I told them they were welcome to hang out and have a bite to eat, and they accepted. Not long after, a local reporter dropped in to conduct an interview with me. I excused myself from my guests and answered the reporter's questions while I made sandwiches and cut up some fresh fruit. I considered us Walkers to be athletes, and potassium was a necessary part of our diet.

When the article came out in the local paper, I felt vindicated. After interviewing several other Walkers, it was the reporter's opinion that the Walk would never have succeeded if not for me acting as the group's nurse, cook and disciplinarian. The guys never made me feel that way, however. There were so many moments along the journey when I wanted to quit and take my kids back to Santa Barbara. I was the only member of the female species most of the time, which felt incredibly lonely. I cried often, just out of sheer exhaustion.

On days when I came back to the group after finishing some difficult advance work, I'd hold a meeting that the others derisively termed "Toilet Paper Nancy Time" because they would interrupt my briefings by threatening to throw toilet paper at me. They also questioned and nitpicked every detail of the itineraries I set up with the media and townsfolk in each community. Mostly, my arguments won out because the Walkers knew these arrangements were necessary for us to gain the resources we needed to continue down the road. But their stubbornness and lack of gratitude wore me down.

One time, I became so dehydrated that I got a bladder infection. A Salvation Army office referred me to a clinic, where I received antibiotics and a stern warning from a doctor telling me to drink more water. The infection took a while to clear from my system, and when I sat down to urinate, I screamed in agonizing pain. The guys stood outside my bathroom window grinning and joking that the sounds I made were, in fact, orgasms. With crude innuendo like that hitting me every day, I wished more than anything that another woman would join up with the Walk.

When we neared the city of Pittsburgh, I handled the usual advance work. I informed the police department and media, setting up the best route for us to travel through the downtown corridor to our designated campsite. But back at camp, the men had other ideas. They held a meeting, led by Indian Bob and Protest Bob, and decided they would ignore my itinerary, whatever it turned out to be, and go their own route. *Bless the male species,* I thought bitterly when I returned and heard about their plans. *How dumb do you have to be?*

I gave several arguments as to why they should stick to the route I'd outlined, but nothing worked. I couldn't fathom their reasons. Why would they send me into the cities ahead of them, only to give me a hard time after I'd set everything up? Perhaps some of them were envious that I got to spend a day driving instead of walking the pavement with the rest of the Walkers. *Ridiculous.* It was simply work that had to be done, and it made diplomatic sense to have the requests made by a sympathetic, motherly figure. I felt dreadfully embarrassed for giving information to the media and the police that would end up being false, but I had to throw up my hands and let the guys deal with their mess. They would find out how bad their plan was soon enough.

Indian Bob proved to be the chief instigator, and the next day he took it upon himself to lead the Walkers into the city. The representatives from the media were beside themselves because we had set up our original route together, and they had to scramble to find us. When they came up to me for an explanation, I simply pointed them toward Indian Bob, who seemed to be holding a grudge against me for some unknown reason. None of the townspeople came to visit us, nor did we receive donations of any kind. The city of Pittsburgh was dead to us. All we could do was walk onward and exit the metropolis with the hope of getting a stronger reception in the next town. The men who plotted against me were suitably chagrined, and for the rest of the journey, I had no further problems with arrogant asses wanting to destroy the careful advance work that I did for the group.

~

AS WE PROGRESSED THROUGH THE WESTERN AND CENTRAL PARTS OF the state, we witnessed a great deal of poverty. The coal mines were shutting down and jobs were hard to come by. Cities were struggling with homeless populations and police were chasing them out of business districts and arresting them for vagrancy, just as they did in Santa

Barbara. Some evenings, Bob and I would stroll out of camp and explore the nearby neighborhoods, and one night, we found a little tavern. We walked through the front door, approached the bar and saw that they were serving beer on tap for only ten cents apiece. *Incredible!* We took advantage, sitting down with the locals so we could hear a little bit about their lives.

The general sentiment was a deep sadness about the lack of work and the food insecurity that went along with it. This was nothing new for Bob and I. We knew poverty. However, the tavern owner had lowered his prices for these folks, doing what he could to help. I came away believing that Pennsylvania had a sense of charity and compassion that few states possessed. They were truly looking out for one another.

After several days without drama, the ever-obstinate Indian Bob decided to put up one more fight. He wanted the Walk to veer southeast straight to Washington, D.C. rather than continue eastward toward New York City, arguing that the trip to the Big Apple was unnecessary. I had already made arrangements to meet up with the National Coalition for the Homeless, which was based in Manhattan and was in the midst of a multi-day protest on the steps of City Hall. They were expecting us. The plan for Washington D.C. was to get there in time for Mitch Snyder's "Housing Now" rally, and I countered that we'd be bored and restless if we arrived too early.

Indian Bob likely had hurt feelings after the Pittsburgh debacle and wanted to finish the Walk sooner than we were supposed to. Thankfully, I managed to sway the other Walkers to my side and got them to commit to finishing the itinerary as we originally intended. Indian Bob stood down, and the caravan resumed its journey down the highway.

Our route turned northeast toward the capital of Harrisburg which drew power from the Three Mile Island Nuclear Generating Station, located twelve miles south of the city. Built in 1974, the station suffered a partial meltdown on March 28th of 1979 - the most serious accident in United States commercial nuclear power plant operating history. Studies concluded that the people in the surrounding townships suffered no adverse effects from the release of radioactive gases and radioactive iodine into the environment. But many locals told a different story... one of health ailments and diseases that were ongoing and devastating. Regardless, the event struck such fear into the hearts of Americans regarding nuclear power that the industry never completely recovered.

To help me do the advance work in Harrisburg, I selected David Gary, a truck driver from Missouri with an addiction to strong coffee. After having suffered so much criticism over the months when I went unsupervised, I decided that having a male representative would appease the chauvinist majority among the Walkers and save me a lot of grief.

My unofficial chaperone and I dropped off a flyer at the police department, then headed to the chamber of commerce. We told them of our cause and of our basic needs, and the ladies in the office suggested that we rest up for two days on City Island. This site was located across the Market Bridge in the middle of the Susquehanna River. It was in the center of the downtown district and would be a good place for the media to wait for us so that they could capture footage of the Walkers crossing the bridge. David and I were thrilled at having secured these amenities, and as we headed back to our group, I knew I wouldn't have any trouble with the two Bobs ever again.

Krystal and Sean proved to be a hit with the media. My son told the reporters that in 1987, at the end of a protest march we'd done from Santa Barbara to the gates of Ronald Reagan's ranch, the sheriff's deputies informed us that in order to see the president, we would have to go to Washington, D.C. One year later, we were doing just that, and Sean said he would hopefully get to see President Reagan when he got there. Krystal was the cutest four-year-old, and the media loved asking her for her perspective on our cross-country adventures.

*Bob and Krystal on the bus in Harrisburg, Pennsylvania (photo by
Bob Levy of the Patriot-News)*

Unfortunately, the other Walkers traded their blood plasma for
cash and purchased gallons of alcohol so they could get well and truly
drunk. They pitched a tent over a picnic table and called it their
M.A.S.H. tent, like the television show. After a few hours of undisturbed drinking, none of them were in any condition to speak to
anyone.

I was enamored of the people of Harrisburg, as many of them came
to visit us during our stay on City Island and they seemed genuinely
interested in our cause. But our departure date arrived soon enough,
and we headed east toward Philadelphia.

The state troopers that we met along the way were fantastic. They
invited us to stay on a piece of property that they owned inside the
Philadelphia city limits, and we asked for a week's time so that we
could repair our support vehicles. My RV had a tire with a hole in the

tread that was the size of a fifty-cent piece, and the only thing keeping it together was the tube.

After we made camp, I tried to convince the two Bobs that my brakes were scraping, but they wouldn't believe me, which was infuriating. They made me drive back and forth through our campsite so that they could listen to the scraping sounds, and they claimed not to hear them, even though I could. The vehicle needed new shoes before the damage required us to buy new drums. Still, they refused to take my word, and I started to cry. Frustrated beyond belief, I got out of the RV, found a belt and began smacking the side of the RV until I depleted my pent-up energy. Then I walked up to those idiots and told them the Enterprise would not be going anywhere until she got some new brake shoes.

Perhaps it was due to the fury with which I wielded that belt, but I finally got my way. The RV received new brakes and a new tire to replace the deteriorated one. Now she stood a chance of making it to Washington, D.C. without failing or hurting anyone.

The media visited our campsite to do interviews, and once the stories made it onto the airwaves, the crowds started arriving. One visitor brought a ham dinner to share with us. Another night, it was spaghetti. One guy pulled up in a truck and told me his wife had sent him to deliver some toiletries to the female Walker. A large box of Tampax was among the items, and I nearly broke down in tears. All this time, I'd been forced out of financial necessity to use toilet paper to stem the flow of my menstrual cycles.

Other visitors brought clothes in such quantities that they piled up in a mound... so many that we could not possibly use them all. We had to donate the extra garments to shelters and thrift stores. Philadelphia was truly the City of Brotherly Love. It was a wonderful feeling. The citizens seemed proud of the efforts we were making to bring the homeless situation to the forefront of public consciousness.

I hated to leave our Philadelphia campsite, but somehow I knew we'd be back in the near future. Our route took us northward toward the industrial cities of Allentown and Bethlehem, then we veered east toward the New Jersey border. Just before crossing into the Garden

State, I entered a town to do some advance work and received a weird reception. The people seemed to be walking around like zombies. No one knew where their police department was. Perhaps they had been programmed not to talk to strangers, but the effect of their ambivalence was scary. Some chemical must have been slipped into their water supply. I returned to the Walkers and told them to forget going into that town. It gave me the creeps.

~

SEAN, KRYSTAL AND I WERE WALKING THROUGH AN UPPER-CLASS development past rows of beautiful homes during one afternoon in New Jersey. When we came alongside a particularly beautiful estate with a set-back mansion and well-maintained front lawn, a Doberman Pinscher came rushing across the grass toward us, spittle flying out of his mouth as he barked up a storm. I took a step toward the property, stared right into the belligerent dog's eyes and bellowed out a loud growl - something almost like a roar. Immediately, the Doberman skidded backward onto his butt, took one last look at me and started sprinting in the opposite direction. If his docked tail had been intact, it would have been tucked firmly between his legs. He glanced back a few times to make sure the dangerous human wasn't following him. That took care of *him*.

Sean had been a stalwart walker this entire time... more than a match for any of the adults in the crew. Krystal hiked in short spurts. The longest distance she traveled in one go was four miles, and she was definitely ready for a nap by the time we got back to the support vehicles.

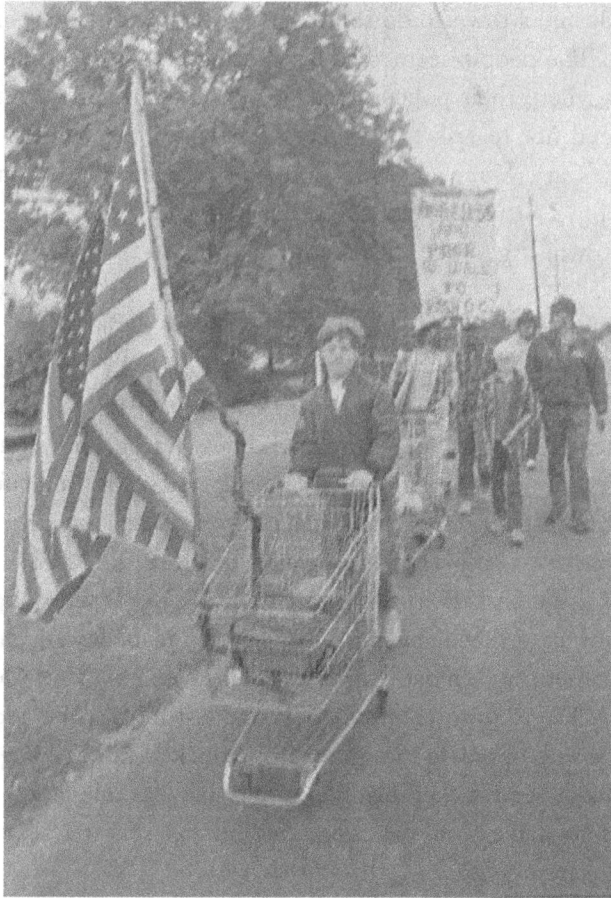

*Jeff Hess, David Gary, Alfred Lee, Sean, Bob Hansen and Indian
Bob in Bridgewater, New Jersey (photo by George Smith)*

Traffic grew increasingly more congested as we approached the terminal for the Staten Island Ferry. It took forty-five minutes to get through the lines and load our people and buses onto the vessel. But the ride through New York Harbor past the Statue of Liberty gave me the chills. I felt immensely proud that our ragtag group had walked across an entire continent and were now able to witness this spectacle in all its glory. The journey east was almost at an end.

We disembarked in Manhattan and proceeded on foot to a park that encircled City Hall. The support vehicles parked alongside the public space in a red zone, hoping that the police would be kind and let us be. Thankfully, they did. The local homeless activists and their supporters from the National Coalition for the Homeless welcomed us into their midst. They'd been protesting for about two weeks by the time we arrived, and they didn't look like they were going anywhere. American flags and hand-crafted signs abounded and were raised into the air whenever politicians entered the City Hall building. Since it was a presidential election year, people felt more motivated than usual to raise their voices and advocate for change.

Michael Stoops, one of the lead organizers of the National Coalition for the Homeless, took our group out for pizza, which felt like an appropriate meal for first-time visitors to New York City. Other than that, we were mostly left to our own devices during the week that we were there. I found a coffee shop across from the park and spent many hours regaling New Yorkers with tales of the Walkers and our misadventures. They needed to hear the stories about our struggles, and a cup of coffee in one's hand is a great leveler; it helped us relate to one another more easily than if we'd simply conversed on the street.

*Joe - a homeless New York resident - and Krystal at City Hall Park, New York City (photo by Newsday/Ozier Muhammad)*

Among the new cast of characters in New York City was a small man of Puerto Rican descent named Pete who was especially inspired by our endeavors and wanted to give us a tour of the metropolis. He showed me how to jump the turnstiles in the subway and make a run for the train so that we didn't have to pay. We rode to Brooklyn and back this way, and I supposed a couple of free rides wouldn't hurt the city. The subway attendants always let it slide.

One day, I decided to take my kids to the top of the Empire State Building. However, once we arrived at the fabled skyscraper, we discovered there was a twelve-dollar fee to use the elevator, and that was too steep for me to afford. Discouraged, we headed back for the Plaza. On the way, we noticed the Disney movie "Cinderella" was playing in a store window, so we stood and watched it for a while. A homeless man approached us and asked for a dollar so he could ride the subway. I turned away from the movie and asked him why he needed money when he could simply jump over the turnstile like the rest of the homeless people did. The panhandler looked at me funny, and I added that I didn't have any cash to give him; I was homeless, just as he was. Surprised, the man proceeded to give me a big, long lecture about being homeless with two children. He said I should be ashamed of myself. I was more amused than angry. Even my fellow homeless people made assumptions about my lifestyle, it seemed.

THE WEEK WENT ON, AND EVERY DAY WITHOUT FAIL, THE protesters lined up along the entrance to City Hall to chant and wave signs at the city representatives as they entered the building. When Mayor Ed Koch arrived for work, they'd yell, "Hi, Eddie!" and he would turn and wave to the crowd. Despite his folksiness, I considered him a typical politician, devoted to what he considered to be more important issues than the well-being of those living on the streets of his city.

I loved being in New York. The buzz of energy never let up, day or night, for it was truly The City That Never Sleeps. After seven days of unending excitement and stimulation, however, it was finally time to head for the United States capital. By now, it was mid-October, and we had three weeks to get to the Housing Now rally, which was scheduled for November 8th. In about two hundred and twenty-five miles, our journey would finally be over.

As we were packing up, an Asian man and his daughter approached us. The father explained that his offspring, Bea, had a hole in her heart, but nonetheless, she wanted to join us on the trek to Washington, D.C. Bea didn't have much time left in the world because of her medical condition; still, she desired to do something with her life that would be both important and memorable. She was a tiny, dark-haired woman in her early thirties and had the sweetest personality, so despite the obvious risks to her health and well-being, no one could tell her no. Her father, who had to work in the city, signed paperwork absolving us of any responsibility should anything happen to his daughter.

Bea was not the only recruit. My friend Eve reunited with the group before we left New York City, and our Puerto Rican friend Pete also decided to become one of the Walkers. He wanted us to call him "Protest Pete", and we readily obliged.

We set off down Route 1 through New Jersey, heading toward Philadelphia and Baltimore. Travel was slow-going this time because Bea was unable to walk at any pace greater than a crawl. She was continuously falling behind. To accommodate, we'd pick her up in one of the support vehicles and drive her a mile or two ahead of the group so that she could move at her own speed. The Walkers would quickly catch up to her, and then we'd move Bea again.

One day in Maryland, we found an abandoned gas station next to a bowling alley and decided to camp there for the night. Bob went off on his own to do some exploring. Sometime later, Bea knocked on the door of the RV and said she was having problems with her heart, but her nitroglycerin was locked up on the bus. It seemed that Bob had locked the vehicle on his way out of camp, and he'd failed to give anyone the keys. *Terrific.*

I brought Bea into the Enterprise and asked her to look after my kids while I went searching for Bob. It was dark outside and I wasn't looking forward to wandering around in a strange town, but Bea's life was potentially at stake. First, I checked the bar in the bowling alley, but there was no sign of Bob there. I headed back outside, looked down the street and saw some blue lights on a building about one-quarter of a mile away. It looked worthy of investigation, so I walked down the road and came to a tavern. Inside, I was shocked to see that the female servers and dancers were not wearing a stitch of clothing. This establishment was a nudie bar, and I was sure Bob had to be lurking around here somewhere.

One of the women came up and asked if I needed any help. I started to tell her that I was looking for my boyfriend so he could return to our campsite and remedy an emergency situation, but then I spotted him. Bob had seen me first and was trying to hide. I supposed he was feeling guilty, and when I strode up to where he was seated, Bob reached out his arm and let out a plaintive *"Help!"* as if he were a captive of his raging hormones. I rolled my eyes and explained that Bea needed her medication fast. He could hand me the keys if he wanted to stay here, and I would watch over the bus until he got back.

For some reason, Bob failed to grasp that this was a medical emergency. Rather than get out of his chair, he asked me to sit down and hold his hand. He wasn't ready to leave quite yet. Too many naked women in his peripheral vision. I relented and sat down for about ten minutes. Then, once again, I told him to give me the keys; he could stay until he was ready to come back. Bob finally let out a mournful sigh and said, "No," then got up and came with me back to camp. Bea got her nitroglycerin and survived to walk another day.

Before we reached Baltimore, Bea became ill with a fever of 104 degrees. We parked on the side of the road so that the Walkers could take a swim in a nearby creek, and I set up a medical tent alongside the Enterprise so that I could attempt to lower Bea's temperature using cool towels and vinegar. I didn't want to give her aspirin since I didn't know what kind of blood thinners she was on, but my administrations didn't seem to be working and I grew increasingly worried.

Just then, a Volkswagen pulled up behind the bus and RV, and two women jumped out. They had heard about us on the news and wanted to talk to me about the Walk. I was a little distracted, so I handed them a flyer and asked them if they knew what to do for a 104-degree fever. One of the women said she was a nurse and was willing to have a look at my patient. I was astounded. It felt like a miracle. Quickly, I ushered her into Bea's tent, and I'm not sure what the nurse did, but once again, Bea started to feel better. I was eternally grateful that help had arrived just when I needed it the most. It was miracles like these that kept our band of misfits perpetually moving forward toward our final destination.

## ❧ 14 ❧

## RALLY AT THE CAPITOL

O n November 7th, 1988, the day before the presidential election, the Walkers finally strode into Washington, D.C. Over nine months had passed since we left Santa Barbara and began our journey across the breadth of America. I had lost a lot of weight over the course of the year - not that I had that much to begin with - but I was so thin now, I looked like a tweaker. More importantly, the dream I had possessed since I was fifteen years old had finally come to pass. We had arrived.

We parked our support vehicles in front of the Federal City Shelter at 425 D Street Northwest. It looked no better than any of the other shelters I'd seen, but its creation was a saga in itself. In 1983, in response to a widening homeless epidemic, President Reagan announced that vacant federal buildings would become available to local governments and charitable organizations to use as emergency shelters. A homeless advocacy group called the Community for Creative Non-Violence, or CCNV for short, secured a one-dollar lease on a former University of D.C. building on D Street, but since the structure had been vacant for some time, it was in severe need of repairs and upgrades. There was no sprinkler system, and there were only four showers for the six to eight hundred people staying each night.

The CCNV and activist Mitch Snyder pushed the government to renovate the building, but the officials they spoke with argued they weren't responsible under the terms of Reagan's 1983 policy. Winter was coming, and Mitch felt that he needed to force the government's hand to start work on winterization before the cold weather set in, so in September of 1984, he began a hunger strike. His demand was that five million dollars in federal money had to be allocated to prepare the shelter for its new purpose. In public, the feds vowed not to respond to such tactics, but as the November 6th election grew closer, they grew worried about the potential for political controversy. They privately urged Mitch to end the strike, worrying that his death could galvanize public opinion against President Reagan on this issue. On November 4th, just two days before the election, the television program "60 Minutes" was set to air a report on the hunger strike, and this motivated the Reagan administration to re-open negotiations. An agreement was made to invest five to ten million dollars into the remodel, and Mitch was rushed to Howard Hospital, where he was informed that President Reagan had personally approved the agreement while on board Air Force One. After fifty-one days without food, his hunger strike officially ended.

Unfortunately, the next year, the administration tried to push the CCNV to accept a three-million-dollar renovation that would turn the building into more of a barracks. Negotiations faltered, and eventually, the General Services Administration announced that the building would be demolished. As the July 10th demolition date grew near, Mitch and the CCNV dug in, vowing to fight eviction even when buses arrived to relocate the residents to another building in an isolated part of the city. Again, the federal government gave in, though it took two more years, two more hunger strikes and a TV movie that featured Martin Sheen portraying Mitch Snyder before the $6.5 million renovations were finally finished.

Mitch himself welcomed us into the building. He was a scraggly, slightly-arrogant individual who never went without his army fatigues in public. Homeless people considered him a hero, and he certainly had a knack for publicity, even if some of it was self-aggrandizing. We held a meeting that night and discussed details for our march to the White House the following morning. A number of people planned to be arrested as part of the Housing Now Rally, and in order to reduce the potential for violence, a representative of the Capitol Police told us at the meeting what to expect if we wanted that outcome. A roped-off area would be created along Pennsylvania Avenue and those who desired arrest could step across the perimeter and be handcuffed. Bail would be set at twenty-five dollars, so protesters were told to have that much cash in their pockets. Between the leftover money in the kitty and some funds distributed by the CCNV, the Walkers had enough bail money to accomplish their goals.

Sean wanted to be arrested, too, but Mitch didn't think it was a good idea for minors to be involved, and I agreed. Besides, someone tipped me off that my old antagonists Peggy and Diane might be attending the rally, and I didn't want to give those witches any excuse to cause trouble. I chose to avoid arrest myself so I could look out for my children, and I put the word out that if the two women came anywhere near us, I would do something to them that I'd likely regret for the rest of my life.

That night, Krystal, Sean and I stayed in the RV instead of the shelter, though it was hard to sleep in anticipation of tomorrow's rally. The event marked the culmination of our epic journey and it was difficult to predict what would happen next. Also, there were signs of drug dealing and other nefarious behavior outside of the former university building, and every time I glanced out the motorhome window, I felt a little on-edge. Although the structure may have been cleaned up, the surrounding neighborhood still bore signs of lawlessness and decline.

The next morning, hundreds of activists gathered outside the shelter. The Election Day procession to the White House was an invigorating climax to our cross-country adventure, and thousands more people met us in Lafayette Square, opposite the glistening presidential mansion. There was a stage where musician Tracy Chapman played to the grateful crowd. Radio personalities like Casey Kasem and Wolfman Jack advocated for affordable housing during breaks in the music, and the gathered citizens chanted, *"Hey, hey, government! The poor pay too much rent!"* and *"Homeless, not helpless!"* Celebrity child pediatrician Dr. Spock took the microphone and declared, "This Reagan Administration, of course, has been cruel. During the last eight years, the health of children has actually gone down for the first time in the 20th century."

*Krystal and Nancy at the Housing Now rally (photo by Washington Post)*

Sean wandered around the park grounds until Mitch Snyder came up to him and asked if he would like to meet Cher. My son was ready and willing. He followed Mitch to a group of secret service agents who'd been hired to protect her, and after introductions were made, Cher invited Sean into her circle of protection. She said he reminded her of her own son, Elijah Blue. The celebrity actress and singer was about to participate in a photo op, walking the remaining distance along Pennsylvania Avenue to a prominent site near the White House, and Sean was told he could join her if he wished. Flanked by bodyguards, Cher took his hand while they chatted and the camera shutters clicked around them. A photo from that moment ended up on the front page of the Washington Post, and Sean refused to wash his hand for several days.

*Sean and Cher at the Housing Now Rally (photo by The Washington Post)*

Meanwhile, Protest Bob and Indian Bob stepped past the barrier set up by the Capitol Police and allowed themselves to be arrested. Along with Dr. Spock and Casey Kasem, they were handcuffed and led into a local gymnasium to be processed. To entertain themselves while sitting on the hardwood floor, they began singing the anthemic Queen song "We Will Rock You" over and over again, stomping their feet and clapping as best they could. I can only assume that it drove the Capitol Police insane.

After the protests and festivities were over, the mania that had sustained my spirits all day turned into a deep depression. I wished that I had my boyfriend to talk to, but Bob had told me that he was going to sleep in the shelter after being arrested and released, and I didn't want to step foot in that facility after nightfall. I holed up in my RV with the children and stewed over our situation while they slept. The chief cause of my funk was that I wanted to be home in Santa Barbara for Christmas but I had no idea how we were going to get there. We had only one hundred and fifty dollars left in the kitty, and those funds wouldn't last long with two gas-guzzling vehicles and numerous mouths to feed. We didn't have time to scrounge the highways for aluminum cans like we did before. The best plan I could come up with was to walk down the street to the Wendy's fast food restaurant and get a temporary job. I'd flip burgers for as many weeks as it took for us to earn enough gas money for the drive home.

Sleep was hard to come by that night. Around 5 a.m., Bob walked out of the shelter, stepped into the motorhome and asked if I would like to get a cup of coffee somewhere. We headed over to Wendy's so we could sit in a booth and ponder over our experiences from the past year. Eventually, Bob looked at me and said, "Let's go home."

"How?" I asked him. "We have exactly one hundred and fifty dollars and two huge vehicles that we can't leave behind."

Bob was unperturbed. "We started this Walk with one hundred and fifty bucks. We'll figure it out." Somehow, despite all the obstacles he'd faced in his life, my boyfriend retained a deep, abiding faith in the universe. It was one of the things I loved about that man. I trusted him, and my depression eased up for a time.

That morning, we gathered all the remaining Walkers around the two support vehicles for a final meeting. With heavy hearts, we told them that the Walk was over. Because of the low amount of funds, only the original organizers who came from Santa Barbara would drive back with us. For those left behind, we had no money to give them, but we agreed to equally share with them all the food stamps we had left. It was a bittersweet moment, but everyone agreed this disband-ment was what had to happen.

The cartoonist Jeff Hess caught a ride to his parents' home in Bettendorf, Iowa. David and Lee went their separate ways. Bea's father came to pick her up and return her to New York City. That left a few stragglers. Protest Pete seemed a bit lost, unsure of where to go next. He, along with a couple of other stowaways, managed to sneak on board the support vehicles and join Indian Bob and the rest of us for the return journey.

That left the ungainly Noel to figure out his fortunes. We secured permission for him to stay at the CCNV shelter and thanked Mitch Snyder for his hospitality. Mitch said that in all his travels, he had never seen a more organized group of homeless people than the Homeless People's Association in Santa Barbara. That meant a lot. With those words in our hearts, we turned our support vehicles around and headed for home.

Mitch was a passionate and troubled man. Two years later, he was visiting Santa Barbara, and I noted how exhausted he looked when he came up and said he needed to return to the shelter in Washington, D.C. I tried giving him a hug, but he felt stiff as a board. "Next time you're here in California," I told him, "you should go on a walk in the redwoods." I could tell the man needed a break from his constant activism. He wouldn't look anyone in the eyes. Something wasn't right.

Not long after, we read the news in the USA Today that Mitch Snyder had hung himself in his bedroom. His monumental efforts to promote homeless rights had not brought him lasting happiness. All the same, Mitch's impact on the homeless community was profound. I can only hope that in some small way, our efforts over nine months in 1988 had an enduring impact that would outlive both Protest Bob and myself.

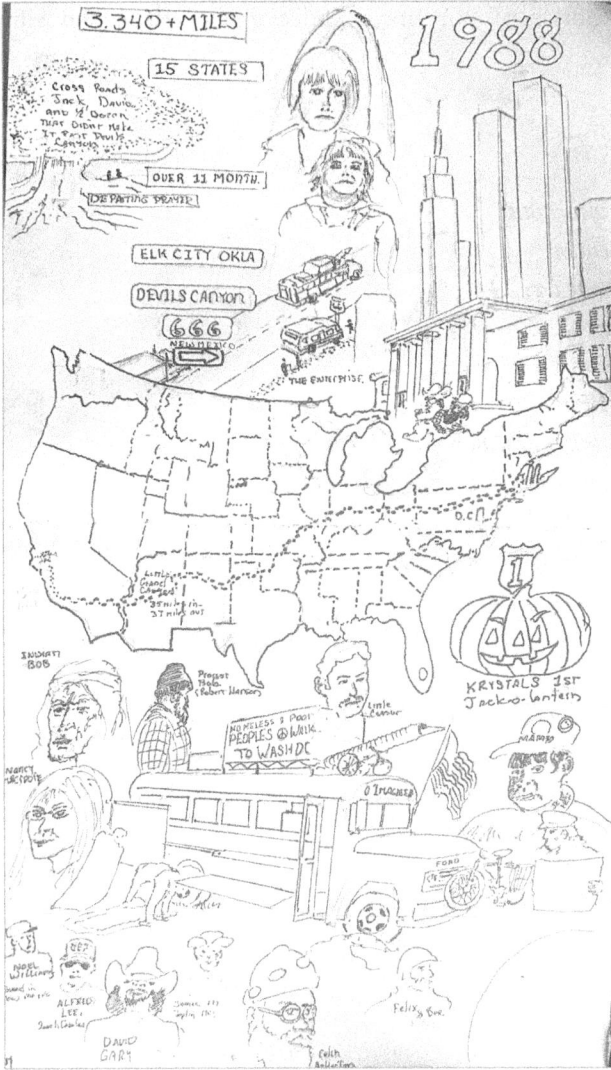

*Drawing by Jeff Hess*

~

PETER MARIN, A WRITER AND FOUNDER OF SANTA BARBARA'S
Committee for Social Justice, accompanied the Walkers for the sixty-
mile segment between Gallup and Grants, New Mexico in March of
1988. When he returned to our hometown, he was inspired to write a

poem in honor of our brave endeavor. It was called simply, *"The Walkers"*.

*No one*
*When we set out*
*Not even we believed*
*We'd make it---*
*Thirteen of us*
*From Santa Barbara.*
*King's Birthday.*
*Clouds low on the horizon.*
*The rainy season beginning*
*Trucks on the highway*
*Step by step down on the road*
*3,000 miles one coast to the other*
*10 months across 2 dozen states.*

*I still remember the feel*
*of the sun on my face*
*The hot nights in the midwest*
*where we bathed at dusk in*
*Farm ponds. I remember the*
*Bridge over the Mississippi*
*The storms in Ohio*
*The leaves underfoot in the east.*
*I remember the wide turnpikes*
*Narrow roads*
*How the air thru which we passed*
*Scoured us until we glowed.*
*I remember how as we climbed*
*In New Mexico toward the*
*Continental Divide*
*The light of the sun came thru*
*The clouds lighting*
*First one part then another*

*of the plain, we crossed*
*Rising at its furthest edge*
*To jagged peaks.*
*At the top of a high pass*
*Rain soaked us*
*Hail bounced at our feet*
*Solitude enveloped us*
*Muting the sounds of the world.*
*A clarity of light surrounded us*
*As if we had come suddenly close*
*To something other than ourselves.*

*Later at night*
*Our bickering began again---*
*The drunken arguments*
*Over money or women or*
*Which roads to take*
*But what did it matter?*
*We slept knowing we had*
*For a moment*
*Entered another world---*
*The one we dreamt as children*
*Must be there.*

*Along the way*
*We picked up cans, sold blood.*
*Ate so much surplus cheese*
*We could not shit for days.*
*By night we saw flares of gas*
*By day sight of cities guided us.*

*In the street, people stopped us*
*Tears in their eyes*
*Pressing change in our hands*
*Or lifting in the air V'd fingers*
*Or fists to spur us on.*

Men joined us crazed by war
Lovers star-crossed
Children sent packing
Parents abandoned
The poor made homeless when
Police tore down their tents
Or stamped their fires out.
We saw men arrested for
Sleeping on riverbanks
Women for wheeling a
Shopping cart down the street.
By the light of our fires we
Heard men speak of lost children
Or the pain of exile
With no hope of return.
In sleep they cried out to us
As do those shipwrecked
Driven wild by thirst
Who see on the horizon
imagined rescuers.

In huge shelters in great cities
We saw 1000 paupers in unison
Turning on cots
Like meat on a spit
Snow falling outside.
I can recite
Culled from our travels
A litany of horrors
A geography of loss
The grieved faces melt into one
The cities' combined skies
Became a single huge roof
Above a chamber of sorrows
Stretching from sea to shining sea.

*Ask me now why we did it and*
*I have no answer. It was not for*
*Housing, tho' we spoke of it.*
*Nor was it for charity*
*Tho' we received it.*
*Nor was it even for justice---*
*At least not for ourselves.*
*We began that is all  and*
*Before we began*
*We were nothing*
*It was only a dream*
*A thing we said idly we'd do*
*And then we were there*
*On the road no turning back*
*Only ourselves to measure*
*Failure or success.*
*I believe now we crossed*
*Not only the country*
*But a far region inside where*
*The soul has its home.*
*The tall mountains wide plains*
*Were part of ourselves*
*Discovered in the great*
*Blanketing silences of the land.*

*I am as you see*
*Still on the streets*
*No wiser*
*No more sober than before.*
*And yet---I tell you I am*
*Not the same.*
*I once saw in New York*
*Buddist monks*
*Walk for peace*
*In stately order*
*Solemnly*

*Beating drums:*
*Boom, boom, boom*
*They walked as if in*
*A slow-motion funeral*
*Boom, boom, boom.*
*It was like the beating*
*Heart of the world*
*And when later I heard*
*They had walked*
*Across the whole nation*
*In the same way*
*I cried.*

*On our walk*
*We had no drums*
*We shambled signs on our backs*
*Shopping cart pushed ahead*
*An American flag held aloft.*
*No doubt we were comic*
*Or sad in the eyes of*
*Drivers who whizzed by*
*Our brown shabby junk-laden*
*Bus lumbering behind us.*

*But we too no less than*
*The monks felt in ourselves*
*Something holy.*
*We too heard in the beat of*
*Our hearts struggling uphill*
*The sound of the world:*
*Boom, Boom, Boom.*

*Now in my thoughts, I dance*
*As the wind devils did in Texas*
*I ride the high clouds*
*As I once rode freights*

*And I step among stars*
*Like a man crossing a stream*
*Stone to stone without stumbling*
*But who will believe it*
*Seeing me familiar on the street*
*My palm out*
*A bottle in my hand?*
*I am on fire with the truth*
*Behind the mask of my face*
*And yet*
*Mute, mute, mute,*
*I cannot tell my tale.*

～

THE TASK OF MAKING IT BACK TO SANTA BARBARA FELT DAUNTING, knowing how much money we'd spent on gas to reach the nation's capital. Someone at the D.C. shelter, however, informed Bob about a program informally known as "Traveler's Aid" that could assist us in getting across the country. We could walk into police stations in various cities, explain our situation, and they'd send us on our way with ten-dollar vouchers redeemable for gasoline at local gas stations. It was their way of encouraging vagrants from overstaying their welcome and taxing a community's social services - a bribe of sorts that ushered the problem along to the next city.

We were happy to take advantage of the system soon after driving into Maryland. As a group, we'd decided to stick to the same route we'd walked to get to the East Coast so that townships would recognize us and not be fearful of the way we looked, even if that meant traveling northeast toward Philadelphia instead of immediately heading west. Also, that path would allow us to reconnect with charitable organizations and media representatives along the way, which would help generate donations of cash and supplies.

I tried begging the guys to go without alcohol for the trip home, knowing that we needed our senses intact to keep these old vehicles moving down the highway. They knew we lacked the funds for booze but argued that we could stop in towns along the way and do odd jobs for spending money. I had to relent. However, I was still adamant that we needed to make it to Santa Barbara by Christmas Eve, no matter what.

After crossing the Pennsylvania border, we parked beneath an over-pass to have lunch in the shade. I served up tuna sandwiches for the gang inside of the RV. One of the men wanted hot sauce and left the Enterprise to go search the other support vehicle. A minute later, he came running back, hollering, "The bus is on fire! The bus is on fire!"

We raced over and saw smoke pouring out from under the hood of The Imagine. Quickly, the guys popped it open and put out the flames, then after the smoke cleared, we assessed the damage. Evidently, a spark had caught the carburetor oil pan on fire, and it was now black-ened and completely useless. Glumly, we returned to our lunches and discussed what to do next. Buying a brand-new carburetor was out of the question. We'd have to drive around looking for junkyards for a used carburetor or we'd need to purchase a kit to rebuild our damaged one. Either way, our kitty of a hundred and fifty dollars was about to diminish much sooner than expected.

We removed the carburetor, locked up the bus and set off in the motorhome to find a junkyard. The first one we came to had the right parts to allow us to rebuild the damaged system. It cost us fifty dollars and came with a bonus gift. Amid the rows of derelict vehicles was a wrecked delivery truck full of Rolling Rock beer, and the owner of the junkyard told the guys they could take as much as they wanted. Soon, the RV was filled with stacks of these cases. I silently cried, as I'd been hoping for a respite from all the problems alcohol had caused over the past year. Still, it turned out to be a blessing in disguise, for over the next few weeks, the blood plasma money that we raised went strictly toward gas instead of booze. I was glad to not have to fight that battle over and over again.

We found a church parking lot and used it for a staging ground while we rebuilt the carburetor. The next morning, we reinstalled it in The Imagine and, to our relief, it worked. We were back on the road again... *but not for long.*

Later that day, I was driving the Enterprise, listening to the Eagles on the radio and staring at the back of the support bus when I noticed that the right rear tires on the bus were wobbling. I got on the CB and called ahead to Bob, "Pull the bus over. We have a problem."

"What?" he blurted.

"Pull the bus over now!" I shouted into the receiver.

Bob found a place to park and we assessed the damage. On two tires, it appeared that the spindles that attached the rims to the axles had sheared off and the pair of wheels were ready to fly off at any moment. I blamed my boyfriend. Bob was a collector of old signs and unusual junk, and he'd been steadily acquiring oddities as we traveled cross-country. The accumulated weight had finally been too much for the poor vehicle to handle.

The bus couldn't move another foot down the highway, so we jacked it up, removed the wheels and considered our options. Someone remembered that we'd bypassed a truck stop not too long ago, so we drove the RV back to see if we could enlist some help. It took the last of our money, but a mechanic at the truck stop was able to weld another set of spindles onto each wheel. We had the tires reinstalled and finally made it to Philadelphia.

The state troopers were kind enough to let us stay on their property within the city limits again. Then the media caught word that we were back in town, and they sent reporters to interview us about our experiences in Washington, D.C. The publicity was a boon to our efforts, for donations of cash and supplies started coming in. I was able to buy some used tires for the RV because the current set was nearly worn down to the tubes.

After a week, we headed westward across the Midwest and into the Great Plains. Along the way, the guys kept a lookout for temporary job opportunities. In one town, a circus needed help taking down their tents and packing them up for the next stop on their itinerary. The men worked long hours that day but only received twelve dollars apiece for their efforts - a disappointing exchange, but it supplied us with gas money at a crucial time.

With the assistance of the ten-dollar "Traveler's Aid" gas vouchers, we managed to limp into New Mexico where our luck finally ran out. There were no blood labs in the state where we could convert plasma into cash. The alcohol drinkers had cut back on their intake after the supplies of Rolling Rock beer had run out, but even with their generous sacrifice, we were still destitute.

In desperation, I placed a call to the Homeless Coalition back in Santa Barbara, and they agreed to help us out. The Legal Defense Center threw together a barbecue fundraiser that netted a couple hundred dollars. They wired the money to us through Western Union and a few days later on the 13$^{th}$ of December, we made it back to our hometown with a hundred and fifty dollars left in our pockets. It was an amusing anecdote - we'd started the walk with a hundred and fifty dollars, left Washington, D.C. with the same amount and ended up with the same number at the end of our long journey. But more importantly, we'd achieved my goal, which was to return home before Christmas.

The cartoonist Jeff Hess was waiting for us at Fig Tree Park. Also, to our astonishment, Colin - the man who had stolen the kitty and left us stranded outside of Terre Haute, Indiana - was back in Santa Barbara. He didn't have anything to say for himself, but we didn't waste time on recriminations. We were just glad to be home. I did taunt Colin, however, that if he'd only waited a few days, he could have taken the seven hundred dollars we'd raised from the fundraiser in Indianapolis.

After several hours spent telling stories and catching up with our homeless friends, I got back in the motorhome and drove to Carrows. There was one more person I needed desperately to see. Thankfully, she was there at the counter - a small, thin brunette whose eyes filled with joy as soon as she spotted me. My best friend Clu got up and flew into my arms, and only then did I feel that I'd truly made it home.

~

TWO DAYS AFTER OUR RETURN TO SANTA BARBARA, BOB AND I WERE driving up Milpas Street in the RV, running errands, and it occurred to me that the hundred and fifty dollars we had left was going to disappear fast.

While we were paused at a traffic light, I turned to Bob in the passenger seat and told him that I needed to start looking for work. If it were at all possible, however, I didn't want to go back to delivering papers. The early morning hours were too much of a grind.

Just then, a pickup truck pulled up alongside the motorhome, and a shaggy head poked out of the window. It was my son's father, Ross. "Hey, Nancy!" he shouted. "Mr. Monson wants you to come in and talk to him!"

I groaned. Bob started to chuckle. "You're never going to get out of the newspaper business, are you?" he teased me.

So I got my old job again. Back to rising at 2:30 a.m. every morning, seven days a week, delivering the Los Angeles Times. Bob started picking up odd jobs as a handyman, and I knew we'd be fine.

The school bus called The Imagine was given to Kim Fickling, who was living on the streets with her two children and needed shelter. She made monthly payments to Bob until the vehicle was paid off.

As the holidays approached, my own family spent most of their afternoons at Fig Tree Park as we used to. That tree was my home, and I wanted more than anything to have a joyous and relaxing Christmas. Soon enough, I would need to contact the district attorney and attempt to answer the charges that had been filed against Sean before we'd started the Walk. But before we ventured into the courtroom and faced the juvenile justice system, I wanted to give my children a proper Christmas.

The guys at the park erected a Christmas tree, and we scrounged up some decorations. The tree was rough around the edges, but then again, so were we. Thus, it was fitting that the police showed up to confiscate our holiday centerpiece.

Bob wasn't having it. He seized ahold of the trunk and would not let our tree go. A tug-of-war ensued between Bob and the cops. The tree moved back and forth across the park grounds until the police finally arrested Bob and threw him in jail for failing to obey a police officer.

The media had a blast with this story, and the headlines read, "The Grinch that Stole Christmas from the Homeless". The district attorney wasn't looking for that kind of publicity, so he declined to prosecute Bob further, even though the police had found a bud of marijuana in his pocket. Bob was sentenced to time served and was released back to the community.

A homeowner from Santa Barbara named Edmund Finucane wanted to make sure the homeless weren't forgotten during the holidays, so he created flyers that said, "Come Meet the Homeless on Christmas Day". The gathering would be held at Fig Tree Park, of course. Ed was a sweetheart of a man who busked with his violin on State Street on occasion and would sometimes invite us into his home for a spaghetti dinner. Perhaps he was simply lonely, but his compassion was nonetheless appreciated.

The night before the event, on Christmas Eve, we placed candles in plastic cups on the buttress roots of the fig tree. Since our ornamental tree had been taken by the cops, these lights would serve as our Christmas decor. We held hands around the fig tree, and a street singer who'd been studying opera graced us with a stunning rendition of the Lord's Prayer.

Afterward, I looked around for Bob because I wanted him to be around when the children opened their presents, but he seemed to have disappeared into the night. Frustrated, I went searching for him. Eventually, I found my boyfriend on Montecito Street partying with some friends. I walked up to Bob and asked him to come spend some time with his family on Christmas Eve. In answer to my request, he simply gave me a mischievous smile and pulled out an unopened half-pint bottle of Jack Daniels. I assumed this meant he was refusing to come back with me, and a wild impulse took over. I seized the container from him, uncapped it, brought it to my lips and tilted it upright. I didn't set it down until I'd drained the whole bottle. It was worth it to see the look of shock on Bob's face since I so rarely touched alcohol. He realized I was serious.

Bob helped me stumble back to the motorhome. I maintained my composure while Sean and Krystal opened their presents, but once they were finished, I knew I couldn't fake sobriety any longer. I told the kids to go play outside with their toys, and as soon as they were gone, I slumped in my chair and put a hand to my forehead.

Bob walked over and picked me up. "Don't make me lie down," I sobbed. But Bob placed me in bed and laid down next to me. I turned and puked every ounce of whiskey all over him. He jumped out of bed and cursed, but I chided him, "I told you not to make me lie down!"

The next morning, I felt terrible, as expected. It was a brutal experience, forcing myself to prepare and play hostess to the hordes of people who came for the "Come Meet the Homeless on Christmas Day" affair. Still, the day was successful in that clothes, food, money and gift-wrapped presents were pressed into the hands of the needy. The greater community had shown up for the event, and perhaps the fame we'd acquired over the course of our walk across America had something to do with their presence and compassion. There was so much more work to be done to support the rights of the homeless, both in Santa Barbara and as a nation, but despite my aching head, I couldn't help but feel a degree of hope.

We were on our way to someplace better... even if it was only one wobbly step at a time.

# EPILOGUE

I f I had the time, I would write a second book to chronicle all the misadventures I endured after returning from the walk across America. So many stories... many of which were not particularly advantageous to my health and sanity, but were certainly colorful.

The courts took Sean away from me and placed him into foster care, primarily because I'd kept him out of school for a year so he could participate in the Walk. He bounced from foster home to foster home, getting kicked out with great frequency due to bad behavior, though he'd excel in Juvenile Hall every time they sent him back to Santa Barbara to await his next placement. On his eighteenth birthday, he was given a suitcase to put his belongings in and released onto the streets. Sean had never graduated from high school and had few skills except the ability to survive one day at a time. He lived homeless for a long time, self-medicating like so many others. From time to time, I asked him to share the RV with me, but he was a big man now and was determined to find his own way.

I continued to live in my motorhome, although the battle against parking tickets was unceasing. Accompanied by my friends from the Homeless People's Association, I engaged in more acts of public protest and street theater. For the Solstice Parade, we built a "Golden

Throne" - a giant toilet meant to publicize the need for public restrooms downtown. Clu reigned over our float as the "Potty Princess", and we gave the parade watchers fake tickets for sitting on the sidewalk. Bob, Colin and Daniel dressed up in serapes and sombreros at City Council meetings, calling themselves the "Bathroom Banditos" as a gimmick to bring more attention to the restroom issue. At one point, Willard Hastings asked me to start a protest against city sleeping laws, so I threw a party for Bob's birthday in De La Guerra Plaza, and then we just never left. We stayed there for four months, holding City Hall hostage until they passed an ordinance creating a distinction between "sleeping" and "camping".

*Krystal in front of City Hall (photo by Kevin McKiernan)*

My work delivering newspapers went on, seven days a week, with just two weeks of vacation per year. Forty-one years in total. Bob and I maintained our relationship throughout this time, apart from a couple of periods of separation that were necessary to establish boundaries and make us realize how much we loved each other. It took a while for us to reach an income level where we felt financially secure. Bob picked up odd jobs as a handyman around town, and his finish carpentry work was stunning. He and I patched and painted numerous houses, and when those projects were hard to come by, we helped senior citizens with the errands they couldn't do on their own.

In 2010, Bob received a call from his mother. She asked if we would like to take over a cabin she owned on Green Valley Lake in the San Bernardino Mountains. It needed some work, she said, and we soon realized that was an understatement. The cabin was falling apart. New drywall panels, flooring and insulation were needed, but Bob, with his skills in construction and finish carpentry, was just the man for the job. We hired three homeless people from Santa Barbara to do the grunt work. After three weeks of hard work and a fresh coat of paint, Bob and I finally had our first home. It was a huge milestone for us. I especially appreciated having a washer and dryer and not having to bring clothes to a laundromat anymore. We fell in love with the Green Valley Lake community, and Bob was thrilled to have a warehouse in which to put his many scavenged belongings. When his mother passed away, ownership of the cabin and the surrounding property fell to us.

Living that far from our friends in Santa Barbara was difficult, however. In 2015, we decided to take advantage of the GI veterans' loans and use them to purchase a house as close to my hometown as possible. The nearest we could afford was a home on the outskirts of Santa Paula on the road to Ojai, but we managed to lock ourselves into a 2.25% mortgage payment and felt pretty good about it. After living most of my life with the specter of housing insecurity looming overhead, it felt surreal from time to time to have a permanent roof over my head. Our home on wheels is still parked in the driveway, and occasionally I still sleep inside her, just to make sure the memories do not fade.

Also in 2015, Bob and I were finally married. Maintaining that relationship was hard work, for we were both stubborn individuals, but underlying our connection was a solid friendship that endured through the decades.

Our child, Krystal, grew up to become an amazing and successful woman. After high school, Bob helped her purchase a VW Westfalia pop-up van, which she slept in to save money while she attended Santa Barbara Business College. Other teens in her socioeconomic situation would have struggled with rent payments and been unable to afford tuition or get ahead in life. But Krystal knew how to live out of a vehicle comfortably, thanks to her unusual upbringing. Now she has both a Master's Degree in Business and a California state real estate license. She is self-employed, managing rental units for clients in addition to the seven homes that she and her husband own. I couldn't be more proud of her.

*Bob, Nancy and Krystal*

I continued to work as the office manager for the Homeless Coalition until it folded in the 1990s. I served on the board of the City and County Task Force on Homelessness and spoke frequently in front of the City Council and the County Board of Supervisors. When the new Cacique shelter and day center was opened, I was appointed to that board, as well. I even started a choir there, and one of the highlights of every year was performing in a Christmas show for our homeless clients. In 2019, I started volunteering for the Committee for Social Justice, a homeless advocacy organization founded by Peter Marin, and I continue to support their efforts to this day as a grant writer, community organizer and secretary of the board.

Challenges will forever face the homeless community, but through the decades, Bob and I, along with our fellow activists, were responsible for many success stories. Thanks to our creative advocacy efforts, public restrooms were built next to the Marshall's department store downtown and in one of the parking garages. I helped create the Safe Parking Program for people that live in their RVs… a program that is still in operation today. The Carrillo Apartments were built to house the homeless, and they operated on a housing-first model, so residents didn't have to be sober before they moved in. Each of the sixty-one units had a furnished studio bedroom and a full bathroom, and residents could take immediate advantage of mental health services, addiction counseling and job training. Low-income housing units were built or established in Santa Barbara County, and with the help of rental assistance programs, many individuals and families have been rescued from homelessness. There are still not nearly enough units to meet the community's needs, but my own son, Sean, found a room in a single-occupancy housing project called the Faulding Hotel, and as he suffers from mental illness, his rent is supported by General Relief.

Sometimes, our achievements can only be measured in anecdotes... in how we have affected individual lives. For example, a few years after the Walk, I drove down to the Jungle parking lot to visit friends and spotted a tan-colored sedan parked amid the other vehicles. A strange person in his late thirties sat behind the wheel. He left his car and walked over to my truck, and it took me several moments to recognize the skinny man because he was so clean and neatly dressed. It was the guy who once had a crush on me: New York. Medication had done wonders for his sanity and well-being. New York told me that he had gone back home to live with his mom and get his life back together. He retrieved a package from his car and handed it to me through my truck window. It was a box of cookies baked by his mother who wished to thank me for showing kindness and patience toward her son. That blew me away. I got out of my vehicle and embraced him. You never know how a little help at just the right time can turn someone's life around.

∾

*Will Hastings, Actress Nichelle Nicols, Daniel Knapp and Don Hamilton at City Hall protest (photo by Kevin McKiernan)*

OVER THE YEARS, PEOPLE HAVE ASKED ME WHAT I WOULD DO, IF I controlled the levers of power, to help relieve the pressures that cause homelessness to arise in our communities. In truth, the problem is beyond the scope of what one individual can do. There are so many aspects. Real estate speculation drives the cost of rent and mortgage payments increasingly higher. Downtown property owners raise the price of monthly rentals above $10,000, forcing businesses to close their doors and increasing the rate of unemployment. Affordable housing projects get pushed back because of NIMBY-ism and the rising cost of materials. Meanwhile, the number of people forced onto the streets grows every year. Who can keep up with it all?

Rather than take the time to understand the basic needs of homeless people, our society shuffles them out of sight, embarrassed by their presence. We fence in our neighborhoods so that these "outlaws" cannot use the amenities. The public bathrooms get shut down, and then citizens scream that the homeless are using their front curbs as a place to relieve themselves. But where do we expect them to go?

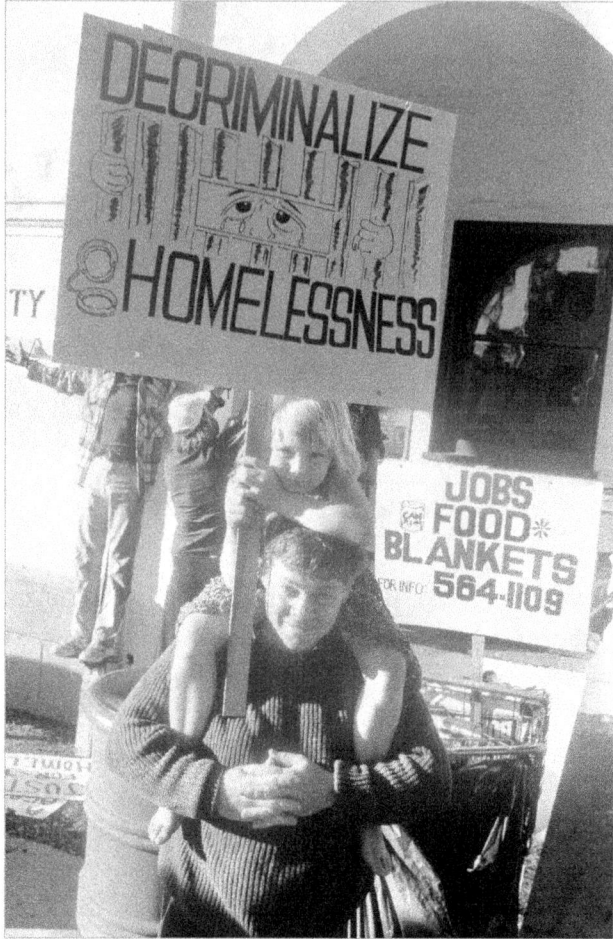

*Krystal and Jeff Hess (photo by Kevin McKiernan)*

This has been a slow-moving and ever-present crisis. We all watched over the years as affordable downtown cottages were demolished to create office buildings. Low-income hotels were renovated and rebranded as tourist accommodations. The combination of high rents and gentrification forced people to scavenge for alternative housing situations, so people climbed into box cars and built hootches in the overgrown and forgotten pieces of property along highways and railroad tracks. We lamented when Kenny Burr was shot in the forehead and Michael Stephenson was stabbed in his sleeping bag too many times to count. People moved into their vehicles so that they could have a locked door and a roof over their heads.

This exodus is not over. Not by a long shot.

As these issues are too big for one person to tackle, even over a forty-year time span, here are my recommendations on how our community can best move forward:

## Look to History

THE GREAT DEPRESSION OF 1929-1939 WAS A DEVASTATING BLOW TO our country. By 1933, over fifteen million Americans were unemployed. Banks called in their loans as customers closed their accounts and withdrew their cash. Men stood in long lines for bowls of soup while holding signs that read "HOPING FOR WORK". In an effort to reverse the economic downturn, the New Deal package of social programs was created by the federal government. Community improvement projects administered by the Works Progress Administration and Civilian Conservation Corps helped restore peoples' sense of dignity, providing employment opportunities while spurring industry back into production. Eight and a half million people found jobs building schools, shelters and highways. Over a billion trees were planted and over eight hundred parks had trail systems built by the CCC. Workers received certificates for the trade skills they'd learned, and many were able to leverage these certifications into permanent jobs.

Today there is a Building and Construction Trades Council in our tri-county area that puts together pre-apprenticeship training programs for interested people. Cities should connect with them to get people back to work in the trades. Employment services should operate in tandem with housing and homelessness assistance programs so that people can more easily return to the workforce and have the critical support they need before paychecks start arriving.

Wouldn't it be wonderful if our federal government created a new workforce program to employ people unable to afford college or uninterested in joining the military? Our sons and daughters could serve this country by doing infrastructure work for one or two years and then graduating with certificates of trade. Just think of the knowledge that future generations could gain instead of having to spend their time trying to survive on the streets.

## Stop Criminalizing the Homeless

IT MAKES NO SENSE TO TURN PEOPLE INTO OUTLAWS FOR THEIR attempts to address their basic needs... for sleeping or sitting on sidewalks and benches. Stores enforce draconian rules about their bathrooms, leaving the homeless with no place they can go if they want to clean themselves up and feel better about themselves. We should be focusing on solutions rather than pushing for more citations and more court and jail time. Tickets are issued to those who can never pay, so infractions turn into misdemeanors, giving each individual a police record that will stay with them for the rest of their life. The cost of code enforcement and cycling homeless people through our judicial system is staggeringly expensive, and by separating the homeless from the rest of society, we breed fear and ignorance of their plight.

## Create Safe Sleep Areas

SIMILAR TO SANTA BARBARA'S SAFE PARKING PROGRAM, WE COULD create places where simple shelters are erected when existing homeless shelters are full. Huge tents are set up at Earl Warren Showgrounds to protect Christmas trees... why can't we do this for our fellow humans during the cold and rainy nights of winter? Currently, the people who run our warming shelters decide for our brothers and sisters on the streets how far temperatures have to drop before they open their doors. Not a single one of us is up to the challenge of sleeping outdoors when it is thirty-five degrees. The threshold should be forty-five degrees, or better yet, an additional shelter should be opened during the cold winter months.

Rather than having people guess whether a particular warming center will be open or not, the homeless should have a guaranteed shelter they can utilize each night between the hours of 7 p.m. and 7 a.m. All the arguing over temperature thresholds would be eliminated. This concept has worked well in the past, and it could work again. These shelters could also be connected to day centers where job placement, health and housing services could be offered free of charge.

## Let the Homeless Educate the Public

EDUCATION IS THE KEY TO PROMOTING THE WELFARE OF ALL mankind, and it is time to invite the homeless back to the table. I shrink when I see homeless people standing outside of meetings where people are discussing what's best for them. They should be fully part of the discussion and allowed to share their own creative ideas and solutions. It is the height of elitism to think the problems can be solved without their input.

## Link Housing Resources to Mental Health Resources

MENTAL ILLNESS RUNS IN MANY FORMS, FROM LIGHT TO SEVERE. THE stresses of street life are enough to try the sanity of even the most positive people after several weeks. The system of social services is a maze, and it is hard enough to navigate it without being mentally ill. Resources are out there, but those who are forced to live on the streets without support systems are usually the last to find help for their afflictions.

*The Protest Walk to Sacramento: David Hopkins, Dee Dee,*
*unknown, Holly Dunn, Bob, Marco*

A close friend came to me with this idea: build a compound that
provides temporary studio apartments for mental health clients. A
stabilization unit for crisis intervention would be situated on the property. Patients could return to their normal apartments or move into
alternative housing after a two-week stay, but they would not be
thrown back out onto the streets. There is currently such an apartment building in Santa Barbara, but the crisis unit is all the way across
town.

The community should be educated more about mental health.
Watching a person walk down the street talking to nobody tends to
frighten people. More often than not, there is nothing to fear. It would

be good to reduce that person's stress with housing and a strong support system because anxiety only exacerbates the symptoms of mental illness. The more secure people feel, the more capable they are of thinking clearly and repairing their relationship with the world around them.

## Provide More Places to Park Vehicles

SANTA BARBARA'S SAFE PARKING PROGRAM PROVIDES A FEW DOZEN spaces for people living out of their vehicles to park overnight in government parking lots. Amenities include restrooms, hygiene services and rapid rehousing assistance. For those who must park elsewhere due to increasing demand for those spaces, protection from police interference would greatly enhance their quality of life. Advocacy organizations like Homes on Wheels are also asking for places for people to safely park in the daytime. A low-cost RV and automobile park could create even greater stability for those in need.

## Revamp the Foster System

MY SON SEAN WAS PLACED INTO THE FOSTER SYSTEM BECAUSE I TOOK him out of school for a year to do the Peace Walk, and they considered that "neglectful." Also, they felt I could not control his behavior and assumed they would do a better job of it. Sean had learning disabilities, but he was extremely bright and excelled at messing with the foster care system. His caretakers would call me, asking for help in figuring out my son, but I refused to help out of spite. The system needs to be more accommodating toward parents who have unconventional living arrangements because even though sometimes removing a child from an abusive home is necessary, the definition of "neglect" is often arbitrary and used as a weapon against the homeless.

When a child is taken from their biological parents, he is supported by the state or county in which he resides. But when he turns eighteen, he is told to pack his bags and go on his merry way because the money given to his caretaker is cut off. I cannot imagine a child of eighteen being considered a full-grown adult, especially one that is released without an education or trade skills that would prepare them for a stable life. My son was turned out onto the streets in this unprepared state, and he was homeless for the next twenty-four years. There needs to be systems in place to better train foster teens for the real world and better programs to help guide and support them during this critical period of transition so that they have the best chance of success.

∾

BEFORE I CONCLUDE, I WISH TO THANK ALL THE PEOPLE WHO helped me through the decades I spent living out of my vehicles.

Mr. Willard Hastings, Esq. headed up the Legal Defense Center, and with the help of Kit Tremaine, he gave us our voting rights back. Willard was open, honest and gentle. He inspired me to volunteer with the Legal Defense Center on Thursdays, answering phones and filing paperwork.

*Dave Collier and Willard Hastings (photo by Kevin McKiernan)*

Peter Marin, the founder of the Committee for Social Justice, who led the organization, implemented classes for the homeless, gave rides from jail and started the Elf Project, which gave mechanical assistance to those living out of their vehicles. The Committee is still in operation and remains a strong voice for social consciousness.

Rogelio Trujillo, who helped us at the Legal Defense Center. His voice at City Hall spurred us on to greater things. Rogelio provided barbecues for the homeless, and his son has followed in his footsteps.

My best friend Clu Carradine, whose support kept me from going off the deep end countless times. She followed me into homelessness but now also owns her own home with her brother in Buellton. A co-founder of the advocacy group Homes on Wheels, Clu continues to shine a light on injustices in our community.

Susan Dunn Cobb was a vehicular dweller who became one of the best activists for the homeless in Santa Barbara history. She now lives on a boat in Florida with her husband.

All the guys from the street who protected me and my children over the years. Wherever you all are, I thank you from the bottom of my heart.

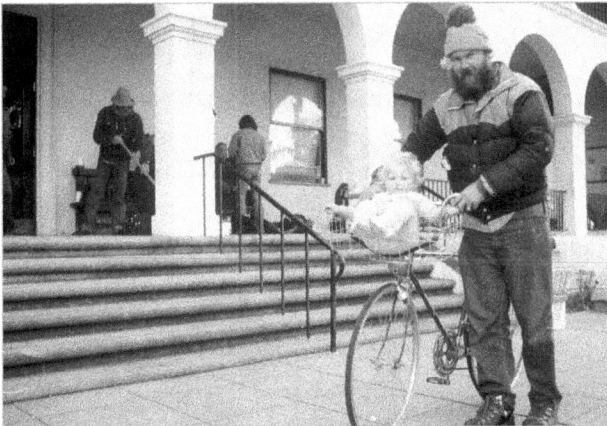

*Bob and Krystal at City Hall (photo by Kevin McKiernan)*

And finally, my husband, Protest Bob Hansen. He suffered a heart attack and passed away in March of 2024 in our Santa Paula home, not long after we sang "Happy Birthday" over the phone to our son-in-law. It was one last moment of shared song and celebration. Bobby was compassionate, stubborn and uncontrollable at times, but he safeguarded me and was quick to forgive my faults. We had a complicated and crazy relationship. Whenever things got bad, I would leave him for a time, but longing would always bring us back together. Bobby, I will always miss you, and I hope we will meet again in the afterlife and continue our friendship.

~

SUSAN COBB TOLD ME THAT THIS BOOK'S CONCLUSION SHOULD BE that there is no conclusion. She is probably correct. The fight for homeless rights and the battle against the root causes of homelessness is ongoing. She also said that the best gift we can bestow upon mankind is to help them see how they need to love others. We need to share the truth in the hope that a light will go off in people's minds, enabling them to reflect and take action so that their lives have personal meaning. Susan went on to say that my own life is deep and meaningful because of the person I chose to become over my many decades on this planet. In her words, I am a living legacy that will transcend the pages of this book, and my impact will go on long into the future.

I cannot speak to the veracity of her judgment. I am just one of many who have fought these battles. Nevertheless, I do hope that the people who read my story will realize that we are all at risk of finding ourselves homeless. It can happen to anyone. But with willpower and compassion, we can make the road a little easier for those who follow.

# APPENDIX A: THE HOMELESS
# PEACE WALK NEWSLETTER

The idea of the Peace Walk Newsletter was proposed during one of the meetings that were held each morning before we hit the pavement. I loved the idea because I thought it would help educate people back home about our endeavors. Also, it gave me an excuse to be absent during the meetings so that I could work on the layout and submissions. I couldn't stand listening to people bitterly argue about who picked up more aluminum cans for the thousandth time.

The overall design was created by me and Jeff Hess, the cartoonist of the Walk, who also drew all the pictures. I did the typing and solicited poetry and biographical information from the other Walkers. Only one issue was ever made. Ten copies were generously printed for us by the Homeless Coalition of Oklahoma in Oklahoma City, and I mailed one to my friend and benefactor, Kit Tremaine. The rest went to the Legal Defense Center in Santa Barbara, which distributed them to members of the Homeless Coalition.

On our return trip from Washington, D.C., we ran out of gas money in New Mexico and were left stranded, but the newsletter helped the Legal Defense Center and the Coalition raise the funds to bring us home.

# HOMELESS PEACE WALK TO WASHINGTON D.C.

Vol. 1

APRIL 88. JEFFERY D. HESS

Copyright c 1988           Homeless People's Walk           April, 22nd

The Homeless and Poor People's Walk to Washington D.C. started from the Moreton Bay Fig Tree in Santa Barbara, California on January 16th, 1988. It's Purpose: To set up dialogue and an information exchange on the subject of homelessness in every city it passes through and to bring about a focus of attention and caring on a level to the plight and problems of the Homeless and Poor populations. It's Goals: To help structure more energy and funding from the Federal Government to the States, Counties, and Cities for the Homeless and Poor of America. To help in decriminalizing homelessness. To help bring order and peace to the many and varied problems among this rapidly growing segment of the American population. And to help bring about solutions that leave room for Human Pride and Dignity. It's Final Goal: will be to make a National Call to all Homeless and their advocacy groups to meet on October 20th, 1988 at Battery Park across from the Statue of Liberty and walk with us the remaining miles to Washington D.C. We hope that many of you will join us either there or at the White House on November 7th. We also hope that when you come that you will bring an American Flag to signify that we all as Americans can still hold onto a part of the true American dream together.

We, of the Homeless and Poor People's Walk to Washington D.C. do feel that our endeavor is well worth the effort we are putting out. We are gaining an education for ourselves about how really terrible the homeless situation is across this Nation. There has been a problem in every city we have come through so far - and we feel that there will be much more to experience. In California it is so easy just to jail the homeless or at least set up ordinances that will run them in and out of the court systems. In Arizona and New Mexico we find a deep-seated prejudice between some of the white population and the Indian Nations. Some of the white people in these parts feel that there is no real problem with the homeless in these two states but if one looks around a little and talks to the Indians, one finds that their honesty brings about the true stories this Walk seeks. We have found many people who are needing help here. People who have no electricity or running water. People who are devastated by the lack of un-employment (50% by the reservation indians) or the lack of any job beyond the minimum wage level and because of this the lack of affordability to any housing market that almost always exceeds their wages. We are running into whole families, moving from coast to coast, looking for jobs to support their children and housing needs. Occasionally we run into what we like to call a "Poverty Pimp" type situation. In other words we find a lot of Federal Funding being wasted or overcharged in some places we have looked at. But most often we find that those who work towards helping people are genuine but could use a little help in adding a more constructive programming to

their establishments. These are some of the observations we have made so far on our journey.

Throughout the many steps that that this Walk has taken, it has encountered very favorable responses to it's efforts. It has met up with a few confrontations by the police. Some start out on a negative note but most of them turn into a positive state after we talk to them. All of the people who stop along the road and at rest areas have given us small donations of money and food with a thumbs-up attitude. It is interesting to note, however, that most often it is the middle-class or the poor who stop and relate to us. Many of the cities have given us radio spots and have invited us onto local talk shows.

In the Malibu area, after a few suspicions were cleared up, the Walk was invited onto the Pepperdine University grounds to talk with a sociology class there. In Los Angeles Homer Gomez, head of the sociology department at Pitzer College, arranged a visit for the Walk to exchange information with his students there and at Harvey Mudd. Donations of canned goods were given and an invitation to take showers.

All has not been perfect on this Walk. We have had to leave room for human error. In Venice a party was donated to the walkers and many of the participants decided to leave the Walk and stay in Venice. That left the original four people who worked at organizing the Walk in Santa Barbara, California. But when the Walk left Venice, five more people joined. In Arizona, at an appropriate place called Devil's Canyon, six walkers decided to split off from the main group and start a walk of their own. They were given $200.00 to help them on their way because they did not like the way the money was kept in a kitty. They felt that it should be split up between all the walkers. We understand that three days after these walkers left they were hurting for money. We wish them good luck and hope that they are doing well. At this time we are holding strong with ten steadfast people. It seems that this is our average amount. But it makes it easier to support this amount of people.

A week outside of Albuquerque, New Mexico, we could feel a high degree of energy eminating from us all. We felt renewed with a ferver that made us walk stronger than we had for a while. We had heard that emotions were running high against a break-in demonstration put on by the Homeless Union in the city that we neared at an abandoned building to show the lack of housing for the people of America. All of us on the Walk became interested in seeing if we could help to re-unify all of the people who were working on the homeless issue in Albuquerque. Colin Atherton and Nancy McCradie went into the city two days ahead of schedule to follow up on the pre-advance work that Peter Marin had done for us. Everything went like clock work. We looked for the social services agencies that dealt with the homeless and the many people involved helped us with our advance work. Learning about a press conference involving Christopher Sproul, the nationwide organizer of the Homeless Union which began in Philadelphia, we showed up to meet him and found ourselves invited to talk about our Walk. So during the course of our two day stay in Albuquerque the media did an excellent coverage on us. The people of the city were very friendly. They met us outside of town and walked through town with us and helped us with some laundry. The University of New Mexico let us camp on their grounds and provided us with showers in their gym. Various social services helped us in obtaining food, clothing and medical treatment. We cannot end this piece about Albuquerque without mentioning a place for the homeless called Saint Martins. Operating a large day center, a clinic for the homeless, a counseling service, and a feeding program, we feel that any one interested in starting up services for the homeless should come to Albuquerque and

take a tour of the place. We found a lack of political clout in the city however, so we suggested to several people that they contact the gray panthers and the league of women voters to see if these two groups might help them to begin a political campaign drive to lay down in front of the local politicians there. It was interesting to note that while we were there the mayor decided to begin a voucher system for people to stay at motels until they could find housing on their own.

We did not stay in the city without any fun. On the grounds of the University, they put on their two day Fiesta while we were there. We wish to give our heart-filled thank yous to the people of Albuquerque for their dialogue and their help.

---

The Homeless and Poor People's Walk to Washington D.C. is now trying to set up a mailing system. We have found what we are looking for with Mail Poxes Etc. U.S.A. We will let you know when the system is set up. We are also looking for a way to set up a checking account for the donations we have been receiving. By the time you receive our second News Letter we will hope to have these two things set up. Please enjoy this News Letter. It is our first one and we are still learning how to do them.

---

We are still moving on Interstate 40. Our next major cities will be Tucumcari, Amarillo, Texas, and Oklahoma City. From there we will change to route 44.

At the time of this
publication, the Walk has
nine members. We wish to
acknowledge all the temp-
orary walkers that have been
with us in the past and who
have left due to reasons of
their own. Below is an intro-
duction of the walk members
who are with us now and the
reasons why they feel The
Homeless and Poor People's
Walk is beneficial to them
at this time in their lives.

blanket wrapped around his
shoulders approached him
and asked for help in find-
a place to sleep. Bob could
not understand why people
were out on the streets with
no place to go. After many
months of work on the homeless
issue in Santa Barbara, he decided to organize a walk to
Washington D.C. He also feels
a desire to learn about America's
homeless everywhere.

Colin Atherton was born
in Canada and lived for a
few years in Florida. He
joined the Walk in Santa
Barbara, California. He
felt that by learning to
become an activist he could
help his friends in Florida.
He came on this walk to get
in shape and do something
positive to keep the issue
of the homeless and poor alive
in this election year.

Robert Duncan, affectionately
known as Indian Bob became a
professional walker when arthritis
discontinued the ability to work
in his field of employment. He
was one of the members of the
Great Peace March two years ago.
He has a great deal of honesty
and integrity about walking and
helps to bring about peace at
times when we are a little tired
and cranky. He is walking on
this march in hopes of having a
vigil in front of a big corporation
to get them involved in finding
inexpensive and non-dependent ways
solving the homeless issue with
dignity. His statement that society
is always judged by the way they
treat their poor and homeless has
been with us since the days of
the beginnings of Christianity.

Robert Hansen has been an
activist and protester for a
number of years in Santa
Barbara, California. He
chose to work on the homeless
issue because one cold night

Nancy McCradie, a resident of
Santa Barbara, California, became homeless with her son to
run away from an abusive and
alcoholic environment. In self-
defence of her situation she
became an activist in the homeless issue and helped start an
organization called The Homeless
People's Association. She joined
the Homeless and Poor People's
Walk in Show Low, Arizona in
hopes that she could help with
the advance work, documentation
and whatever else to turn this
walk into a worthwhile endeavor.
She also feels the need to educate herself about problems of
homelessness across the Nation.

Sean McCradie, a twelve year
old felt the need to gain an education that he could not get in
the public school system at this
time in his life. He did a walk
to Reagan's ranch on a childrens
Peace Walk two years ago in hopes
that he could talk to the President
about World Peace. He was told
by the guards at the Ranch gate
that they were not allowed to give
any messages to the President at
his ranch. And the only way to
get a message to the President
would be to go to the White House
in Washington D.C. So, here he
is as always very hopeful that
he will get his chance.

Krystal Freedom is the daughter
of Robert Hansen and Nancy McCradie.
She was born August 23rd, 1984. At
three and a half years old, she is
a regular bombshell. Energetic and
high-spirited she says that she came
on this walk to be with her mom and
dad and Sean. She also wants to
ride a horse

"Irish" came to this Walk
after recognizing Sean McCradie
at a rest stop in New Mexico
outside of Gallup. He has been
around and in the Santa Barbara
area at times and knew Sean.
Because he is homeless, he feels
that if this Walk will help the
homeless out then he is all for
it.

Jeffery Hess was born in Pleasant Valley, Iowa. He served six years in the United States Navy. After his discharge, Jeff became a regional director for a rescue mission in Los Angeles. After a time, disgusted by a drug problem in the mission itself, he left and wandered into Ted Hayes and an organization called Justice Ville. He worked for a time as a homeless activist. Hearing about the Homeless and Poor People's Walk, he decided to join. He enjoys cartooning and is portraying the Walk through

his art form. He is on the Walk to help himself build a significant and better understanding of the family future and the future of all mankind.

David Gary, a newcomer to this Walk, joined in Grant, New Mexico. He is very hopeful that America's Government will wake up and do something for it's Homeless and Poor people.

## GET A JOB!

GOOD NEWS; we have a job. Some places pay 40¢ a pound, others pay 63¢ a pound. Our job is picking up aluminum cans. The people on the Walk decided that as long as we had enough money for food and gas, the can money would be split between us all. Most weeks the total is $25.00. People buy what they want--and this can lead to disunity in the camp. But as long as they are private and don't bring heat on the Walk, we feel that it is all right. But we have had our share of problems! $2.00 or $5:00 isn't much, but just "IMAGINE"

Written and submitted by:
Robert Allen Hansen

This Newsletter would like to publish a poem that was presented to this editor by an anonymous street person who hitch-hiked all the way from Florida hoping that it would be published as soon as it was needed. We feel that the first edition of The Homeless and Poor People's Peace Walk to Washington D.C.'s Newsletter should be the publisher. We hope that you, our readers, will enjoy it.

---

The sidewalk streets are old, the people's stares; on the edge of being cold.
"Beware" I was told "where you walk, the shirt on your back may be stolen"
The cracks in the concrete, the asphalt strewn around to make up the streets.
At the corner; stood the bus-stop seats.
A lone man sucks and chews his cigar, while waiting, standing on his feet.
I walked up to him with gear on my back, seeing he was searching for a light, I struck a match and brought it to his face;
He puffed his stogey with a sense of inner taste.
Looking at his pocked face, I could see signs of traumatic fear and rejection;
His eyes showed images of society's reflection.
"My friend" I did begin "Will this bus take me to the Brandon corner, near the rescue mission?"
He replied: "Down a block and up three corners, take a left...
Look for the modern day mourners.
They will be sitting there, or could be standing, some leaning on the wall, some asleep on the landing."
Then he turned and swayed, took a few steps, looked back my way.
His eyes met mine, they seemingly shined.

Without a word, a look, an utterance, or a glare,
He proclaimed: "Peace my brother, do not despair.
Though the world seems grim, and life is getting bleak,
Analyze and observe, strive for what you seek.
Search for truth, and reach for your beliefs,
Use the wholeness of your mind, and you...
...shall be complete."

EMC

---

## HOMELESS LINGO DICTIONARY

1. BULL: a) railroad police
   b) Jail guard.

2. BURN ONE: To smoke a joint.

3. DIRTY FACE: One who rides the rails/hops a freight.

4. EAR BANGING: An hour of preaching christianity before being fed.

5. GESTAPO: Undercover Police.

6. POLLIES: Handmade cigarettes.

7. PANHANDLING: A way of raising money by asking for it; some might call it fund raising.

8. POVERTY PIMP: One who makes money off of poor people/such as; a social service.

9. SALLY: A nickname for the Salvation Army.

10. SHORTS: The tail end of a cigarette. example; "Save me shorts"

11. SIX-UP: Warning of Police in the area.

12. SPREAD YOUR HUSTLE: "Ask someone else"

13. <u>TAYLOR MADES</u>: Store-bought
cigarettes.

14. <u>THREE HOTS AND A COT</u>: a)
Jail. b)The rescue Mission.

15. <u>TROLL</u>: One who lives under
the Fig Tree or a bridge.

16. <u>WING NUT</u>: a) Mental Patient
b) One who lets himself be
hussled to win friends

The idea for this dictionary
was submitted by Homeless
Walk member: Colin Atherton.
Lingo and definitions submitted by all members of the
walk.

---

THE NIGHT BEFORE THE SPLIT.
POETRY BY COLLIS

A QUART OF BEER
IN GOD'S CANYON
WITH SYMBOLS OF
THE DEVIL AROUND

AN OPEN REVOLT
AGAINST THE WALK
PROFOUNDIT'S .ABOUND

. FINALLY SLEEP
BUT I KNOW THAT
SOMETHING IS UP.
MAYBE IN THE MORN-
ING THINGS WILL WORK
OUT OVER A COFFEE
CUP.

ART BY JEFF HESS

---

THE CHOOSING OF THE SEED CORN

at dawn before
the sun has risen
over Second Mesa
the people gather on
the night dark desert
around the pit they
dug the day before.
the suns fierce heat
will force them into
shade when he is in
the sky so now they work
in haste, dig deep
down in the earth
and pull the ears
of corn from out
their smoldering bed.
wrapped in aromatic herbs
and grasses the two most
perfect ears are passed
from hand to hand
so all can see
they have been chosen
as the Seed Corn for
the crop to come.
and now they must
be guarded with great care
until the time for planting
corn has come and then
the perfect kernels
will return to sleep
inside their Mother Earth
and sun and rain and wind
will work their miracles again.

The Homeless and Poor People's
Walk to Washington D.C. feels a
special affection for the author
of this poem. Since we are in
New Mexico at the time of this
publication, we find that the
words portray a true picture
of the people here. We wish
to give our thanks and good wishes
to Kit Tremaine by publishing
her work once again.

## A DAY IN THE LIFE

EVERY morning at daybreak
Colin Atherton will be seen
unlocking the bus, groping for
a match to light the stove and
put on the coffee. Sleeping
bags spread on the ground in
various places only rise and
fall with the breath of their
occupants. When the coffee is
ready, Colin will go into action, harrassing the sleepers
until they are arroused enough
to throw something at him.
Milling around like a bunch
of sloths at 7:30 A.M., the
walk members throw brackish
barbs at each other until
the coffee they call "mud"
does it's work. Everyone
then goes into action, rolling up bags, eating the gruel
they call breakfast, and discussing the plans for the day.
At 9:00 A.M. the walk is ready
to proceed. Walking in two
mile incraments, the walkers
look down the road for the
support vehicle that has all
the truckers fascinated and
think about the sip of water
and the energy snack they will
slurp up before continuing.
At lunch time, weary but feeling high on lots of oxygen,
they will sit around and rest;
nursing blisters and shin-splints.
Maybe their exhaustion will bring
about a little in-fighting and
jealousy of the people who are
driving the support vehicles.
But they will go on, mindful of
their goals and do the job that
is required of them. In the
evening when the mileage goal
is completed, they begin to
think of the many truckers who
honk to inspire them, the many
people who stop along the road
to talk to them, the treasures
they have found, and the beauty
of the changing scenery they by-
pass during the many steps that
they take. A meeting might take
place each evening and snide jokes
will be told until they finally

wind down and fall asleep with
with the exhaustion that makes
them sleep so well. 8:00 P.M.
is bedtime; (yawn) goodnight.
Tomorrow is another day.....

Written and submitted by:
Nancy Jean McCradie

---

One of our walkers was given this
little reflection on the road by a
well wisher. It was copyrighted in
1986 by the Antioch Publishing Co.
in Yellow Springs, Ohio. It is call
ed DON'T QUIT. We feel that it is
appropriate to our own feelings as
we walk down the road:

When things go wrong as they sometimes will,
When the road you're trudging seems
all uphill,
When the funds are low, and the debt
are high,
And you want to smile, but you have
to sigh,
When care is pressing you down a bi
Rest if you must, but
don't you quit.


Success is failure turned inside
out,
The silver tint of the clouds of
doubt.
And you never can tell how close you
are,
It may be near when it seems afar.
So, stick to the fight when you're hardest
hit—
It's when things go wrong that
you mustn't quit.

We, the undersigned, have read and do support the purposes and goals of the Homeless and Poor People's Walk to Washington D.C. We send our best wishes with them.

PURPOSE AND GOALS: To help in structuring more energy and funding from the Federal Government to the states, counties, and cities for The Homeless and Poor of America.

To help in the Decriminalizing of Homeless People

To help bring order, peace, and reasonable solutions to the many and varied problems among this rapidly-growing segment of the American population. And to help bring about Solutions that leave room for human pride and dignity.

| Name | city | state |
|------|------|-------|
| 1. | | |
| 2. | | |
| 3. | | |
| 4. | | |
| 5. | | |
| 6. | | |
| 7. | | |
| 8. | | |
| 9. | | |
| 10. | | |
| 11. | | |
| 12. | | |
| 13. | | |
| 14. | | |
| 15. | | |
| 16. | | |
| 17. | | |
| 18. | | |

# APPENDIX B: IN MEMORIAM

Living on the streets takes a toll on the human body and psyche. We go to sleep at night wondering if we'll be alive in the morning, and yet regular people fear us. They classify us as outsiders, outlaws, alcoholics and drug addicts. Don't they realize that we live lives of constant fear ourselves? We are just as human as they are, and many of us grew up in Santa Barbara.

These are just a few of the worthy and eccentric souls I've encountered during my decades of homelessness who either died on the streets of this city or spent much of their lives there. They have affected me in profound ways, and I wish I had space to tell the stories of so many more of them. Even though these men and women have left the planet, they will remain in my heart forever.

## Frank Cooper

Frank was a member of the Homeless People's Association. A quintessential gentleman, you could put a picture of Abraham Lincoln next to his face and not be able to tell the difference. We all wanted to dress him up in a top hat and black overcoat and have him march up State Street during the Summer Solstice parade, but he never let himself be persuaded. The man loved his beer and would share count-less cans of "quarter pounders" with his compadres. When the cops came patrolling downtown, he would warn the other homeless that there were "raccoons on State Street".

One morning, I was delivering my bundles of L.A. Times newspa-pers to the Santa Barbara Liquor store when I saw Frank staggering down the street. I thought his behavior was curious because it was too early in the morning for him to be drunk. The liquor store wouldn't open for quite some time. I needed to continue my deliveries, so I didn't drive up and check on him. I just had to hope he was okay.

Later that afternoon, some of Frank's friends found him at the bottom of Milpas Street, close to the railroad tracks. He told them he wasn't feeling good and, concerned for his well-being, his friends wondered if they should call an ambulance. Frank said he was going to lie on the ground for a while, but if they could fetch him a beer, it might improve his health and spirits.

By the time they returned, Frank had passed on. The autopsy showed that he'd died of double pneumonia.

## Colin Atherton

Another sincere gentleman, Colin hailed from British Columbia, and he would proudly display the papers that proved his dual citizenship. A bartender by trade, he eventually succumbed to an addiction to the very drinks that he'd served. Colin was a skilled panhandler and enter-tainer. He'd sit in his wheelchair and captivate the crowds of people who came to party in the clubs on lower State Street. "Got a quarter for me to kill Rush Limbaugh?" he'd call out, and laughter would inevitably ensue.

Always an adventurer, Colin joined us on our walk across America in 1988. He liked being an organizer and would often help me do advance work in the cities along our route, preparing the citizens and social service organizations for our arrival. We'd find a restaurant and a phone book, jot down the important phone numbers and then call the media, police and local nonprofits. If the community had a stab lab, we'd figure out the details. Everything would be done to maximize how much recuperation the Walkers would experience once they entered the city.

Colin's low moment was when he ditched the Walk outside of Terre Haute, Indiana, taking three hundred dollars from our kitty with him. That was the money we needed for gas and supplies, and he nearly left us stranded. Luckily, we had fifty dollars stashed elsewhere, and that got us to Terre Haute where we limped into a shelter and tried to recoup our losses. The media covered our story, and donations from the community started coming in.

When the Walk was over, we found Colin waiting for us back in Santa Barbara. We forgave him. It's best to leave grievances in the past.

Colin aided in our street theater efforts by helping carry the "Golden Throne" - a giant toilet, painted gold - up State Street during the Summer Solstice parade. During that event, Clu, dressed as the "Potty Princess", knighted him as "Sir Colin, the Anal" because of his uptight personality, and she referred to him by that nickname from that point onward. He was a member of the "Bathroom Banditos" - a trio comprised of Colin, Bob and Daniel who wore serapes and large Mexican hats to City Council meetings in order to drum up publicity for the need for public restrooms. His legacy was that a bathroom was built next to Marshall's department store downtown along with a second restroom in one of the parking garages.

Ultimately, Colin drank himself to death, passing away in his wheelchair on the 500 block of State Street. A few days before he died, Colin pushed his wheelchair up to me and softly asked, "Is it alright if I call you Nanny?" I knew that he had a crush on me. Nevertheless, I broke down and gave him permission, adding that only my closest brothers were allowed to call me that. He would be missed.

## Edwin Kozdrey, Jr.

Courageous, talented and extremely intelligent, "Prez Ed," as we affectionately called him, got himself elected to the role of president of the Homeless People's Association in the 1980s. He knew a bit of law, so he was a good person to lead us through our many legal battles. Ed came up with and executed many strategic acts of civil disobedience over the years, to the city's consternation. The mailbox at Fig Tree Park was just one of his plans, and he proudly stood next to it, taking questions from the media about voting rights before the city government tore it out of the ground.

Prez Ed had to leave us for a while to help his father run his hydraulics business in Blythe, California. There, he met his beautiful future bride, and to this day, I still carry their wedding photo with me. Their marriage ended in tragedy, for one evening, Edwin came home from work and found his wife cut into pieces and strewn about their living room. Her former husband, released from prison, had tracked her down and murdered her.

Edwin understandably had a mental breakdown. He returned to Santa Barbara a broken man. In his depression, he began to push around a shopping cart loaded with his possessions and whatever recyclables he could scrounge up and convert into cash. Using the deposit money from aluminum cans, he loaded up on alcohol, drinking to forget the awful images that haunted his memory.

During a major summer heat wave, Edwin collapsed while pushing his cart across Cabrillo Boulevard. Heat stroke and dehydration had been his undoing. We miss you, Prez Ed.

## Michael Brook Tice

Michael, or "The Right Reverend", as we called him, was a big, boisterous man with red hair and a full beard. I met him during my early days at the Jungle lot when he pulled in with his camper, introduced himself and asked for a safe space to rebuild his engine. He was raised by a religious fanatic mother who taught him to preach when he was a little boy. She took him to Christian revival meetings, spiritual events and city street corners, putting out a donation hat and profiting from her son's fiery orations and deep biblical knowledge. He maintained a preacher-like presence even in adulthood.

When I knew him, Michael was the sweetest and most intelligent man. He was also gay, so I was never harassed by him like my other male acquaintances. We quickly became fast friends, and he introduced me to the world of CB radios which, for those who lived out of their vehicles, was important for socializing and survival. He and his good friend Steve Bagnall were fierce protectors of me and my family, especially Sean, keeping him safe from Child Protective Services when I needed to go to work. Michael had some mental issues, but he took medications to dampen the worst effects. Anxiety attacks still got the better of him sometimes. He and Steve could work each other up into a panic if left to themselves, and it would be up to me to reassure them and calm them down.

Eventually, Michael grew tired of the stress of police visits and political activism. He and Steve took their campers to the Rincon so they could live a more peaceful existence, and Clu and I would have to drive down there to visit our Irish rebel. Even then, Michael still frightened the cops from time to time with his famous Tarzan yell.

In the 1990s, Michael finally moved to a small cottage in Oroville, California. He was a "water baby" and loved the river up there. He made jewelry, took care of a lovely garden and had lots of friends. He was happy. Diabetes came in strong towards the end, however, and caregivers tended to his needs at home until he passed away in 2022. Clu and I grieved when we received the news. Michael was full of life and such a fun guy to be friends with. I will forever miss him.

### Steve Bagnall

Steve met my friend Clu and started dating her when they were both working for the City of Santa Barbara's parking district. In 1981, his back was broken when he was hit by a car while crossing the street. He was left there to die, but a Good Samaritan called an ambulance for him, and he woke up in Cottage Hospital. Unfortunately, Steve had to spend the remainder of his life dealing with the fallout from that injury. He was a brilliant, fun and witty guy who loved animals, especially his Australian Shepherd dog. Though he was gentle, Steve also possessed a strong sense of justice and was intensely loyal to those he loved. He lost his job after the accident, then lost his apartment due to his lack of income, so he moved into the Jungle lot with his pickup truck and old camper and quickly became part of the family. He and Michael made a great team, coming up with endless ideas about how to distract the cops and keep them off our backs. He was also a talented builder and could fix or design anything.

His relationship with Clu didn't survive for long after the accident, but they remained dear friends, even though Steve had to grapple with failed surgeries, laminectomies, hospitalizations and addictions to prescription pain medications for the rest of his life. He broke his back a second time during a tractor accident at a ranch he was working on in Ojai. When he lost his ranch housing, Clu and her friend Roy invited Steve and his two Australian Shepherd dogs to live in a shack on their Goleta property.

After Steve recovered, he needed work, and Clu connected him with her longtime friend Colleen, who needed a handyman who could clean the facilities at her dog grooming business after hours. Steve and Colleen soon realized that they had known each other as children. He'd had a huge crush on her when he was twelve, but then his parents moved away and they lost contact. Reunited, the two of them hit it off so well that their friendship quickly drifted towards romance, and they were married on New Year's Eve in Las Vegas in 1990.

After a quarter of a century together, Colleen succumbed to cancer-related illnesses in 2015, and Steve was shattered. Although Clu and others stepped in to help, Steve was dealing with the loss of his health and mobility at the same time, and he went into a tailspin, attempting to eat himself to death. He suffered horrendous conditions in a run-down Medi-Cal nursing home in Santa Barbara - the same place that Ed Finucane reported to the state for infractions in 2011. As his legally-designated next-of-kin, Clu did what she could to improve the quality of his treatment, but ultimately, Steve died of hypertension and congestive heart failure - a.k.a. a broken heart - on May 26th, 2023. He was a good human, a dear friend, and the physical world won't see his like again.

## Edward McCutcheon Mannon

Slightly brain-damaged from birth, Edward managed to survive on the streets of Santa Barbara. He was quite the musician and carried a guitar around constantly, though he could also play the clarinet, saxophone and flute. Edward smoked copious amounts of marijuana to help him cope with his tremors. His biggest fault was his temper. He couldn't control his behavior when he got angry. In a sense, lashing out was Edward's way of crying when life got the better of him.

I was introduced to Ed one night while I was sitting in Carrows with my best friend, Clu. He became like a brother to me, and we jammed on our guitars together now and again. Edward wrote song lyrics and loved to steal my cigarettes when I wasn't looking.

One evening, Clu arrived late to a party at Brian Eccles' house, looking quite rattled. She explained how she'd been hitchhiking to the party when the man who picked her up tried to rape her. Clu managed to fight him off, dive out of the car and escape. Hearing this, however, Ed went off like a nuclear warhead. He grabbed a souvenir Gurkha knife that belonged to Brian's parents and went running through the upper Garden Street neighborhood fit to kill. Thank god he never found the perpetrator.

I handed Ed a pencil and paper one day and told him to write down his thoughts the next time he was about to go off on someone. "It's mightier than the sword," I told him.

Whenever Ed became disruptive during our weekly HPA meetings, I would assign him the role of facilitator. He did marvelously at that job and kept the discussions running smoothly. Unfortunately, during City Council meetings, Ed would often erupt in a screaming hissy fit when he was faced with the injustice of laws criminalizing the homeless. Cuss words would explode from his mouth, and the police would have to escort him out of the chambers. Eventually, he learned to leave on his own before his behavior got out of hand.

My world feels a bit emptier now that Eddie is not in it. I miss our talks and our guitar sessions.

One night, I bought him dinner at Carrow's. We were calmly conversing when another homeless man sitting at the counter decided to goad Eddie into a fight. Ed fell into the trap and quickly became uncontrollable, loudly hollering threats until the manager came over. I tried to explain that the man at the counter had started the commotion, but the manager didn't like how Eddie looked or sounded. He asked my friend to leave the restaurant. Angry and hurt,

Ed ran out the front door and then turned to spit at the establishment.

I informed the manager that he had just kicked a millionaire out of his restaurant. It was true: Ed's father had passed away, leaving his children with a 4.6-million-dollar estate. "Really?" was all the manager could say.

When Ed first received his inheritance, he moved into the Faulding Hotel but eventually grew sick of paying rent. The hotel managers also wouldn't permit him to smoke pot in his room, so to regain his freedom, Edward moved back onto the street.

One of the final things Ed did with his money was purchase an electric bike. He mounted it without wearing a helmet, and when he took off, he was unable to maintain control. He fell, hit his head against the curb and shattered his skull. Edward's family had to make the painful decision to take him off life support, as his brain was scrambled and would never recover.

Ed's possessions were distributed among the homeless and scattered across town. I claimed a walking stick that Edward had made after he saw a stick I'd created and wanted one of his own. It sits in a corner of my cabin on Green Valley Lake - a rightful resting place for this token from my dear friend.

### James Magruder

I cannot say enough about my adopted son, James. He grew up in Montecito, just outside of Santa Barbara. As a young adult, he camped among the veterans in the Jungle - the wild, untouched and sometimes marshy strip of reeds and brush that grew between Milpas and Santa Barbara Street along Cabrillo Boulevard. James himself was just as wild. He was taken under the wing of "Old Man Clifford", one of the Vietnam vets, and he adopted much of their lifestyle. James brought in several friends - Mark, Smitty, Indian Lee and Hopper - and together they cooked food and drank the quarts of beer they affectionately called their "quarter pounders." His group was also part of the Homeless People's Association and would speak in front of the City Council about how unjustly the city was treating them.

James and his friends would accept their tickets when the police passed them out, but they consistently refused to show up in court, so on Warrant Day, they'd all head to jail. Incarceration wasn't all bad; they knew how to "keister" marijuana in order to sneak it into jail so that they and their cellmates could have a little fun.

Continually rebellious, James was a natural leader, and collaborators were easily sucked into his plans. One day, he climbed a thirty-foot pine tree in the Jungle and built a platform where he and his friends could relax and hang out without being disturbed by the police. It worked; the next time the cops entered the Jungle to hand out camping tickets, James called out, "Come and get me, Piggies!" from his treetop perch. The policemen swung their flashlights around but failed to look upward the entire time.

One of James' friends who escaped the streets shared an amusing story about him. James was exploring the town one afternoon when he spotted a set of keys left in a door lock by a Parks and Recreation Department employee. It was like finding a pot of gold. On that keyring was the master key to all the public restrooms in Santa Barbara, including every one that was normally kept locked to keep out the homeless. People on the streets would still exercise their natural functions just outside the locked doors or in the nearby bushes because they had no other choice. As city policies go, preventing access to restrooms was both inhumane and had obvious consequences.

Before James turned the keyring into the Parks and Recreation office, he made copies of all the restroom keys, giving a few to me in case I ever had a bathroom emergency. I passed one of those along to a preacher named Hank so he could unlock the bathrooms in Pershing Park where he led services and fed the homeless on Sundays. He would faithfully lock them again before he went home. Hank loved this gift, for he was a scrappy rebel who refused to stop his Sunday services, even when the nearby hotel owners complained and the City demanded that he vacate the area. "I don't care!" the preacher would shout. "Jesus is my boss, not the City!"

One cold and rainy evening, James, Hopper, Julie and a few others decided to let themselves into the bathroom of the Cabrillo Boulevard bathhouse. It was a real treat to be able to stay dry and warm for once, but everyone went quiet when they heard a rattle at the door. It was after hours, and they'd locked the door from the inside so that no one could come in, even if they had their own key.

"This is the police!" someone yelled from behind the door. "I know you guys are in there!"

The cop hammered on the door a few times, but nobody in the bathroom moved. Finally, the officer shouted that he was going to get his dog. James and his friends listened for the cop's fading footsteps. Then Julie unlocked the door and tossed the key into a nearby trashcan. She darted back into the bathroom and waited. Soon enough, the cop returned with his canine co-worker and kicked the door open. The homeless gang faced him with innocent expressions on their faces.

"All right," the officer began, "how'd you get in here? Who has the key?"

Julie looked over at James. "Do you have the key, James?"

"No," said her friend, attempting to keep a straight face. "Hopper, do you have the key?"

Hopper denied possession, passing the question to another homeless individual. They continued to gaslight the officer while the man waited patiently for the charade to finish. His dog barked incessantly the whole time.

James finally asked the cop, "Is that your dog?" When the officer confirmed ownership, James went on. "Is it true that dogs are a reflection of their owners?"

"I'd agree with that," said the cop.

"In that case," said James, "I think your dog is the biggest asshole of them all!"

That sealed it. They all were carted off to jail. When they were released, the gang returned to the bathhouse and sifted through the contents of the trashcan for the key, but unfortunately, the can had been emptied. They didn't worry much because they'd made multiple copies. After the City received a handful of reports of similar bathroom activity, however, the Parks and Rec Department went and changed all the locks, and the pot of gold went empty.

*James writing tickets for sitting on the sidewalk during the Solstice Parade (photographer unknown)*

James continued to wage mischief against the city government. He was part of the protest at City Hall in 1989 that sought to amend the legal definition of "sleeping" versus "camping". Our legal team had requested that we keep our protest ongoing, and I told them that if we received food support, people would stick around. The Legal Defense Center contacted Comic Relief - a national anti-poverty charitable organization - and they provided the food and funds to sustain our efforts through the next couple of months.

The protest was slightly insane. Every morning, the police would walk into De La Guerra Plaza and make sure we were sleeping and not "camping". They'd roust us off the public sidewalks, and we'd move onto the park lawn for the day. One evening, James discovered that a window in the City Hall building had not been closed and locked properly, so he decided to climb inside with some friends and explore the rooms and hallways. Seeing an opportunity for a practical joke, James retrieved a mannequin that we'd used during a previous protest and placed it on the mayor's couch inside her office. They returned to the window they'd used to enter and made sure to lock it. Then they headed to the front lobby so that they could make their exit. Before leaving, James noticed a cardboard house that was part of a display, and he relocated it to the front steps as one final act of tomfoolery.

When the government employees showed up for work on Monday, all hell started to break loose. The mayor, Sheila Lodge, was frightened to see the dummy on her couch, for it represented a violation of her privacy and potentially her safety. Within the hour, the police swarmed the protesters and started to question them. They pulled me aside and interrogated me for thirty minutes. "Who did this?" they demanded. But I knew nothing. The only thing I could tell the cops was how funny I thought it all was.

James' chief claim to fame was his ascent of a streetlamp pole during a protest when President Reagan came to Santa Ynez to cast his vote. He hung a sign on top that read, "Homeless can't vote in the USA," and was subsequently arrested. James was an unrepentant rascal who unfortunately suffered from pancreatitis because he drank too much. After a long life of activism, his pancreas finally burst and he passed away in Cottage Hospital in 2007.

### Daniel Knapp

The best of the best. Bob Hansen and Daniel adored each other. The two of them spent hours brainstorming ideas for guerrilla street theater, which was one of the most effective ways to educate the general public. Every member of the HPA had skills in this department, but Daniel was the best actor in the bunch. He could strike up a conversation on any topic, and he often held court outside the Art Museum or at the bus stop in front of the El Carrillo Apartments - a site that the City Housing Authority built for the chronically homeless to help them escape the streets.

On top of his theatrical skills, Daniel was a fine musician; countless chords from his blues guitar wafted through the streets of Santa Barbara during his time there. His cover of a Moody Blues song can be heard in the documentary "Streets of Paradise."

The first time Daniel found himself living on the streets, it was because a janitorial business that employed him fell apart. He approached the Homeless Coalition, looking for work, and we hired him to drive a van we had purchased. He would take people to out-of-town protests or ferry them to their medical appointments. Because of his social skills and charisma, Daniel met a number of politicians and celebrities over the decades and persuaded them to support our cause. In later years, whenever Bob and I left Santa Barbara to work on our cabin on Green Valley Lake in the spring and summer, Daniel would hitch a ride with us and stay as our guest for a while. Eventually, the novelty of peace and quiet would wear off and we'd drive Daniel to the Greyhound station in San Bernardino and send him back home.

Our friend's luck ran out one day when he got into an altercation at Alameda Park with a meth user. He was severely beaten and kicked in the head numerous times. Even so, Daniel was unwilling to tell the cops who committed the crime. He tried to heal from his injuries on his own, but a few weeks later, he had a severe brain aneurysm. They took Daniel to the hospital, and he was placed in a coma while the doctors worked to repair the damage from the stroke. When his brother arrived a week later, he took one look at Daniel as he lay there on life support and determined the man would not want to live like that. He gave the order to pull the plug on him.

However, instead of dying, Daniel woke up from his coma. He was unable to move anything but his right arm and leg, but over the next few days, he learned to communicate with us by using just his hand. He'd give us a thumbs-up for *yes* and pound the bed with his fist for *no*. Sometimes, Daniel would simply flip us off when he didn't like what we were talking about.

I felt certain that after months of therapy, Daniel's body would heal and he might come back to his full self. But his family couldn't grasp that Daniel was fully conscious and wanted to live. They didn't want to go through all the time and effort to see if he'd recover, so they took Daniel off food and water and placed him in hospice care, hoping that he would pass away quickly. Since we weren't family members, the decision was out of our hands.

We sat at Daniel's bedside in hospice and played him The Eagles and The Beatles, occasionally letting him take hits of weed through his nostrils. I never saw my partner Bob cry as much as he did for his dear friend. Daniel howled back, communicating his emotions as best he could. Two weeks passed this way, and my daughter Krystal held Daniel's hand as he drew his last breaths. Then she and I wrote his obituary for the Santa Barbara Independent. Daniel's ex-wife, his son and his sister came from far away to attend his memorial service. It was terribly sad... such a waste of a good man. His son, Danny, went on to become a musician and continued his father's musical legacy.

### Linda Archer

Linda was a bank manager who started using cocaine and became addicted to the point that her work deteriorated and she was fired. She landed on the streets of Santa Barbara and did her best to survive. I got to know her because she would camp behind the newspaper warehouse where I worked, near the junior high school.

Linda began to prostitute herself for money, and she never looked homeless. She almost always kept her clothes neatly pressed and could blend into any middle-class situation. Her one quirk was that she never smiled. Perhaps this was because she had to always be on her guard, like most women who lived on the streets. Linda couldn't tolerate the shelters, but she never caused a fuss or asked for assistance. Unfortunately, when death came for her, she was unable to call for help in time.

Linda was found along the railroad tracks, bludgeoned to death by a tree branch. Rumor has it she refused to surrender her food stamps to her attacker, and she paid the price. After several years, investigators finally found her killer, and he is now serving time in federal prison.

## Michael Stephenson

On August 4th, 1985, Michael curled up in his sleeping bag in the gazebo of Alameda Park and fell asleep. That happened to be the night that a few prep students from a military academy in Santa Barbara decided to dress up in commando-style clothes and go out into the streets with their Marine K-bar knives, looking for some gang members who had harassed their classmates. They found Michael lying in the gazebo, and one of the men slashed the poor man's throat. He was stabbed seventeen times. The last words Michael managed to croak out were, "No, my friend, oh no!"

The military brats went back to their academy and told their classmates that they had "bagged a Mexican." Thankfully, they were turned in by their peers. In court, one of the attackers said, "It was just like sticking a pig," and they were sent to prison for a long time.

The homeless community was scared to death after this tragedy. Many of our supporters joined us for an Easter sunrise service to honor the life of our friend, Michael, who died at just twenty-nine years of age. Michael Stephenson, painter of houses, you are dearly missed.

# ACKNOWLEDGMENTS

I wish to thank the following individuals:

Peter Marin - a writer, educator and a good friend - for his fellowship in working with the homeless. He not only spoke for them, but also *with* them, which is, in Peter's view, far more important. Peter has asked me to say this on his behalf: as much as the homeless may need help, they also need good side-by-side company and street-level allies in their various and seemingly endless struggles. Peter urges us to ask ourselves, *Who sees those in need? Who hears them when they speak? Who meets them as equals face-to-face?* Nothing, he believes, matters if you don't include the homeless in your pursuit of solutions.

Also, Willard Hastings, the head attorney at the Legal Defense Center. He worked tirelessly on behalf of the homeless, helping them fight their tickets in court, and he was instrumental in securing their right to vote in California. Willard was an honest and wonderful human being with no hatred for anyone. He had a wonderful sense of humor and his barbecues were just another avenue he used to share his resources with the community.

Alison Adams, another dear and close friend from the Legal Defense Center. Alison worked side-by-side with Willard Hastings and Peter Marin to help the homeless. She was elected to the Democratic Central Committee and ran unsuccessfully for City Council. An appellate attorney by trade, she is still writing briefs and continues to work from home. She recently gave the keynote speech at one of the Committee for Social Justice forums.

Bryan Snyder, the editor of this book, who worked tenaciously to try to make sense of my writings and bring clarity without losing sight of the true facts behind my adventures.

Jeffrey D. Hess, a visual artist who joined us on the Walk and whose illustrations are featured in the 1988 Homeless Peace Walk Newsletter. He is well known for his comic strips and caricatures, and several businesses that operated in Santa Barbara displayed his mural artwork on their walls. Despite facing numerous health challenges, Jeff remains a loyal, stalwart and capable man with a heart of gold. Currently, he lives on a desert compound in Cibola, Arizona with BJ and Betsy, his Labrador puppies, and his benefactor, a sheriff who picked up Jeff while he was hitchhiking and gave him a mobile home in which to reside on his property. Jeff still works for Search and Rescue along the Colorado River, and I am honored that he agreed to pull out his pens and markers to create the cover art for this book.

Clu Carradine, my best friend, who supported me every time life spun me in a new direction. She is a wonderful advocate for those without a roof over their heads because she, too, became homeless due to gentrification. Even now as a homeowner, Clu continues to use her writings to admonish government officials about the way the homeless are treated in this county. For this book, she stayed up late on several nights, fixing names, doing research and suggesting deletions to keep me out of trouble.

Don Hurzeler, who was Bob's teammate in track and field when they went to Pierce State College and broke national records for the mile relay. He is a published author and provided insights that helped sharpen the focus of this book in its early stages.

Susan Dunn Cobb, who lived in a school bus with a cabin built upon its roof and raised six children on the streets of Santa Barbara. She became a wonderful activist and published a book dealing with her years spent advocating for the homeless.

Finally, I must mention Michael Brook Tice, Linda Miller, the members of Homeless People's Association and the Homeless Coalition, and everyone who works hard providing services to help get people into housing.

www.ingramcontent.com/pod-product-compliance
Lightning Source LLC
Chambersburg PA
CBHW062046270326
41931CB00013B/2966

* 9 7 8 1 9 5 8 8 6 0 1 2 0 *